Praise for *On Human Potential*

TALENT DEVELOPMENT 3.0

"This new publication, provided to help regular K-12 classroom teachers traverse the talent development journey with their students, offers exceptional insight into the importance of early identification and nurturance of talent in all domains. Furthermore, it provides specific guidance in how to go about doing those tasks. One chapter, for example, provides specific examples for using a Talent Development Record to create a profile and shows a comparative example of how two students may look similar in some respects but in fact are quite different in respect to needs that should be addressed. Another chapter on provisions lists important STEM opportunities that are available nationally to service talented learners, along with an explanation of why they are appropriate for such learners. Not only does the book make a case for finding and serving talent, it argues strongly for discerning the differences between strengths and talents in the process, providing a clear sense of why the top 5% may need a different diet from the top 15%.

The book also looks systematically at talents in different domains, focusing more on artistic, creative, and psychomotoric talent than academic as so many other resources tend to do. By so doing, it provides teachers avenues to understand artistic and creative talent in their students that would otherwise be overlooked. The book examines leadership talent, talent in the performing arts, and talent in specific sports to illustrate the specific ways that talent may be manifested in quite different and specific domains. Kay also uses case studies to illuminate her points about the need for support on the talent development journey, highlighting two female scientists whose lives were very different, based partially on the support levels they received at key stages of their lives.

By taking a characterological approach to issues of looking for talent, Kay grounds the work in everyday encounters teachers have with their students.

Inquisitiveness, for example, is seen as the lead quality in looking for scientific and other talent areas as well. Kay demonstrates how this quality leads to the beginnings of the talent development process and allows teachers to understand how talent begins to emerge. The book also offers a developmental perspective, providing teachers at all levels the data needed to advance a talent agenda for students in need, regardless of age.

On Human Potential: Nurturing Talents and Cultivating Expertise represents an important breakthrough in examining the talent development process in the school context, how to find it and how to respond to students who exhibit advanced behaviors in specific domains. It is a 'must read' for busy practitioners who want to be guided in their work with talented learners and offers practical advice to other educators and parents who want to ensure that students who show abilities in areas of learning have opportunities that match them.—**Joyce Van Tassel-Baska, EdD, College of William and Mary**

"This book fills a gap in the gifted education literature by focusing on the development of talent in those domains currently identified in the federal definition. I particularly liked the discussion related to converting strengths into talents. Being able to observe specific characteristics and achievements to create a multi-dimensional portrait would support educators' cultivation of talent in each and every learner."

—**Susan K. Johnsen, professor emeritus of Educational Psychology, Baylor University**

"As a student of Dr. Sandra Kay, I remember how moving and unusual it felt to have a teacher focus on understanding and encouraging the potential in my little self. For me, this included her generously reading and responding to endless pages of my early creative writing that I would type in my basement and vulnerably deliver to her desk. Now, many years later, as a parent grappling with how to guide my own child toward opportunities that match her interests and abilities, Dr. Kay's wisdom on identifying and building expertise, and her Talent Record as a tool, offer a blueprint for moving forward."

—**Dorian Block, senior staff associate and director, Exceeding Expectations project, Mailman School of Public Health, Columbia University**

"Sandra Kay's book is a timely and badly needed corrective to the shameful disregard that educators have shown over recent decades for meeting the needs of gifted and talented students in regular classrooms. Using innovative, simple-to-implement methods, and providing clear guidelines and exemplars, Kay empowers teachers, schools, parents, and communities to unite in recognizing, tracking, and fostering the unique abilities of our most precocious and creative students."

—Michele and Robert Root-Bernstein, authors, *Sparks of Genius* **and** *Inventing Imaginary Worlds*

"Every classroom K-12 is an opportunity to discover and develop talent. There is potential in children and it is our obligation as educators to understand how this potential can be nourished and guided. While developing expertise is complex, it follows patterns and Sandra Kay helps us understand these patterns. Through her experience, knowledge, and caring for students and teachers, she challenges us to accept this wonderful obligation to guide students from potential to expertise."

—Nicholas Colangelo, PhD, dean and director emeritus, college of education, University of Iowa, Belin-Blank Center for Gifted Education

"Providing a graceful, down-to-earth tri-part intertwining of research from multiple disciplines with tenets of professional educational practice with principles of positive parenting, Sandra Kay's *On Human Potential: Nurturing Talents and Cultivating Expertise* is a resource that any adult who is in any way involved in the development of a young person must read. Foundational to this book is the undeniable necessity for schools and parents to collaborate for identifying, nurturing, and optimizing young people's greatest abilities. Just as the aegis of special education promotes schools and homes working together to ensure that the needs of students with disabilities are accommodated, this book delineates a powerful, evidence-based systems approach for ensuring that children mature in a manner likely to bolster and promote their individual talents."

—F. Richard Olenchak, PhD, head, Department of Educational Studies; professor, Educational Psychology and Research Methodology; professor, Gifted/Creative/Talented Education, Purdue University

"Although our society desperately needs to inspire a new generation of problem-solvers, creators, and innovators, much talent goes undeveloped in many classrooms. In this vitally important book, Sandra Kay offers insight into the talent development process and provides a roadmap for teachers and others to ensure that each student's capabilities are recognized and developed to their fullest potential. Teachers and parents everywhere, as well as school administrators, counselors, and educational policymakers, should not miss it!"

—Linda Brody, EdD, director, Study of Exceptional Talent; director, Diagnostic and Counseling Center, Center for Talented Youth, Johns Hopkins University

"In spotting children with gifted potential and guiding their development, no one plays a more critical role than their teachers. In her new book, Dr. Sandra Kay provides teachers with empowering tools to both identify and to nurture budding academic and non-academic abilities. Some such talents are within the classroom bailiwick and therefore teachers' responsibility to provide; some fall outside it, either because they are not included in the academic curriculum or because they are already so far advanced. In these pages, teachers will also learn to develop realistic expectations for their students' optimal achievement, and—in partnership with parents—to map wholesome and successful pathways. This is a most welcome addition to pedagogic toolboxes."

—Nancy M. Robinson, PhD, University of Washington professor emerita of Psychiatry and Behavioral Sciences

"This book very effectively demonstrates a way for educators, parents and students to document and record a student's strengths and accomplishments using a Talent Record system in order to encourage each student's meaningful growth. This is a valuable tool that is greatly needed in order to meet the needs of so many students whose potential, creativity, curiosity and gifts must be nurtured and developed. It's a must read for anyone who cares about gifted and twice-exceptional individuals!"

—Lois Baldwin, EdD, former teacher and administrator, Gifted Special Education Program, Southern Westchester BOCES, New York, and co-founder/president of AEGUS (Association for the Education of Gifted Underachieving Students)

"In addition to its being a powerful text for teachers in training, Dr. Kay's important book recommends itself as an ideal text for teacher professional learning communities. Professional Learning Communities, or PLCs, describe a group of teachers who meet regularly over a sustained period of time to work collaboratively to improve their teaching and their students' learning. This is a book one does not simply want to assign to teachers to read. Rather, sustained study, over a school year, wherein teachers read portions of the book in groups together, will tune teacher apprehension of talent in their students and enable teachers to become the 'talent scouts' envisioned by Dr. Kay. Some monthly meetings will be devoted to Dr. Kay's research, and others will be focused on specific talent domains and their associated records. Teachers in the group might alternate assuming the role of leader, becoming the month's expert based on immersion in Dr. Kay's text. At the end of the year, the groups of teachers working with *On Human Potential: Nurturing Talents and Cultivating Expertise* will have instantiated the book's ideas into teacher classroom practice, with the attitudes and tools necessary to document the talents of their students."

—Dr. Rosemary Steinbaum, dean, instruction and staff Developer, Joseph Kushner Hebrew Academy/Rae Kushner Yeshiva High School, Livingston, NJ

"Dr. Kay has dedicated her educational career to fostering enriching opportunities in the lives of students. Since no two gifted children are alike, the use of the Talent Record allows for better identification of students and more focused classroom instruction. This book goes beyond the basic multiple measures for assessing students' potential for talent. It highlights the importance of talent development and allowing students to set their own goals, in order for school systems to recognize and support their individual expertise. In an era of accountability this is an excellent book for today's educator."

—Elsie Rodriguez, superintendent, Monroe-Woodbury Central School District, Central Valley, NY

"Sandra Kay does a superlative job carrying out a difficult task: Bridging the huge gap between the scientists busy in their Ivory Towers and the practitioners working hard in the trenches. Moreover, she pulls this off across a wide landscape of abilities, from creativity to leadership and beyond. Impressive!"

—Dean Keith Simonton, distinguished professor emeritus of psychology, University of California, Davis; author, *The Genius Checklist: Nine Paradoxical Tips on How You Can Become a Creative Genius*

"This book provides confirmation that it is our responsibility to recognize and cultivate the interests and abilities of our talented youth. The author includes poignant examples of creative individuals, in-depth strategies for talent development, and an array of resources. I highly recommend this book to both parents and educators because it affirms our knowledge about and interactions with talented youth and provides concrete next steps to support their needs."

—Marcia A. B. Delcourt, PhD, coordinator, EdD in Instructional Leadership Program, Western Connecticut State University

"Sandra Kay's book provides school administrators with an exceptional insight into the need for Talent Profiles for all students. Dr. Kay provides guidance on how to achieve a course of action to meet these needs. With school leaders spearheading this movement, staff and students will benefit greatly from the models, strategies and specific suggestions provided in this book."

—Marcia M. Norton, EdD, professor emeritus; former department chair, Department of Educational Leadership, SUNY New Paltz; former principal, New York State and the Department of Defense (DOD) Schools

"The depth of the information here—an update on misconceptions, issues up for debate, and sources of information, a synthesis of research, along with samples of behaviors and sets of possibilities associated with the arts, would also be of enormous help to arts educators and others eager to support and guide each student's artistic growth and development. If public schools embraced the process and tools presented here by Sandra Kay, students who have artistic and creative potential would benefit greatly because it places the arts on a level playing field with other strengths and talents."

—Karen Lee Carroll, EdD, dean and professor of art education emeritus, Maryland Institute College of Art

"Dr. Sandra Kay's new book, *On Human Potential: Nurturing Talents and Cultivating Expertise,* offers the reader a thoughtful and practical dive into important topics associated with educating gifted students. She has had an illustrious career as a prominent educator, evidenced by years of working in schools, and as a professional academic, who earned an Ed. D. from Columbia University's famed Teachers College. Her combination of experience and formal training is quite rare in the field of gifted education and her new book provides the details and insights to prove it. Because of her unique expertise, when I have faced complicated issues in the educational lives of gifted students, I have sought out Dr. Kay's wisdom. The book details a practical (theory driven) approach to talent development called Talent Profile. It is a perfect construct reflecting Dr. Kay's remarkable career. Only she could create this thoughtful approach to guiding the practice of educators."

—Tracy L. Cross, PhD, Jody and Layton Smith Professor of Psychology and Gifted Education, College of William & Mary, executive director, Center for Gifted Education & Institute for Research on the Suicide of Gifted Students

On Human Potential

On Human Potential

Nurturing Talents and Cultivating Expertise

Sandra I. Kay

ROWMAN & LITTLEFIELD
Lanham • Boulder • New York • London

Published by Rowman & Littlefield
An imprint of The Rowman & Littlefield Publishing Group, Inc.
4501 Forbes Boulevard, Suite 200, Lanham, Maryland 20706
www.rowman.com

6 Tinworth Street, London SE11 5AL, United Kingdom

British Library Cataloguing in Publication Information Available

Library of Congress Cataloging-in-Publication Data

Names: Kay, Sandra I., author.
Title: On human potential: nurturing talents and cultivating expertise/Sandra I. Kay.
Description: Lanham, Maryland: Rowman & Littlefield, [2019] | Includes bibliographical
   references.
Identifiers: LCCN 2018043328 (print) | LCCN 2018055588 (ebook) | ISBN
   9781475842937 (electronic) | ISBN 9781475842913 (cloth: alk, paper) | ISBN
   9781475842920 (pbk. : alk.paper)
Subjects: LCSH: Learning ability. | Creative ability. | Motivation in education.
Classification: LLC LB1134 (ebook) | LCC LB1134 .K39 2019 (print) | DDC
   370.15/23–dc23
LC record available at https://lccn.loc.gov/2018043328

Printed in the United States of America

Contents

Foreword

Talent Record System

I'll never forget eighth-grade student Michael T.—although at the time he seemed easy to forget. I was new to teaching and could barely pay attention to anyone who didn't exhibit challenging behavior or academic needs, and Michael was quiet, never disruptive. Because I was overwhelmed, and because I had no signs of his interests, I didn't make much effort to create a relationship between us.

Mid-semester, his mother sent a note saying that Michael would be out the following week because he would be touring as a member of a renowned youth orchestra. Armed with this new information, I got some insights into Michael's priorities and how I might reach out to him. Concurrently, my impression of him changed dramatically from puzzlement to admiration. I'm not proud of the attitudes I've described here, but my experience is reflected in Sandra Kay's outstanding work described in this book, arguing that most teachers are not familiar with the range of their students' accomplishments outside of their subject area, much less outside of school.

Several studies have questioned the feasibility of differentiating instruction for special interests, abilities, and creativity as a goal for classroom teachers. Dr. Kay argues that teachers already note what needs improvement (to achieve proficiencies) why not add strengths, interests, and accomplishments demonstrated that go beyond expectations? Having a profile available of children's interests and associated activities (which show persistence and commitment) is invaluable for developing individualized (i.e., differentiated) assignments and projects.

Chapter 3 allows us to look at two children who appear to have similar records. With additional information added to a Talent Record we start to see how they differ and how each could evolve in the coming year. For example, Dr. Kay presents the case of a child who might be considered potentially gifted in mathematics because the student sees beauty or patterns in numbers. However, artists also like patterns and symbol systems. Whatever entries her future mathematics and arts teachers make in the file may guide the student and her parents to seek additional electives and out-of-school activities.

Talent Records include norm-based indicators of accomplishment that help put children's talents and strengths into perspective and to indicate the kinds of opportunities they may need to meet higher level (regional, national, or international) goals. For example, if a child is performing well locally in sport or math or chess, how well is he or she doing compared to others of the same age in the same domain? The benchmarks provided in the Talent Record system inform the public about what experts in the field consider to be yardsticks of talent at various degrees of rarity and what kinds of behaviors students can exhibit that would elicit entries into a Talent Profile. A set of benchmarks of excellence is especially valuable for families without "connections" or who may not be familiar with what's needed to participate in talent development in various fields. The Talent Record is also a great resource from which young people can build a resume for internships, mentorships, or college applications.

You might ask yourself, "How would the average teacher or parent be familiar with indicators of accomplishment for sport, music, humanities, and STEM?" How, for example, would an English teacher know if it is big a deal to win a state science fair or sporting event? Further, teachers don't have exposure to a large enough norming group to know how exceptionally creative or advanced a student might be. Although benchmarks change over time, Dr. Kay's deeply researched indicators help guide teachers in how to interpret individual profiles of student accomplishments or creative contributions in their class as well as how to add to the record in the realm of the teacher's expertise.

A further nuance handled masterfully by Dr. Kay is demonstrating that the trajectory of talent varies by domain. Some domains have plenty of research on early indicators of talent. Other domains, such as diplomacy or the social sciences, require judgmental maturity and sufficient exposure to a range of human behavior to show and develop talent. Also, in the performance domains, you need some height or lung capacity before you can accurately demonstrate talent in a specific sport or musical instrument.

I met Sandra Kay a few years after I moved back to New York and sought out active members of the scholarly and advocacy communities in the state. Sandra was way ahead of her time concerning children's creative potential in the arts and academics, recognizing and delineating the myriad impediments to supporting students' creative productivity.

Sandra and I shared many of the same mentors from our days at Teachers College, although I was from an earlier cohort of students. Both of us were encouraged to explore domains of talent rather than giftedness as a global concept. Our work has always concerned what you do (being gifted in math, art, sport, etc.) more than who you are (being a gifted person). My studies have focused on the development of both musicians and scientists with a special emphasis on the psychosocial, and Sandra's more in visual arts and creativity with a cognitive focus on instruction and learning. I'm so excited that Dr. Kay's work will be more widely available because it fills a real void in gifted and talented education.

The treasure trove of ideas in this book should also lead to additional research on predictors of talent and more exploration of talent trajectories in domains. As I followed Sandra's efforts to record creative and academic achievements of students in her classes, Michael T. would always come to mind. With the advent of this book, new and even more experienced teachers burdened by large class loads and not enough time to get to know each member of their classroom community will have a helpful tool to serve them. Everyone who encounters Sandra Kay's Talent Record process regrets not having learned about it sooner.

—Rena Subotnik
Director of the American Psychological Association's
Center for Psychology in Schools and Education

Preface

Culture of the mind must be subservient to the heart.

—Mohandas Gandhi

It was an "Aha" moment—an event you immediately know will define the rest of your life in significant ways. I remember exactly where I was standing when the Talent Record (originally called Talent Profile) idea came to mind. I was leaving an elementary school building after what I knew had been a pivotal meeting for the life and happiness of a child.

On leave from the school district that had been the center of my working life since completion of my undergraduate degree, I had returned at the request of both the parents and school for this meeting where teachers, administrators, school psychologist, and parents met to consult about one child. Despite three years of classroom-based evidence collected and defended by three grade-level teachers in addition to my evidence accumulated over three years of working with this student in a gifted and talented program, it still took over two hours to reach the decision to skip the child one grade level to create a less restrictive environment for that child's emotional and intellectual needs.

Seeing all this consultation with fresh eyes, I witnessed an example of the remarkable concern most educators have for their students, including their former students. Everyone cared deeply, but there was no way to bring together all of the teachers' perspectives on a child's behaviors, strengths, or needs unless this type of special meeting occurred. In fact, such types of meetings are required at least annually for students with Individual Education Plans (known as IEPs) that address special education requirements necessary for their success.

At the same time that it became painfully clear that this student was finally receiving what she needed to succeed, I also realized there wasn't any other way to communicate all of the insights gleaned over five years of schooling by multiple experts that I had just witnessed during that three-hour meeting with nine adults. The inherent evaluation systems regarding students' academic progress lacked an efficient method for maintaining a record of everyone's perceptions of a child's strengths and accomplishments to determine the best environment, curriculum, and instruction for each individual. In fact, there was no place to record a child's strengths and accomplishments that exceed expectations and may require special accommodation.

Experience in all grade levels over many years as a district coordinator of gifted programs provided the opportunity to watch thousands of children develop from kindergarten to high school graduates (and beyond), offering a developmental perspective of emerging talents. This longitudinal perspective on a child's exposure to many learning environments coupled with my simultaneous enrollment in a doctoral program in special education with a focus on gifted education provided the necessary expertise to see this gap in efficacy and efficiency.

The need for a Talent Record for all students as a solution to many educational problems entered my mind just as I exited that school. The cumulative record would save so much time for planning optimal matches for all students, every year. An efficiency expert might have a field day figuring out the cost effectiveness. The gap that most interested me was the opportunity the Record would provide for shared communication that sets up all children with the best-case scenarios for continued personal growth. Because, as I have said before, "That that does not grow, dies." We cannot allow curiosity and wonder, and the joy those feelings provide, to die.

That moment inspired many summers and weekends of further study on the current research on expertise that I had begun during my doctoral work on the figural problem-solving and problem-defining behaviors of three levels of expertise in the visual arts within an adult population. With background as a visual art educator, I had been most curious about the discrepancies between Catherine Patrick's (1935a,b) early research on the problem-solving behaviors of artists and nonartists and the later study conducted by Getzels and Csikszentmihalyi (1964, 1976) with creative and less creative art students at the University of Chicago.

In the latter study, the researchers based their work on the former, yet, using many of the same variables, they found opposing results and came to different conclusions. Combining the research on creativity with the work on expertise that was just evolving, interest in the interaction of developing expertise and creative processes guided me to select each of the populations that had been studied by these forerunners to see if any explanations might emerge.

The discoveries made in that research study led me to question if there were also developmental stages in children's creative thinking and, if so, in what ways might creative thinking be cultivated in K-12 environments. I was invited to be a Visiting Scholar at Teachers College, Columbia University, to continue this dialogue with the scholars I had the honor of having as mentors: A. Harry Passow, A. J. Tannenbaum, Elizabeth Hagen, Maxine Greene, Morris I. Stein, and Howard E. Gruber. This environment enabled my thinking and craftsmanship as a scholar to continue while I remained a practitioner.

My work on this Talent Record as well as defining the concept of Elegant Problems are the products of those years (1989–1999) and longer with Dr. Hagen as she continued to assist in the development of the Talent Record throughout its piloting in a K-12 setting. As coauthor of the Cognitive Abilities Test (CogAT), Dr. Hagen's exceptional expertise in assessment of intellectual abilities guided the early development of this record of talents.

With the philosophical support of the school district's administration, particularly the assistant superintendent of curriculum and instruction, efforts were made to collect data for Talent and Aptitude Profiles for the students participating in a special program. The immediate purpose of these records was to inform meaningful facilitator/student discussions for independent inquiries.

One of the goals of the program was to bring together students with the same intensity/perseverance/interest/enthusiasm for learning so they could find peers with the same values if not precisely the same interests while they all were instructed in skills empowering consumers of ideas to become successful producers of ideas.[1] Understanding and respecting each other's areas of talent was another specified goal of the program.

It was a small step to the realization that the students in the program were not the only ones that needed to appreciate what was involved in developing expertise in each talent domain. For many, recognizing what knowledge and skills are necessary to advance athletic or artistic talent to the next level of expertise was far easier than understanding what was needed and how to develop expertise in leadership, creativity, or academics. Unfortunately, all of the valuable research conducted on developing expertise in both adults and children was not informing practice.

Teachers working in the gifted/talented program, the parents/families, and the student completed annual talent scout forms providing documentation when necessary. The whole community of administrators, coaches, music experts, community and religious leaders, and especially the parents helped to build the beginning list of attained achievements as situated within charted possibilities in that particular endeavor. Parents of those children we had identified for the program who had accomplishments achieved outside of school in very specific domains such as preparing to be an Olympic skier or the creativity demonstrated by a successful young entrepreneur were extremely helpful in mapping that category with some of the achievement possibilities by collecting all documentation on the talent domain(s) in which they excelled. A child's desire and effort focused on accomplishing a lemonade stand matters.

This grassroots effort inspired and fortified by the research efforts of many scholars can be recognized in this applied synthesis. Despite subsequent years of work sharing this around the country and the world, this project remains at its initial stage. There will always be more to add to the research that informs practice, and this, hopefully, will never end. Because scholar colleagues as well as teacher colleagues around the country have frequently asked for this book, I hope readers will continue the conversations and investigations in three potential directions.

The first direction remains central to the original goal for the Talent Record: to help others provide all children with an annual snapshot of their demonstrated strengths in relation to the expertise that can be found in their pursuits so as to encourage each student's meaningful growth. Meaningful growth is not just about developing talent. The benefits of these annual snapshots are many and will be discussed in chapter 2.[2]

However, the true worth of the Talent Record is in communicating and illustrating a child's current position on a developmental continuum. Like the worth attributed to a picture, this assessment clearly and succinctly illustrates the environment of talents each child has explored and to what extent accomplishments have occurred in each student's chosen areas of strengths.

This idea turned out to be even more useful than expected. The value to the students as they pursued their own independent inquiries was often in how the chart invited further conversations leading their curiosity and wonder to direct future investigations that continually increased joy and skill. Having the tool available to all teachers and family invited continuous additions each year from multiple perspectives that informed the pupils of potential strengths they might choose to pursue. The value of having a record of talents increases with age.

The second direction I hope this Talent Record takes is as a communication tool that unifies every faction of and every contributor to a child's world. The substantially increased value education could have as a curator of a cohesive, creative collaboration of family, community, talent domains, and resources to meet the needs of all children's developing expertise would please efficiency experts as well.

The longitudinal experience of working with students who were so different from their classmates also illuminated the crucial role of peer groups from which friendships emerge by highlighting the painful moments when a child lacked them. This observation is not new, and has been periodically emerging in popular culture stories.[3] The need for a friend who "gets you" seems critical, if not paramount to happiness. If this record is used to transport a child's universe to include some place where a potential core friend might inhabit, be it a science lab, a creative writing workshop, leadership class, or computer programming summer camp that alone is worth the effort. Social growth seems to also mature developmentally when children enjoy an optimal match in environment.

In uniting all resources for this Talent Record system, an altered education could level the playing field among and between talent domains. Presenting teachers with a record of advanced accomplishments has, without fail, altered the conversation about placement by all those viewing it. A form that presents all talents literally on the same page also expands the perceptions of everyone who encounters the child, elevating the annual conversation to a starting point that might otherwise take three or four years to manifest itself as a pattern for the school to address.

In doing so, it also provides a magnifying glass on what is and what needs to be with regard to providing opportunities for talent development for all children in all areas and in multiple environments. The obvious gaps in opportunities for some students to advance in their area of strength and interest will be an important part of the conversations.

This might fuel further research findings to provide more/better developmental characteristics of early talent development, but its efficacy is in its ability to instantaneously provide a vivid portrait of a child who needs access to creative writing opportunities and skills or an optimal curriculum in lieu of the grade level math class planned.

Equally important, staff development is built in. Teachers seeing the need to know more to address the accomplishments of specific children they are to receive will try to incorporate advanced skills/interests in the assigned curriculum. This could lead to an authentic entrance into the advanced level of teaching expertise I labeled as *instructional strategist*. A first step toward this level of expertise is in using concrete methods of recognizing and acknowledging the unique potential of each child and his or her emerging talent in any or multiple domains, even those domains unfamiliar to the expert in front of the classroom.

Moving from a teacher whose focus is on content and curriculum to an instructional strategist who bases his or her strategy decisions with regard to each child's strengths, proclivities, and interests tends to provide both students and faculty with all the rewards of creative teaching. That would be the ultimate goal of this stage of teaching, experiencing the extreme joy from the challenge of finding successes through meaningful instruction. Expertise is required to reach teaching as an art form. This quality of expertise is one easily recognized by other teachers, parents, and students. It is a quality that takes informed practice.

This then is a third potential direction for the book, finding ways to continue the conversations and investigations on teaching expertise going from the teacher stage to what I propose is an intermediary stage as an instructional strategist. This could lead to a third phase described as scholar/practitioner that some universities propose as the ideal terminal degree for expertise in teaching. Fortifying the structure of the concept of scholar/practitioner requires finding legitimate, concrete, and recognized ways to unite the academic world of research with K-12 education practices so the communication can continue to inform each other from both directions.

Teachers who become instructional strategists and then become practitioners/scholars are able to define Elegant Problems[4] facing education and develop the research questions and empirical procedures to find elegant solutions in collaboration with others studying expertise. Visiting Scholar positions need not be the only way to obtain this opportunity. Studying this proposed developmental stage model of teaching would also add to the research on expertise in teaching. Practitioners/scholars can help define and direct worthwhile educational improvement that is especially meaningful to learning in situ.

SEEKING BEST PRACTICE

Studying expertise within the field of cognitive science has always been fascinating.[5] My specific interest is in best practices for facilitating the pre-novice phase, the phase that occurs prior to the moment a student chooses to pursue a talent, as that seems the most mysterious. How an individual decides what to pursue, with all the required effort and skills needed to develop that interest into talent, then talent into expertise, is germinal to the role of the expert teacher who has become the instructional strategist in K-12 classrooms.

Knowing what and how experts perform in a chosen field can help everyone recognize at least some of the requirements necessary for long-term preparation toward elite performance. These requirements may be subject to each specific context or type of talent as well as to the position the learner holds on the continuum of expertise from appreciators to beginners to novices and beyond.

As with any worthwhile instruction, beginning with the level of the learner and knowing what direction to aim for when developing next steps provide a richer and more meaningful contribution to the evolution of the child, not just the child's interaction with a curriculum. At extremes, this might take the form of a physical education teacher reaching out to a child who prefers to live in his or her head, by making a personal connection to use mind control to reduce stress in the body through breathing and exercise. Children competing in creative problem-solving tournaments or spelling bees benefit from direct instruction in the similar strategies used to calm and focus elite athletes. Knowing these commonalities helps everyone relate to each other. It also helps intellectual beings care for their bodies.

Developing new skills is pertinent to every stage of developing a talent. When looking at the pinnacle of elite-level talent in adults working in diverse fields, Jarvin and Subotnik[6] describe different stages leading to the final stage, experienced by very few, of artistic productivity. Various skills and abilities were found at the core of each stage of development, and the stages and skills differed between each domain/area of study. Preparation of children for these experiences may or may not follow the same pattern.

NOTES

1 Tannenbaum, 1983.

2 Benefits to the students are discussed later. With regard to the benefits of this type of assessment, see Howe, 1996. His statement that it was "important to obtain continuous records of people's lives" (p. 260) gave greater credence to this idea of profiling talents in a developmental way. He also inspired me to conduct the research on student's perceptions of their own feelings toward their talent development successes simultaneously with the outside observations recorded on the Talent Record to help others know what is most important to each individual. See Whitehead, 1929 for philosophical underpinnings.

3 Tietz, 2011.

4 Kay, Ch. 7 "Teacher as Choicemaker" in Simpson et al, 1998.

5 Kay, 1989.

6 Jarvin and Subotnik, 2010.

Acknowledgments

This book is dedicated to all who continually flamed my curiosity and wonder about improving the art of learning and teaching. There are too many to list other than to say my most significant mentors for this work were the K-12 students and their parents, those dedicated colleagues I have worked with across the country as well as those educators I met along the path from Teachers College to the national and international professional organizations nurturing professional development. Effective professional development is a two-way street. Mine was paved with treasured friendships.

Special gratitude for the actualization of *On human potential* is felt toward the students, parents, and teaching professionals who allowed me to anonymously quote them or describe circumstances that can be used here to improve instruction for others, as well as the many friends, colleagues, and former graduate students who encouraged and challenged me to write this book. I remain forever grateful for the encouragement of Dr. L. Ciota, assistant superintendent of curriculum and instruction, to apply my research as a visiting scholar at Teachers' College to our district's gifted programs. Great administrators cultivate expertise.

Additional thanks to Margie Kitano, Bernie Dodge, Valerie Wolzien, Rena Subotnik, and Virginia Morris for comments and suggestions on earlier drafts; Geoffrey D. Smyth of Roland Gebhardt Design for their collaboration in designing user-friendly forms for the Talent Record including the tables for this book, and Tom Koerner and Emily Tuttle of Rowman and Littlefield Publishers for their help and guidance.

Introduction

Perspectives on Talent Development and Expertise

No one is an expert on everything. No matter what our aspirations, we are bound by the reality of time and the undeniable limits of our talents.

—Nichols[1]

Elite performance, be it in basketball or ballet, inspires awe in the fans who appreciate the pursuit. Within that population of appreciators are also those aspiring to reach an advanced level of that expertise someday. Direct connections between those at the pinnacle and these early dreamers tend to be too few in most endeavors.

Beginners receive immediate, short-term guidance from parents, coaches, and teachers as to what and how to improve. Those support teams garner knowledge from a variety of sources: a family member already in the chosen field, other parents, local leagues or instructors, and organized support groups like PTAs or local dance schools.

The parents/guardians of the child who demonstrates interest in mathematics will most likely go to the child's math teacher for advice on how they can correctly encourage that interest. The parents who find they have an imaginative, think-outside-the-box child, who likes to take things apart and sometimes also to build things from spare parts, might seek help from anyone.

Few outside the specific area of expertise will know what answers are best, especially for those at the interest level or that initial entrance level of talent development where interest seeks the company of skills. This is true for each specific endeavor.

No one knows everything about all of the valued talent domains that are or will become available to young people. Many teachers do what they can to feed budding interests. Significant research and opportunities for talent development have provided evidence and program options to better meet specific needs of students in specific areas.

For example, the gifted education program founded by Julian Stanley at Johns Hopkins University provided advanced university programs and mentoring for young mathematical talent as early as middle school. This and other programs like it have significantly contributed to the lives of many children. But not all capable children can take advantage of them, nor is every resource geographically available to all of the children who would benefit.

Talent development aimed at elite expertise, whenever it occurs, is an intriguing topic.[2] Access to Internet resources provides a tremendous boon to information gathering about many subjects. It also offers misinformation.

As a mild example, a meme claiming the need to dedicate "10,000 hours" to a skill in order to become an expert has trickled down to informal conversations among parents of middle school basketball team members during breaks in their children's game. Yet, practice alone, no matter how many hours, is not enough. The decades of research behind this catchy idea actually reveal something more important, different kinds of practice.

TYPES OF PRACTICE

Ericsson describes three types of practice beginning with the practice everyone knows: one finds an interest worth pursuing and repeatedly practices the basic skills necessary until one develops a level and automaticity found to be acceptable. He labeled this type of practice "naïve practice."[3] Despite further years of practice, improvement will not occur unless further progress is sought. In fact, researchers found automated abilities actually deteriorated gradually if focused attention on improvement was not ongoing.

Given that most coaches, trainers, and teachers work very hard at designing practice lessons, the characteristics of the second level of practice defined as "purposeful practice" merit description. It is the step between naïve and deliberate practice. Feedback on whether you are doing something right or wrong and how to fix the wrongs usually requires someone else with the expertise one seeks.

Succinctly summarized, purposeful practice requires one to move past one's comfort zone in a focused way, make a plan for reaching clearly specified goals, and design a way to monitor one's progress as well as maintain motivation. The complex roles of parents and teachers assisting at this level have often been described.

"Deliberate practice," the third type of practice defined by the research, is informed by demonstrated expertise by the best performers in a field. This includes the established training techniques found to be effective in each pursuit as well as anything else these practitioners do to excel at exemplary, if not boundary-breaking, accomplishments.[4]

Most significant within this level of training was the cultivation of a mental representation that provided the expert with a personal map. Mental representations or patterns of information found in experts across many domains have been identified at this advanced level of expertise. The quality and quantity of these mental representations are considered more useful and powerful than intelligence, memory, processing speed, or visual spatial abilities in achieving the highest rankings in a field.[5] They are also extremely domain-specific contributing to the ongoing debate about whether general skills are or are not involved in attaining expertise.

Here lies an example of the problem at hand: Communicating the knowledge we do have regarding talent development and expertise needs improvement. The difference between thinking that 10,000 hours of any kind of practice is the key to advancing expertise while other factors involved in the same studies were found to be far more significant is just one example of the disconnect between research findings and standard practice.

Improvement on the quality and quantity of the knowledge we actually do have regarding talent development and expertise in order to properly focus the energies that are spent on getting there is valuable as well. By uniting research and practice, parents and schools, communities and gatekeepers, local and national venues, a more useful map can be drawn, shared, and updated. This map can help to eliminate misinformation as well.

EXPERTISE OF TEACHERS

The study of expertise has, and will continue to make, a significant impact on the "who, what, when, where, and how" of learning and instruction. How great an impact and how quickly the research can accurately be translated into practice will also depend on several factors. Beginning scholars are often warned that new knowledge that could directly improve practice takes approximately 10 years between findings and actual implementation. Computers have not yet made as big an impact at decreasing this timeline to reduce this gap as one would think possible.

No doubt, the studies on expertise in children are difficult to design so that the knowledge taught through a specific curriculum can be sifted from the new instructional strategies taught in that domain. With training in educational research this can be addressed from the classroom.[6] Informative empirical studies conducted by researchers who are requested by leaders of specific programs and foundation-funded are often rich in findings.[7]

An excellent empirical research study conducted by an educator in her classroom found that metaphorical thinking could be taught to five-year-olds if instruction was given in appropriately small steps called scaffolding. The finding challenged developmental expectations defined by the field.[8]

Instructional clues for further exploration by teachers in classrooms can contribute to the field of education when scientifically studied and published. In fact, significant educational researchers such as A. Harry Passow, Elizabeth Hagen, and Paul Torrance have suggested that the most important research on teaching and learning would come directly out of classrooms.

Yet, those who work in the classroom do little, if any, classroom research. There are many teachers who do ask the questions but do not have the means to find the answers so they depend on principals, or educational researchers and policy makers. Questioning and the desire for scientific information about instructional strategies that work in each specific context distinguish the perceptions of the instructional strategists, those performing at an advanced level of teaching expertise, from the perceptions of a teacher.[9]

Accurately describing the context of studies that address the interactions of teaching and children's learning requires researchers to provide all of the details of the context of their study. Any pertinent variables including the presented curriculum and specific instruction that was conducted are necessary before any findings can be useful to replication studies in other classrooms. Reflecting on the instructional strategies used in relation to the specific curriculum presented and simultaneously addressing both allows consideration of the interactions to better inform experts in teaching.

To be true to scientific inquiry, the constraints of any study must also be accurate and explicit when a researcher or policy advocate argues for or against protocols and procedures in public education. To highlight the large effects of either inaccurate problem defining or slight inaccuracies of details, let's examine the sentence, "Indeed, international studies have shown that a differentiated curriculum is harmful to achievement and equity."[10] This statement would send many concerned educators to the footnote provided to see what grade levels were involved. Was it just in elementary? What subject area? How many classrooms found this to be true? What countries were involved in the study, and how did the United States do?

Readers find the footnote quotes a 1992 conclusion from one study by the U.S. Department of Education. That footnote states, "Use of a differentiated curriculum based on tracking is negatively associated with student performance on the international assessments and also reduces opportunities for some students to be exposed to more advanced curriculum."[11] By leaving out the specific context of "tracking situations," the statement in the text implied that differentiated curriculum is harmful in all situations.

The quoted 1998 study, supported the de-tracking in the lock step method once used, which led to the opening up of honors/advanced placement (AP) courses to all who "want to do the work," which had major classroom ramifications. Although many parents were thrilled for the opportunity and believed their child was willing to do the work, high school teachers across the country complained that they no longer could complete the AP curriculum at the pace originally designed. In fact, some decried that half the original content had to be eliminated. The organization running the national AP standards altered the curricula to accommodate the new requirements of their new, much larger market of learners. Some colleges no longer accepted AP courses for college credit or raised the score required for that college credit.

Although students were no longer locked out of an honor track because they didn't qualify in fifth grade or whenever the poorly designed tracking began, implementation of the concept of de-tracking, like any well-designed acceleration procedure, would have been better served by simply providing ways to enter advanced tracking whenever it was an optimum fit for the child (and addressed a way to fill any knowledge gaps needed to be successful that would likely exist). Proposing a spiral curriculum to advanced learning is one solution that would solve both problems. These issues frustrate many expert teachers, confuse beginning teachers, and continue the disservice to learners, just different learners.

DEBATES FROM THE DOMAIN OF EXPERTISE AND CHILDREN

Uniting the debates found among those researchers studying elite expertise with observations gleaned from educational practice highlights issues in common between the pinnacle of adult performance and the routes taken from early signs of potential talents in children.

Debate # 1—Domain-Specific Abilities vs. General Abilities in Expertise

The focus on domain-specific abilities found in much of the research literature on adult experts is in sharp contrast to the K-12 educational system's focus on developing general abilities. Education is based on children "transferring" general skills such as reading or comparing/contrasting ideas to domains other than the one initially introducing those skills.

Cognitive science research studies of children often find this to be the case too. An excellent exemplar is the early studies of the relationship between knowledge and memory in children that found changes in the fundamental types of cognitive processing in those children trained in chess.[12]

In this example, the researchers compared other children with chess-playing children in their performances on learning and memory tasks related to chess. Training in memory strategies such as *rehearsal* and *grouping* was found to transfer to other learning situations in those students who were taught them through chess instruction.

The same results were found when teaching multiple strategies for increasing memorization skills as a fun challenge to begin each class in a one-hour pullout gifted program for third graders. We found these students would automatically practice, improve and transfer the skill to their studying habits. This was so effective, classroom teachers asked for the lessons to use for all their third grade students.[13]

Perhaps there is a continuum of abilities that evolve from general to specific. Perhaps each stage of any expertise beginning at the first stage focuses on different abilities as Benjamin Bloom and others have proposed. For example, a few advanced strategies found in adult experts involve knowledge-based features such as perceptual knowledge coupling, perceptual chunking, and knowledge organization. These qualities often distinguish the adult expert from the novice or the intermediate level of expertise in many fields.[14] These are advanced domain-specific abilities not yet relevant to beginners.

Because certain abilities and requisite characteristics have been found to be very different among various talent domains and occur at different times when studying adult experts, a chart was created of patterns emerging from multiple research studies on elite adult performers.[15] With research it is possible that a similar pattern may be found in children, as their general abilities are cultivated further toward the specific abilities required later on.

Relevant to this discussion is the fact that some of the research on advanced expertise that cites domain-specific abilities qualifies those abilities as separating second-string experts from those at the very pinnacle of expertise in a field and those who expand the field.[16] Is that where domain-specific abilities take over? Or is the debate a superficial artifact of the way studies are designed and both general and domain abilities are necessary? There is much to be learned from starting with individual strengths and monitoring any evidence of the potential beginnings of talent development in children.

For the sake of children and the instructional strategists who are trying to meet the needs of these children by using best practices,[17] the notion of developing general skills prior to the domain-specific ones may remain relevant to child development or the pre-novice state despite the research findings on adult expertise.[18]

Debate # 2—Early Deliberate Practice in Children Can Create Ability Where None Was Evident

"In short, perfect pitch is not the gift, but, rather, *the ability to develop perfect pitch* is the gift—and, as nearly as we can tell, pretty much everyone is born with that gift."[19]

Some new research from cognitive science, specifically neuroscience, suggests that the flexibility or adaptability of the young brain is far greater than anyone thought, even specialists in early childhood. One leader in the study of expertise sees these findings as suggesting that the rewiring of any child's brain, if done prior to about age six, would permit almost everyone to achieve perfect pitch.

This would drastically change our understanding of what has been perceived as innate abilities or gifts. No doubt there will be various reactions to Ericsson's conclusion that there is no such thing as a predefined ability. However, these findings just *suggesting* that the possibility exists are a game changer. If learning can be a way of *developing* potential, not just maximizing inherent capability, a new operating system will be needed in education and beyond.

Hopefully, as researchers emphatically debate the strength and limitations of these conclusions and conduct many more studies, we do not lose sight of the importance of early exposure suggested here. Early and ample exposure to the field of choice by a young person is portrayed in subjective autobiographic/biographical studies of experts presented in the following chapters. Surprisingly evident too are the signs of strengths and interests that emerge very early in children once there is a tool for communicating them. Adding physical indicators found in neuroscience research that suggests that if the brain is not "rewired" by that early age, the capacity to do so is lost becomes evermore noteworthy:

> This loss is part of a broader phenomenon—that is, that both the brain and the body are more adaptable in young children than in adults, so there are certain abilities that can only be developed, or that are more easily developed, before the age of six or twelve, or eighteen. (Ericsson & Pool, 2017, p. xvii)

One can feel the earth shake beneath one's feet. Whatever opinion one has of these claims, the subtlety of Anders Ericsson's decades of work on "deliberate practice" deserves much more direct attention by those interested in advancing talent development. The effectiveness of purposeful and deliberate practice is given its due because of the findings that the human body and brain develop new abilities when challenged. Actual structural changes in the brain of developing experts in various domains are found in some of the ongoing neuroscience research.

In fact, physiological differences seem to provide objective evidence to support the absolute need for an optimal match of educational opportunities for all students. Larger structural changes in the brain have been observed with greater challenges up to a point. There are also findings that suggest pushing too hard for too long causes ineffective learning and/or burnout.

Best Practice

Should educational practice at some point actually adopt a philosophy that we all can learn anything we desire with the extreme effort required of deliberate practice, this communication tool will, in my opinion, increase in usefulness. Either way, recording that which is evident along the K-12 continuum of developing talents toward possible expertise and using it as a foundation or blueprint on which the child (with an adult support team) can choose to build future efforts in a focused way are a worthy objective. Currently, any step can be planned out/altered as needed on the Blueprint page suggested as part of this system. Comprehensive studies of individual talent records reflecting emerging expertise might provide fertile ground for germane hypotheses. Certainly, more specific research is warranted.

Initially, this communication tool was designed to preserve and foster the joy and wonder experienced by young people who have found their passion, while helping others identify an idea worthy of pursuit, not because it is a 21st-century skill to know what one does well but to foster the joy it brings to do something well, especially something that takes effort. Apparently, this goal remains the North Star throughout the development of adult, elite expertise:

> I have spoken very little of this here, but expert performers get great satisfaction and pleasure from exercising their abilities, and they feel a tremendous sense of personal accomplishment from pushing themselves to develop new skills, particularly skills that are on the very edges of their fields.

He goes on to say,

> When everything else goes well they experience a level of effortlessness similar in many ways to the psychological state of "flow" popularized by Mihalyi Csikszentmihalyi. This gives them a precious "high" that few people other than experts experience. (p. 257)

(Ericsson & Poole, 2017)

Here, in a discussion about elite expertise in adults by a renowned scholar on the subject, Ericsson also describes the precise reasons that the joys of wonder and curiosity in children continually fuel their talent development. So from his end and mine, the intrinsic reward appears to remain the same.

ORGANIZATION OF THE BOOK

This book is organized to open with an introduction to the research fields that inform practices in the classroom. Beginning with early childhood stories of a few renowned creative adults who discovered their lifelong passion between the ages of 10 and 14, *Chapter One: Measuring What Matters Most: A Strength-Based Approach to Education* provides some useful background research on talent development and expertise that promotes a strength-based approach to education. An argument is made that there is a need to provide all children with an individual Talent Record that integrates strengths and abilities from various contexts, talent fields, and levels of accomplishment, to provide a comprehensive and longitudinal accord of a student's developing talent areas as compared to an objective measurement tool that is based on the expertise of that specific pursuit.

Chapter Two: Going beyond " 'A Pleasure to Have in Class": Evaluation That Informs* describes stories and anecdotes discussing eight purposes the Talent Record can address to provide evaluation that informs in a comprehensive way. By looking at assessment as multidimensional and dynamic, it becomes a tool of growth and focus for every student and all those charged with their care.

Chapter Three: Components of the Talent Record: Chronicling the Development of expertise introduces the Talent Record by comparing two students with the exact same test scores on an ability test. By building each layer of information collected in each of six talent domains, then adding data on behaviors and all of this for each year of school, the magic within each child unfolds. A discussion of Reference Set of Behaviors within each domain is particularly helpful in seeing the similarities and differences in the behaviors associated with less familiar domains such as creativity, leadership, or psychomotor/kinesthetic ability. Once the foundations are in place, an explanation of the chart for degrees of exceptionality is provided. In fact, these forms/tools are illustrated.

Chapter Four: Recognizing Emerging Expertise looks at the support roles found in schools with *teacher as a talent scout* for the elementary, middle, and high school years. Mostly through stories, and a few case studies, specific issues are raised and addressed.

Chapters 5–10 each looks at emerging signs of each originally identified talent domain: *Chapter Five: A Look at Intellectual Aptitude (IA) Surfacing, Chapter Six: A Look at Emerging Specific Academic (AC) Ability, Chapter Seven: Early Sightings of Creative/Productive (CR) Ability, Chapter Eight: On Materializing Leadership (L), Chapter Nine: Sampling of Visual/Performing Arts*

(AR) Abilities, and *Chapter Ten: Early Sightings of Psychomotor/Kinesthetic (PK) Abilities*. Combining quotes/stories from experts in the domain with sample stories of the development of several students, a short introduction to the talent area is offered prior to some examples of useful resources for advancing in that talent domain.

In *Chapter Eleven: So What?—Some Roles of Families, Schools, Communities, and Government in Fostering Talent Development*, the spheres of potential contributors to the monitoring of emerging talents in children are enlarged. Addressing the many facets of a child's world, the possibilities of cultivating talent scouts in each who might add an observation or witness a notable accomplishment enrich opportunities for significant observations. Sample Talent Profiles used in a staff development workshop on curriculum differentiation illustrate their power in moving the conversations from that of a teacher toward that of an instructional strategist.

The appendix provides a few guiding samples of autobiographical information on a few renowned adults to practice creating partial Talent Records from text such as letters or journals encountered when collecting information about students.

NOTES

1 Nichols, 2017, p. 14.

2 See especially Connell, Sheridan, & Gardner, 2003; R. Subotnik's work is listed for examinations of maps of the territories. Clark, 2008; Howe, Davidson & Sloboda n.d., prepublication draft; Wallace, 1989 and Zuckerman, 1977/1996.

3 Ericsson, 2017, p. 14.

4 Ibid., 98.

5 Ibid., 232.

6 Bruer, 1993.

7 Amabile and Kramer, 2011; Eadie, Sutton-Smith, & Griffin 1983.

8 Castillo, 1998.

9 A term I coined to distinguish the professionals who have moved beyond mastering curriculum to focus on mastering instructional strategies—employing a problem-defining skill known in the medical field as abductive reasoning to diagnose (Patel & Ramoni, 1997).

10 Hirsh (2016) in *Why Knowledge Matters: Rescuing Our Children from failed educational theories,* p. 11.

11 Hirsh, p. 229.

12 Chi, 1978.

13 Kay, 1991.

14 Kay, 1989.

15 Jarvin & Subotnik, 2005.

16   Chi, Feltovich, & Glaser, 1981; Chi, 2006; Ericsson & Pool, 2017.

17   Shore et al., 1991; Knowing 'If and What' to propose as additional or replacement curriculum is too open-ended for many teachers to feel comfortable doing even when directed by useful resources such as Renzulli & Smith's IEP guide for the gifted.

18   Ericsson & Pool, 2017; Subotnik et al. 2011.

19   Ericsson & Pool, 2017, p. xvi.

Chapter 1

Measuring What Matters Most

At age eleven, I began Euclid, with my brother as my tutor. This was one of the great events of my life, as dazzling as first love. I had not imagined there was anything so delicious in the world.

—Bertrand Russell[1]

It is said that Andrew Wiles, the mathematician who solved Fermat's Last Theorem after 30 years of work, was 10 years old when he was introduced to and inspired to try to solve it.[2] The famous painter Willem de Kooning was a full-fledged member of the Academy of Holland at the age of 12.[3] Peter Jackson said he became "a filmmaker for life at the age of 9" in his interview for the remake of King Kong.[4] Newman Darby, the inventor of the sailboard, built his first boat at age 12.[5] Inventor Danny Hillis built his first computer in fourth grade and designed his own invention lab by age 12:

"I wish I had my drawing from when I was 12 years old and was laying out what I hoped would be my invention shop," he says. "Because it corresponds almost exactly to what's here."[6]

Brian Behlendorf, one of the pioneers of the open-source Web server community, has two parents who met working at IBM. Describing his childhood, he states:

The public school was very competitive academically, because a lot of the kids' parents worked at the Jet Propulsion Laboratory that was run by Caltech there. So from a very early age I was around a lot of science in a place where it was okay to be kind of geeky. We always had computers around the house. We used to use punch cards from the original IBM mainframes for making shopping lists. In grade school, I started doing some basic programming, and by high school

I was pretty into computers. . . . I graduated in 1991, but in 1989, in the early days of the Internet, a friend gave me a copy of a program he had downloaded onto a floppy disk, called "Fractint". It was not pirated, but was freeware, produced by a group of programmers, and was a program for drawing fractals.[7]

WHEN DOES TALENT BEGIN?

As this introduction suggests, one way we have of looking at the childhood of an expert in any field is retrospectively via biographical stories or auto-biographical perceptions.[8] If one reviews historical records,[9] biographies, and autobiographies to inform our understanding of developing expertise, life's journey for many eminent contributors to our world often includes the discovery and initial introduction to the chosen field of study between second and fifth or sixth grade.[10]

No doubt there are also examples of elite talent that did not begin at these early ages. The point here is simply that it has, therefore it could. Recording evidence of emerging talent for many years in a small sample of several thousand students and watching them become adults, suggests it happens far more often than anyone would guess.[11]

Difference between Strength (Natural Resource) and Talent

It is important to differentiate between the terms *strength* and *talent*. In most instances, an individual's strength describes an attribute as compared to other attributes within this individual and this individual only. *Mathematics was her greatest strength* is an example of the comparison of a person's demonstrated thinking in math to other areas in which behavior or performance might be observed (e.g., science, dance, leadership). This is the perspective most parents have of their children. They see an area of strength in their child from observations that might be confirmed by outside sources like report card grades or comments by others.

So, when parents ask a teacher how well their child with straight A's is doing, the meaning behind the question is "What do you think? Is there enough *strength* to encourage additional enrichment or an advanced program?" or "Is there anything else we can do to support her if she wants to pursue mathematics?"

This is also what is usually being asked with the question, "How well does he or she do compared to others?" This question usually has nothing to do with "others"; it is about taking the next step. These parents are seeking advice with regard to talent development: Is there enough strength to encourage developing that strength and, if so, how do they help cultivate it?

From Strength to Talent

Strengths do not automatically convert to talent in a particular area just because the behaviors identified in talented adults have also been found in children. For example, a behavior such as *often sees beauty in numbers or patterns of numbers* has been found as a support for the development of elite talent in highly creative mathematicians such as Polya, a hero in mathematics. Some children will comment on this beauty as well.

Yet, at this time, there is no evidence that all children who find beauty in numbers or patterns might or could become mathematicians. Artists like patterns and symbol systems too. Additionally, strength in mathematical computations (*learns basic skills immediately, almost intuitively*) without strengths in creative thought might lead to a different constellation of mathematical talent.

To add to the complexity, a creative strength (e.g., *will do anything to avoid boredom*) may be at the basis of inventive play with numbers, but is not sufficient on its own to develop creative talent in mathematics. This necessary but not sufficient condition or quality is not a new concept to gifted/talented education.[12]

Talent, on the other hand, is the capacity for exceptional performance in a domain. The achievement may appear effortless (sometimes called a gift), or it may take extreme efforts. Either way, the outcome is exceptional as compared to others within that talent domain. Evidence of talent requires actual achievement in that talent domain.

Difference between Interest and Talent

Potential talent can be found with or without the necessary interest that plays a pivotal role in the cultivation of these proclivities. Because talent requires serious effort to develop, motivation is required. Educators do come across children with demonstrated strengths and/or exceptional achievements in an area such as mathematics (or basketball or music), but given the opportunity for exciting challenges, the students do not find engagements in this field joyful or interesting.

Without interest, the degree of sustained effort required most likely will not be met later on as challenges become more difficult. Whether we call it passion, intrinsic motivation, or interest, this quality is most useful in directing the journey as individuals map and then explore their own territory of talents. The importance of the learner's voice as the guide in the choice of direction taken cannot be overstated.[13]

One researcher called the experience of matching learning interest and optimum level of challenge "flow."[14] Flow is that wonderful state of engagement that melts away the rest of the world, where one loses track of time, oneself, and one's surroundings outside of the activity immediately at hand. Once experienced, it is this state of being that inspires the intrinsic motivation required to sustain efforts toward the continuous personal growth necessary to acquire competence and later expertise.

WHAT DO DEVELOPING EXPERTS LOOK LIKE?

A look at the development of expertise in various talent domains provides an account of some characteristic behaviors found as an important condition of an expert's approach within his or her field. This novice-expert research, combined with research in gifted/talented education as well as the independent talent domains, provides fertile ground for accumulating a wealth of information from anecdotal evidence of behavioral strengths in various domains such as creativity, leadership, or the arts.

These strengths may be applied to developing talents in any chosen talent domain or field of study. A combination of observed behavioral characteristics and actual achievements recorded by everyone involved in the development of each child would provide a rich, multidimensional portrait of the cultivation and the evolution of talents in each and every individual. This would help us identify the best match of opportunities and environments for every child as he or she develops.

In this vein, historical stories are interesting and can suggest hypotheses. Retrospective biographical research highlights personal interactions with a talent domain. For example, in reading articles or stories about successful and prominent people in business, one frequently reads about the fact that one remembers having had a lemonade stand as a young child. Do all people who have a lemonade stand as a child go into business? We do not know until someone does the research on a very large sample of the individuals inside and outside of the business community. But, is having a lemonade stand at the age of 5 or 10 an indicator of a desire and the requisite effort to try out a business thus making it a noteworthy childhood achievement? This book suggests that this might likely be so.

The Pivotal Bloom Study

A landmark study of elite talent in adult athletes, artists, and academics identified three developmental stages of advancing talent:[15]

- The first stage of talent development involves falling in love with the subject through exploration and play.

- In the second stage, the person learns the skills and develops accuracy in understanding the underlying principles to become an expert.
- In stage three, the learner is socialized into the discipline by a master teacher who assists the learner in finding a personal niche through new ways of looking and participating in the field.

These stages are not age-specific and, in fact, vary among the disciplines. For example, the trajectory for mathematical talent begins much earlier than that for history. However, more than a few biographical sources suggest that many noteworthy producers of ideas in every field had found their passion by age 11. *Children tend to be in fifth grade at age 11.* The importance of multiple assessments of observed strengths during the elementary years is underscored by the need to identify noteworthy passions in any subject area as this indicates the first stage toward talent development.

More remarkably, developing expertise at an advanced level (Bloom's second stage of talent development) can begin *before kindergarten* enrollment in areas such as chess, playing some musical instruments, the visual arts (drawing in particular), some sports, and the domain-specific knowledge required in an academic field. Each September every kindergarten teacher in any school across this country (or any other) may be meeting a potential or future chess master, Olympic gold medalist, or Nobel laureate. In fact, every teacher at every grade level faces this same possibility.

Bloom's study of 120 talented individuals specifically included swimmers, tennis players, sculptors, concert pianists, research neurologists, and research mathematicians. He not only identified the three stages of developing expertise across talent domains but also described the patterns of support he found in all of the parents and teachers within each of these stages. The amount and quality of support and instruction from parents and teachers were a major factor in all of these successful adults.

For example, in the early years, parents (or a relative) encouraged the curiosity of children from a very early age: answering questions with great care, reading, model building, and trying independent science or technical projects were central to family activities. Further interest in a particular talent area was encouraged without holding expectations of the child's level of achievement. First teachers were found to be nearby and have good relationships with children and were not necessarily outstanding in the field. Learning was presented as a form of fun, progress was expected in small increments, and the joy of accomplishment provided motivation and developed self-discipline.

The second stage or middle years of developing talent required parents to assume the major roles of manager of time schedules, planning practices, lessons, and chauffeur availability. Teachers at this stage were usually not as local, were more renowned, and emphasized precision and accuracy in all aspects of the talent field. The student was expected to demonstrate a total commitment to the field.

The third stage or later years of talent development required most of the individual's time to be spent in the talent field, with emphasis on perfecting highest level of talent, developing a personal style, and understanding the larger purpose and meaning of the talent. Other advanced learners provided much of the learning through relationships and comparisons.

This trajectory, especially if the amount of parental support is not as available, strengthens the reason for a school record with early communication of behaviors and achievements in all the talent domains:

> Research on award-winning adolescents and highly eminent people in many fields of competitive accomplishment shows the huge potential of learning environments. Motivating environments and early talent discovery lead to further talent development and even more exposure to more stimulating environments. Highly accomplished individuals master the necessary knowledge, and they persevere and commit themselves to their work. Continued effort and motivating environments developed by parents, teachers, mentor, peer groups, and educational and employment opportunities foster both high academic learning and real-world accomplishment.[16]

Walberg's earlier research, which suggested these emerging patterns, included a study of the biographies of over 200 eminent men.[17]

Further Research on Expertise

Research has also supported the belief that exceptional performance appears implausible without extensive practice.[18] Some have argued that world-class performance requires a minimum of 10 years of deliberate practice.[19] One longitudinal study comparing the hours of weekly practice of expert and amateur pianists from age 2 to 26 found the amateurs to maintain a practice schedule of between zero and five hours per week throughout their pursuit. The experts, on the other hand, continually increased their deliberate practice to almost 35 hours per week.[20] It is difficult to argue against the fact that the many hours of access to a computer as a teenager had to contribute to Bill Gates's success at an early age.[21]

On the other hand, there is more to the development of expertise than just accumulating practice hours. For instance, novices do not have as much information in permanent memory, nor can they process that information as efficiently.[22] Some of the skills that distinguish a novice from an expert have been studied and found to be different in kind (qualitative) as well as different in amount (quantitative) in adult populations.[23]

Longitudinal research is another way to study developing expertise. These studies look at exceptional performers through specific methods that strive for historical accuracy by collecting information across time. Terman's famous study followed a large number of high-IQ children throughout their lives.[24]

Often credited as starting the gifted education field, this study provided initial insights regarding the importance of educational opportunity (especially for those from low-income families through public education) and the importance of pursuing one's passions to attain satisfaction in life. It was a first glimpse into the complexity of navigating from potential to adult productivity. Terman's student Catherine Cox, and then others, led the continuation of the study.

An analysis of the major longitudinal studies indicates that exceptional performance is a complex picture of cognitive and noncognitive elements.[25] Findings from multiple retrospective studies of eminent leaders, scientists, musicians, athletes, and sculptors conclude the following:

> In sum, the results of these retrospective analyses showed that individual differences in basic cognitive abilities were not the crucial determinant of outstanding professional careers. Instead, non-cognitive factors such as motivation, concentration, and endurance, together with support of parents *and educational systems* [italics mine] were mainly responsible for exceptional performance in later life.[26]

The findings from these longitudinal studies reflect many theoretical models of talent development. Several of those theoretical talent development models identify developmental stages that require an emphasis on different factors at different times.[27] Research focused more on the development of elite talent in specific domains, such as music, offered details and factors required at this highest level of expertise.[28]

Whether it is the initial step that focuses on the development of enthusiasm for a domain and leads to a degree of competence[29] or it is developing from an expert to achieving the next step toward "scholarly productivity or artistry,"[30] we are continually learning more about cultivating these natural resources. Research increases the body of knowledge in this emerging field.

HOW IS *POTENTIAL* TALENT IDENTIFIED?

Quite some time ago a theoretical model of talent development described five variables that identified the internal and external factors that transformed potential into the development of gifted children: general aptitude, special aptitudes, nonintellective factors, environmental factors, and chance factors.[31]

More recently, the importance of these contexts for achieving success such as the month in which a hockey player was born (chance) or historical, economic, or cultural contexts that feed success or failure (environment) have been eloquently highlighted as important outliers.[32]

There are many models or conceptions of talent development that have been proposed over the decades.[33] Each model identified observable behaviors associated with each talent domain for the purpose of identifying *potential* in that domain.[34] Dr. John Feldhusen was an early influential leader in the field of research on talent development in gifted education.[35] His description of emerging talent supports the idea of having a cumulative record:

> In conclusion, it is clear that the term "talent" should be used to denote the increasingly specialized aptitudes or abilities that develop in youth as a function of general ability, g, or intelligence, and their educational experiences in home, school, and the broad community. Talent grows as youth develop specific skills, interests, and motivations. Increasingly the general talent domain defines a more specific occupation and increasingly merges with expertise.[36]

The TIDE (Talent Identification and Development in Education) proposal suggests four general domains for talent development in schools. These four domains—Academic-Intellectual, Artistic, Vocational-Technical, and Interpersonal-Social—are addressed, more or less, formally or informally in schools throughout the country. Although two areas where students can excel in school (with or without formal recognition or opportunities) are missing: Creative and Athletic endeavors, Dr. Feldhusen and two other excellent researchers worked on two important rating scales to assess general talent areas: *The Purdue Academic Rating Scales* and *The Purdue Vocational Talent Scales*.[37]

Perhaps the most widely used rating scales are those developed by Dr. Joseph Renzulli and his team: *Scales for Rating the Behavioral Characteristics of Superior Students*.[38] The 10 scales are often found in the identification tools used in many school districts seeking to identify students for gifted programs. Earlier, Paul Torrance developed a *Checklist of Creative Positives* (1969) that assesses strength or talent in the area of creativity. Specific intellectual talents are addressed by Calvin Taylor's model of thinking skills and subsequent Talents Unlimited Program (1978). Standardized rating scales for leadership have been developed as well.[39] By identifying characteristics of scientific ability and providing necessary factors for further development in special programs, high school chair of science Dr. Paul F. Brandwein began a successful science program in 1945.[40]

As may be evident, there is a wide, historic research base in which to obtain standardized behaviors that indicate potential talent for use in a talent identification process. To move this knowledge from its role as a static measure (e.g., identification for programs) to a dynamic assessment (a position from which to grow) alters perceptions for the world of school. Identifying supportive behaviors in every child provides educators with a history of cumulative competencies that can inform present and future endeavors. Combining these hallmark behaviors with a running record of accomplishments attained could provide a blueprint for further development toward the *child's chosen* talent area(s) for developing expertise.

HOW ARE STUDENTS' *ACCOMPLISHMENTS* IN ALL TALENT DOMAINS CURRENTLY IDENTIFIED?

The natural culture of a healthy school environment is one that celebrates all achievements accomplished by all children and adolescents. From daily announcements proudly stated over the loudspeaker by a school administrator to the discussions in teacher's lunchrooms, educators *do* extol the immediate successes of their charges. Yet, these accomplishments evaporate from a child's history almost immediately. Why? I propose that the reason (though not the solution) is simple. A formal method of evaluation that records and communicates accomplishments attained or strengths observed does not exist.

Researchers from a variety of fields and perspectives agree that there are many factors that contribute to the successful development of talent and expertise, and that what happens in schools matters.[41] Sometimes, what happens in schools *significantly* matters. Creating opportunities for alternate paths to the same playing field has always been a goal of public education in the United States.

The idea of recording talents is informative regardless of the definition of talent development chosen by the institution.[42] The 1972 U.S. Commissioner of Education's definition for gifted/talented children provides an inclusive and applicable model that is functional and was federally endorsed although the current revision excludes psychomotor ability:

Children capable of high performance include those with demonstrated achievement and/or potential in any of the following areas, singly or in combination:

1. General intellectual ability
2. Specific academic aptitude
3. Creative or productive thinking

4. Leadership ability
5. Visual and performing arts
6. Psychomotor ability. (p. ix)

The Talent Record (with Talent and Aptitude Profiles) proposed here is a cumulative record that describes and visually synthesizes a student's exceptional behaviors and achievements from kindergarten to Grade 12 in any relevant field of activity in which these young people are active at home, at school, and/or in the community. The purpose is to integrate information (behaviors and achievements) from various contexts, talent fields, and level(s) of accomplishment to provide a comprehensive and longitudinal record of a student's developing expertise in the domains pursued.

In the context of this system, the term "strength" remains an observed behavior that is useful as anecdotal evidence of potential. A behavior is acknowledged on the Talent Record because that behavior has been recognized in educational research as necessary or useful for the entry level of a talent domain. Therefore "a strength" is a behavioral characteristic that has been found in the constellation of skills, proclivities, resource pools, or intrinsic motivational studies necessary to the development of a specific talent. For example, parents and teachers identifying the behaviors associated with mathematical talent when the child is involved with mathematical activities (as described in the Reference Set of Possibilities presented later) would build a foundation for discussion of the next best step for cultivating this area of expertise.

SUMMARY

Despite the fact that we can see what some may describe as a gallery of gifts (gifts of opportunity, chance, interest, perseverance, abilities, and support systems) that are necessary for the realization of talent and expertise, an educational community can do far more to help actualize potential when assessments become a communication tool for development of that potential. The behaviors identified in talent development research provide a list of strengths that are: (1) observable and (2) found to support achievements in a particular talent domain among experts in that field. Combining a record of these strengths in multiple domains with achievements in any domain as they emerge would provide an informative cumulative record.

Although some research suggests that "Achievements early in life predict and influence later accomplishments,"[43] the Talent Record is designed to *record*, not predict, at present. If by recording observed strengths and achievements found in a child that are inherent in adult experts in a talent domain *we do not predict the future but merely curate the past and present*, teachers can help students build on their current level of expertise so that they will be, at the very least, aware of more than their weaknesses as they approach adulthood. Knowing what one does well is a required 21st-century skill. Others will gain a realistic view of their current level of talent in a given domain.[44]

As importantly, all educators will have some evaluation tools to use to communicate what is seen in the glass that is half full. Like the pebble dropped in still water, the positive effects of this approach can ripple through current practice.

NOTES

1 Russell, 1967, pp. 37–38.
2 Doskoch, 2005, p. 4.
3 Scrivani, 1988.
4 *Newsweek*, 2005, p. 64.
5 Small, 2005.
6 Levy, 2005, p. 54.
7 Friedman, 2007, p. 98.
8 The November 2005 Smithsonian special anniversary issue on "35 who made a difference" cites four specific examples of early recollections of the inspiration behind the contributions made: Margaret Burbridge, proved the origins of the elements come from the stars: "Burbridge first became aware of the stars 82 years ago, at the age of four" (written by Bartusiak, p. 34); Richard Leakey, leader of the Hominid Group: "After one 'I'm tired, I'm bored' lament, his exasperated father shouted, 'Go and find your own bone!' This he did at age 6" (written by Morell, p. 40).; Daphne Sheldrick, owner of an animal orphanage in Africa: "Daphne Jenkins grew up on a Kenyan dairy farm. At the age of 3, she was given a young bushbuck to nurture" (written by Chadwick, p. 51); and designer and director Julie Taymor:

> Her major tools are puppet and mask. . . . She was drawn to their powers even as a child. And when Taymor was 16, she finished her Newton, Massachusetts, high school a semester early and studied in Paris at L'Ecole de Mime Jacques LeCoq, where she worked with masks, learning, she told Smithsonian in 1993, "how to transform myself into a non-human object" as well as "how to infuse an inanimate object with character" (written by Rothstein, p. 52).

9 See Robinson & Jolly (2014) for an exemplar of investigations of historical records for biographical research.
10 Autobiographical profiles of talent development, although subjective by nature, can provide some clues as to the achievements deemed significant enough to recall by the individual. These perceptions, especially from those seen as heroes

by some, can serve as a "story" worth telling through the recreating of the partial Talent Profiles that emerge from the autobiography itself. See the Appendix for sample profiles of renowned experts compiled from primary sources and autobiographies such as S. Wolzniak's autobiography as an example of technology in the psychomotor domain.

11 See Kay 2002. Also social media allows far more longitudinal contacts from former students thanking teachers that made a difference, thus suggesting a new way to collect data to someone looking for a useful study.

12 Tannenbaum, 1983.

13 Csikszentmihalyi, Rathunde & Whalen, 1993; Dewey, 1938; Kanevsky & Kay, 2006; Kohn, 1993

14 Csikszentmihalyi, 1990.

15 Bloom, 1985.

16 Walberg, 1995, p. 175.

17 Walberg, 1988. Also see Sosniak, 2006 on retrospective interviews.

18 Ericsson, Perez, Eccles, Lang, Baker, Bransford, Vanlehn, & Ward 2009; Exceptions do exist such as the child prodigy Michael Kearney who held the distinction of the youngest person (age six) to receive a high school diploma among other achievements in the *Guinness Book of World Records* (Schneider, 2002). From the research on child prodigies (Feldman, 1986; Goldsmith, 2000; Milbrath, 1995), one might conclude that a prodigy needs to come with the stock disclaimer that past performance is no guarantee of future success. They are too unique to represent the whole developmental perspective of the relationships among giftedness, expertise, and exceptional performance studied (Schneider, 2002; Sternberg, 2000).

19 Ericsson, Krampe, & Tesch-Römer, 1993; Snow, 1980; Ericsson, 1996.

20 Krampe & Ericsson, 1996.

21 Gladwell, 2009.

22 Walberg, 1995.

23 Ericsson & Charness, 1997; Feltovich, Spiro, & Coulson 1997; deGroot, 1965; Kay, 1989; Subotnik & Jarvin, 2005.

24 Terman, 1916.

25 Benbow, Perkins, & Stanley, 1983; Bloom, 1985; Csikszentmihalyi et al., 1993; Gruber, 1978; Gruber & Richard, 1990; Tannenbaum, 1983; Schneider, 2002; Subotnik & Arnold, 1994.

26 Schneider, 2002.

27 See Subotnik & Jarvin, 2005.

28 Subotnik, 2000.

29 Bloom, 1985.

30 Subotnik & Jarvin, 2005.

31 Tannenbaum, 1983.

32 Gladwell, 2008.

33 Feldhusen 2001; Renzulli, 1978. See Feldhusen, 1995 for a brief review of the contributions of many of the major early models and Subotnik & Jarvin, 2005 for additional models.

34 Karnes & associates 1978; Kitano & Kirby 1986; Subotnik, Olszewski-Kubilius, & Worrell, 2011.

35   His encouragement to develop this Talent Profile included his editorial invitations to early articles.

36   The "g" in this quote represents "the g factor," a phrase that describes the constellation of attributes different researchers describe differently to capture the concept of general intelligence. In particular, see works by Guilford (1956), Spearman (1927), or Cattell (1971). Feldhusen, 1995, p. 13.

37   Feldhusen, Hoover, & Saylor, 1990.

38   Renzulli, Smith, White, Callahan, & Hartman, 1976.

39   See *The Leadership Skills Inventory* by Karnes and Chauvin, 1985 and *Rating Scale for Leadership* by Roets, 1992.

40   Kough & DeHaan, 1955.

41   Bloom, 1985; Brandt 1985; Ceci, Barnett, & Kanaya, 2003; Clark, 1979; Csikszentmihalyi, Rathunde, & Whalen, 1993; Feldhusen, 1995; Gagné 1993; Gagné et al. 1996; Gardner, 1985; Gladwell, 2009; Gruber & Richard 1990; Kaplan, 1979; Passow, 1982; Renzulli, 1978; Robinson, 2017; Subotnik, 2000; Simonton, 1988; and Tannenbaum, 1983.

42   Kay, 2001a, b; See Kay, 1996 for an earlier version using a different model.

43   Walberg, 1995, p. 171.

44   In time, if adopted by all, these records could prove to be a useful research tool for testing predictive hypotheses as well.

Chapter 2

Moving Beyond
"A Pleasure to Have in Class"

The expert in anything was once a beginner.

—Unknown

I fancy that most of those who think at all have done a great deal of their thinking in the first fourteen years.

—C. S. Lewis[1]

Reflecting a well-accepted principle in educational measurement, E. P. Hagen observed, "The best single predictor of future achievement is past and present achievement."[2] Often considered the father of modern education, John Dewey proposed that an individual's strengths and accomplishments are at least as important as knowing one's weaknesses.[3]

Yet formal evaluation of student learning in schools is designed to address only the latter. Report cards measure the percentage of what "is learned" regarding what is taught on a subject or class curriculum. However, notice that receiving a 60% on a report card is perceived as a failure rather than the fact that 60% of the measured course content had been learned. The primary record of a child's progress is the report card, and that, for the most part, focuses on the negative rather than a child's positive achievements.

"Has been a pleasure to have in class" is a common exception to the trend of emphasizing only areas that need improvement in handwritten report card messages. Merely reflecting a subjective emotional response to a past social context that has no chance of being relevant again, this is often the only positive comment found on report cards. Knowing one's child is a pleasure is useful and enjoyable and is not the problem here.

The problem is that it is too often the only positive comment on a report card and, unfortunately, is meaningless with regard to accounting for growth in achievement. Where the need for any specific improvement usually states the achievement goal involved and what needs to be done to get there, nothing like this exists for the child who has aced the subject and wants more. This includes the child who may have achieved the highest grade without effort or advancing any skills, yet may not receive the "pleasure to have in class" evaluation if he or she was left bored all quarter.

Report card comments in secondary school do not change much in terms of options even when surveying positive options available on computerized grading programs. "Has been a pleasure to have in class" is one of a handful of comments regarding personality or effort in a predetermined list of options seeking something positive to say.

The only potential for any positive feedback about a child's interaction with the content in a child's cumulative school record is found on report cards that have a place for comments. If one has the opportunity to review a child's annual report cards across the years, or review a grade level worth of report card comments by thousands of teachers from a variety of schools in several states, or review all the report cards from an entire school district, the observations are likely to be the same:

(1) there are far too few comments made;
(2) almost all written comments seek an improvement; and
(3) in both handwritten and computerized options for choice of comments, strengths or observed talents are not addressed or listed as an option.

In private schools where teachers write letters describing strengths and activities rather than give out grades, the amount of information collected and shared is significantly different.

Evaluation experts tell us that what one selects to measure is important, so why not measure student's natural abilities through demonstrated strengths and proclivities? With a measurement system that provides this information for all children in various milieus, there would be a solid context in which to view exceptional behaviors and emerging talents.[4]

To clarify, individual Talent Records chart measurements of observed strengths and developed talents in specific domains of expertise determined by educational policy and research. They provide a cumulative record of talents, encouraging the possibility of systematically cultivating our nation's greatest natural resource—the potential of its school children.

The need for an evaluation system that records anecdotal evidence of the behavioral strengths and accomplishments achieved throughout childhood and adolescence can preserve these observations of talent and potential rather than allowing them to evaporate. This strengths-based approach to education is perhaps the most comprehensive way that education could address 21st-century skills.

If the education system encouraged such a curatorial dialogue among teachers for cultivating our nation's greatest natural resource, more conversations about strengths and talent development could take place in schools. If the educational system also functioned as the curator of input from family and community observations including achievements in religious organizations, student organizations such as 4H or scouts, and employment opportunities, a holistic portrait of each child could evolve. Identifying outside-of-school factors especially enhances the possibilities of identifying strengths for individuals marginalized in a school setting (e.g., at-risk, learning challenged, in rural or urban populations).

This seemingly simple switch from seeing the glass half empty—what wasn't learned, what is not done well—to also looking at the substance that has filled the glass thus far is a complex systemic addition to current evaluation methods. Luckily, awareness alone can make a difference. Of course, there are many obstacles to any systemic change, especially one that adds the evaluation of strengths and talent development to the current evaluations taking place. Two major obstacles are removed here by (1) providing a system of assessment of developing strengths and talents based on available research and (2) instituting a procedure for chronicling that development and the degree of that development. The first step can begin with an insightful observation describing a valued characteristic written on each report card by each child's teacher(s) every quarter.

Development and implementation of this system reveals many ways that a holistic portrait of strengths can be useful. From the individual to the global view, it

(1) Becomes a communication tool between family, community, and school
(2) Provides students and their advocates with an assessment of past trends in strength development from which to identify appropriate short-term and long-term goals
(3) Provides students with feedback and benchmarks to encourage opportunities for further improvement
(4) Helps teachers target some learning activities toward individual strengths and interests to maximize student motivation
(5) Provides teachers with necessary data for selecting skill groups based on student performance
(6) Provides opportunities for communication and integration of information between and among disciplines offering a level playing field that

encourages the valuing of unfamiliar talents through a language and chart of equivalent accomplishments among athletics, arts, and academics

(7) Can be used as a curriculum-planning tool to forecast needs of a school or district

(8) Allows schools to recognize and support excellence by assessing it as part of a student's school record.

A closer look at each of these uses is provided in more detail here.

TALENT RECORD AS A COMMUNICATION TOOL BETWEEN AND AMONG SOCIAL CONTEXTS

To understand this strength- or resource-based assessment system, some assumptions need to be stated. First of all, all students need to know what they do well, how well they do it, and what it would take to improve to the next level. Knowing one's strengths is an important part of choosing a meaningful life. In many cultures, personal skill development is all about contributing to the community by cultivating one's own natural abilities.

A child's contributions to religious, community, and family systems can inform the school in important ways. In many cultures, an individual's strengths are embedded in his or her family and community strength, and individual commendations are not part of daily practice. By including family and community in the creation of every child's record of strengths, this tool has the potential to support diverse cultural values.[5] This holistic portrait provides all children (and their families) with the opportunity to collage the fragments of their activities outside of school with those within the school. Everyone benefits by the team approach.

A RECORD OF PAST ACCOMPLISHMENTS

The second major assumption is that there is a complex developmental process that involves a variety of factors, as a child's innate resources are cultivated to emerge as a talent or some advanced level of expertise. All learning involves a combination of biological and environmental variables. Children, almost from birth, tend to self-select the environment or sensory stimulation that is most interesting. This self-selection reflects the biological "resource pools" of attention, abilities, proclivities, intrinsic motivation, and perseverance.[6] Whether it is an infant consistently responding to music with total attention or a five-year-old choosing to be engaged in playing chess or building blocks, these internal resources appear immediately and are observable behaviors.

Parents or guardians can provide useful information regarding their child's "resource pools" and proclivities. They often do so to the kindergarten teacher. It may, via word of mouth, reach the first-grade teacher. Rarely does it get to the fourth-grade teacher. Even if the accomplishment is such that it makes newspaper articles or the attention of the principal and is celebrated at the moment, the teacher who receives that student two or three years later is not likely to connect that information to that student.

Over time, parents/guardians very rarely continue to provide detailed information about their child's accomplishments, especially if the accomplishments occur outside of school. However, when the information is requested on an annual basis and incorporated on a record of talents that communicates directly with the teachers and other school staff who can use that information to benefit their child, there is every reason to participate. The strength of the Talent Record increases with age.

STUDENT GOAL SETTING

In a recent visit with a friend known since kindergarten, the conversation, as it tends to do with people who have known each other for a lifetime, revisited memories of our childhood—in this case, our 6th grade class. With fond thoughts of the teacher, this friend proceeded to share her struggle with reading and her position in the lowest reading group due to a then undiagnosed learning disability. When asked if she knew what reading group I was in, she proceeded to inform me of where everyone else in the class stood as well. In contrast, my memory of her was as our greatest female athlete and quite a leader in most informal play activities. In fact, she became president of the class for all four years of high school. But what seems to matter most to her life-long self-esteem was her personal perception of her lack of academic accomplishments rather than her talents. In her mind, what she could not easily do well still defined her.[7]

The lack of connection between the internal perception of a sixth grader such as the one described in the previous quote and the external perceptions of the peers or adults surrounding each child is far more prevalent than one might expect. In the midst of developing the Talent Record and identifying levels of achievement for all of the opportunities students pursue, the question arose as to these students' current self-perceptions. Classroom discussions on talent development led to the realization that understanding students' perceptions of their own talents was essential to implementing this assessment in the course curriculum.[8]

The first study of 138 high-achieving students in grades 3 through 12 in a pullout gifted program revealed the tendency for young students to prize the accomplishments that required directed effort toward a designated goal that exceeded their current expectation level. Specific examples provided by most of these students were in the fields of music or sports, fields where levels of achievement are predetermined and personal growth is monitored against a specific set of standards. In fact the necessary effort/challenge, not the level of expertise attained by the students in a particular field, seemed to be their main consideration when determining satisfaction.

In other words, if a high level of accomplishment was reached without effort, it was not perceived by that individual as equal to the higher ranking given to a lesser accomplishment in a field that took much more effort to achieve.

Two examples of high school students' responses to the survey highlight the complexity of these results. For a very intellectually able 11th grader, receiving six positive critiques on her creative story from writing peers in a CTY distance-learning course she took in seventh grade was cited as the most important adolescent achievement. Nothing else came close. Although her list of accomplishments included state and national academic achievements and awards that included creative writing, since third grade personally connecting with her age-level peers had always been difficult.[9]

The second example: A ninth grader with an extensive list of achievements, including state-level athletic awards in two sports, noteworthy academic achievements (particularly in language arts), and national chess tournament ratings, cited getting 100 in math on his eighth-grade report card because he worked so hard to make it happen.

Another interesting outcome from this first study was a difference in students' perceptions regarding goal setting in competitions. Analysis (post hoc) of the responses regarding competition could be categorized as either achieving a personal best (competition against self) or competing against others. Approximately three-quarters of the responses from students identified as performing in the top 5% of their class perceived achieving a personal best as the goal of competition in all competitions, whether it was an academic, athletic, music, or any other competition. (More on competition is found in chapter 4.)

Recording talents and levels of achievements in all domains on one document that grows with the student provides rich information on each individual *to that individual*. The tool can be poignantly used to encourage seeking personal best with regard to competition rather than the "win or lose" state of mind that inhibits healthy competition strategies at the elite levels of performance. Focusing the development of a talent on the next step toward achieving expertise invites the seeking of challenges. A Talent Record also provides a concrete platform for the student to consider his or her most meaningful immediate goals based on personal interest.

STUDENT INTEREST/MOTIVATION

Knowing that degree of challenge seems to be highly related to attaining personal satisfaction regardless of talent domain suggests that more opportunities for academic challenges are necessary for some children from elementary to secondary ages. Seeking to see if this might only be true for students identified with advanced talents, the second study to use the survey instrument was conducted with an entire middle school population (grades 6 through 8) through a newly formed advisory program.[10] Around 938 of 1,573 advisees responded to the achievement survey.

Of these, 718 surveys listed an accomplishment they had hoped to achieve during the current year. From the 718 accomplishments noted, 494 had to do with raising their academic standing. Comments ranged from passing to the next grade level to getting into accelerated math. Making or maintaining the B or A Honor Roll was the most often cited response.

Around 220 surveys left this last question blank, and nine students stated they did not know of an accomplishment they wished to have achieved during the year. Nearly 77 students listed a goal in athletics. Around 108 responses were placed in an "Other" category that included personal, religious, artistic (mostly music), and social goals.[11]

The results of that study suggest that a desire to improve academic performance is a commonality among a majority of these middle-level students. Whether the student set his or her benchmark at achieving a passing grade, being listed on the B honor roll, or qualifying for an accelerated course, most students had the motivation to improve themselves by way of a benchmark. This makes sense, as the need to grow is paramount to being human.

It also confirms the growth mind-set motivational theory.[12] As in athletics and other areas of talent development, students tend to use some standard to measure personal growth toward a goal. Any individual's personal growth can be stymied by lack of practice in goal setting, perseverance, and motivation in classes that cannot provide the necessary growth opportunities, whatever the content of those classes might be.

We know from other research that it is important to conduct these kinds of studies of intrapersonal variables such as intrinsic motivation.[13] Research on the successes and failures of talented teenagers took a very comprehensive look at this complex concept of motivation.[14] In that study, several factors were found to be associated with talent development in talented teenagers. These included:

(1) Recognition is given for a skill that is considered useful.
(2) Expressive and instrumental awards are requisite to the process.
(3) Development of a talent is based on the presence of optimal experiences.

The Talent Record can provide the kind of "selfie" that motivates and inspires with the reassurance of adult encouragement. The need for experiences and recognition along the way as one cultivates one's talents emphasizes the usefulness of keeping a record of students' strengths and achievements. If nothing else, the record can provide some answers to their questions of "How good am I?" or "How good can I become?" in a more systematic way.

INFORMS CLASSROOM INSTRUCTION

At the most basic level, the insights gleaned from the Talent Record offer teachers pertinent information for planning curriculum modifications and enrichment opportunities specifically geared to the individual's strengths. For example, the child who has won the third-grade essay contest in a district could be encouraged by the fourth-grade teacher to pursue opportunities in creative writing. This usually occurs when a student remains in the same small school with seasoned teachers aware of the previous year's winners.

However, this is actually left to chance as the child might encounter a new fourth-grade teacher or move to another school. Additionally, the middle school or high school English teacher would benefit from knowing that a child, some years before, received district recognition for creative writing. This fact might be used to rekindle a flame that may not have burned recently but is smoldering until it is encouraged again.

At the very least, teachers would be given the opportunity to acknowledge students for their accomplishments in fields not necessarily recognized in school. Whether there is an Olympic hopeful in the class or a child who maintains a professional acting career while attending school, these are facts that would enlighten most teachers' delivery of instruction and choice of assignments.

Noting the level of accomplishment attained may also enlighten decisions regarding the degree of acceleration in a content area. For example, if a seventh grader participated in a national talent search such as the one sponsored by Johns Hopkins Center for Talented Youth and scored within the top 1% of high school seniors taking the SAT, one would not consider a mild modification such as designing math problems for classmates as a reasonable solution for further instruction in mathematics. It would become obvious that a more radical approach to differentiation such as skipping mastered course work or mentoring with a mathematician would be in order.

With this type of achievement receiving an extreme ranking and other students' accomplishments ranked at moderate or basic level as described in chapter 4, new teachers would become sensitized quickly, if not immediately, to the need for different degrees of differentiation within the same talent field. An individual's skills as evidenced through achievements cannot become any more authentic. Using this authentic assessment to develop appropriate instruction within the given parameters of policies (informal and formal) regarding grouping and acceleration enhances opportunities to meet individual needs.

Having multiple talents adds overwhelming complexity to those students who must eventually make choices and decisions that focus more attention toward one chosen talent.[15] Although students who must choose between significant talent areas are sometimes the brunt of sarcasm because of their embarrassment of riches, these students, like other students, need confirmation of the level of each talent attained thus far.

They also need clarification of their aptitudes, abilities, and special achievements in each of their talent areas to help them decide their best course of action for the future.[16] The insights of multiple instructors in each of the advanced fields as well as a talent development team would provide students and families with facts and procedural information needed to make the best choices for the student.

A COMMUNICATION TOOL BETWEEN AND AMONG DISCIPLINES

The Talent Record aims at providing communication and integration of data between and among disciplines. Recording all top-quality performance assessments on one form encourages valuing accomplishments among academics, the arts, and athletics, as well as creativity and leadership pursuits.[17]

The need to better recognize and support excellence in all domains has been an area of concern in gifted education.[18] Although the Marland definition of gifted and talented children, with its recognition of multiple domains of excellence, was nationally endorsed by a majority of educators as early as 1972, public perception and (too often) practice continue to this day to associate gifted and talented education solely with intellectual aptitudes or general academic talent. This could easily change with a tool that recognizes excellence in each of the domains with comparable or equivalent advanced levels of achievement.

The impact of this tool to change these perceptions became immediately apparent during the early research phase. Seeking input from various specialists and sharing the goal of providing a level playing field for all student endeavors increased conversations between disciplines and provided a common dialogue for those involved in academics, the arts, and athletics.[19] This district-wide team approach fosters mutual respect and understanding among the multiple worlds within a school.

Recognition of the degree of accomplishment attained by a student in any field of endeavor is understood best when defined by the common language of a chart of equivalents (see Table 3.5). It also helps to identify simultaneous emerging talents in varied domains.

The second way this communication tool is most impactful is in helping teachers to identify ways of using the Talent Record to help their students in academic classrooms. During in-service workshops, some classroom teachers have asked what they could do to build on accomplishments in areas where they have no expertise such as sports or music. This often leads to great professional development discussions about interdisciplinary connections or themes that are multidisciplinary.[20]

For example, elementary-level students engaged at regional, state, or national competitions in any extracurricular talent field would benefit from a parent-teacher conversation regarding individual needs. These families are, by necessity, very organized, and most would greatly appreciate an opportunity to assist their child to excel in both worlds.

A poignant accommodation that a teacher can offer is facilitating smooth transitions by reducing conflicts between the student's academic schedule and the demands of another talent field. This is not a trivial contribution. Most children who know due dates early can plan to submit their semester or year long-term projects early so these obligations do not conflict with preparing for a huge meet or competition.

Opportunities for enhanced communication take on a larger complexity during high school years where talent development becomes more focused and time-consuming. A high school physical education department chair once asked if there was a way that students who were engaged in a sport that required many hours of practice every day after school might be allowed to substitute a study hall at the end of the day in lieu of a gym class. This would provide the students with time and in the best-case scenario, an academic coach (study hall teacher) to be available so that they could get their homework done and have access to academic help prior to practice. It's a magnificent idea that simply needs administrative support to arrange the scheduling!

Rather than a rule penalizing students with poor grades by removing them from a team, a school could be proactive with built-in study halls that provide the structure and resources to meet required academic success. Setting up students for success by removing potential obstacles is a valuable organizational goal.

Beyond facilitating a child's athletic talent, the encouragement of the classroom teacher to make connections or allow the student to build bridges between the curriculum and his or her developing expertise adds depth and breadth to the learning environment. Brainstorming possible relationships, teachers can make connections between say, gymnastics and the academic grade-level requirements.

For example, the fact that the sixth graders study the human body in science brought on a flood of possibilities for connections with using gymnastics as an example. A fourth-grade teacher became enthralled with the associations between this area and his science unit on movement and energy. The opportunity to study the history of gymnastics as a research topic for social studies would have delighted one student, as it was the self-selected topic in her enrichment class.

Relationships between science and music (e.g., study of wind), biographies of musicians, musicianship, and competition or historical movements in music, are just a few of the possibilities that the classroom teacher might suggest to a music student as possible topics for a classroom writing or research assignment. Making connections between what is taught and a student's interests is one of the joys of teaching.

INFORMS CURRICULUM PLANNING/FORECASTING

Evaluation is a key component in curriculum planning. Yet, without the evaluation of a child's progression along a developmental continuum in a specific talent area, classroom teachers lack adequate information to plan and provide appropriate curriculum modifications that address an individual's strengths or accomplishments. By providing teachers with a cumulative record that describes and visually synthesizes a student's prior exceptional achievements in any field of activity, the Talent Record is a tool that can directly service students and all those involved with their care.

Directly servicing students includes the work of administrators who may never meet the child. But their administrative decisions have far-reaching implications for curriculum planning, and reviewing Talent Records as an important part of scheduling/program planning could reduce conflicts and enhance opportunities. Consider how knowing the number of athletes/ scholars or musicians/scholars would assist secondary administrators in arranging schedules to accommodate those students' dual needs.

The review could also highlight the degree of curriculum modification that is most appropriate for advanced individuals. For example, where one student with a 99% average in an eighth-grade advanced science class may be placed in a ninth-grade advanced course, another with further accomplishments on record may best be served by skipping directly to AP physics. Thus, the Talent Record may be used as a tool for objectively determining more accurate placement in accelerated or honors classes or specific modifications of classroom curriculum.

However, even when a child is capable emotionally, physically, and intellectually to transition between elementary school and secondary school, the scheduling of the class may not be workable. Scheduling at the elementary school is often done horizontally. That is, a classroom teacher designs a day around specials and lunch but the learning day is usually created on one horizon. Secondary school schedules are designed vertically. Minutes of the school day from beginning to end are no longer up to the teacher or team but are predetermined and inflexible creating the vertical axis of the day based on time. Availability of classrooms and teacher's schedules construct the constraints that define course offerings for every grade level.

Savvy administrators know that smoother accommodations occur when outliers such as special populations and special courses, often described as singletons, are scheduled prior to the design of classes that are offered more than once. The higher the degree of student expertise required for the course, the more likely it may become a course offered once per year, semester, or even on a biannual basis in a particular high school. Courses such as select chorus or Latin are clear examples. With sophisticated schools joining forces to offer a specialized course electronically to multiple sites, coordination involves intense teamwork across districts requiring these courses to be scheduled prior to anything else.

Highlighting this complexity, the introduction of a class in Mandarin Chinese was going to be offered by a NYS BOCES as a trial satellite course for interested sixth graders in the entire county. Because many school districts were involved, the county provider would predetermine the time of day and day of the week it would be offered. Many students in the enrichment program that focused on self-directed inquiry had specifically requested instruction in this language, so going about matching the interest with the opportunity was simpler than the district expected.

However, had the principal not been aware that this unique option needed to be scheduled prior to all else for sixth graders because the time and dates of the class were predetermined by the broadcasted instruction, it would never have been successfully provided. None of the potential participants were willing to give up their select chorus or band classes or their regular enrichment classes to partake in this language course that had to be held during the school day.

These kinds of issues make scheduling the bane of many secondary administrators. So years of advance notice for the requisite area (or areas) of acute acceleration for a child's uninterrupted progress from elementary through high school can help administrators facilitate long-term planning. For example, the advanced chorus class and the AP physics class are typically scheduled at different times of the day in high schools.

So if a middle school child is coming up to the high school for instruction in AP physics, the time of day that the course is offered needs to conform to constraints such as busing and hours of that child's school day. In other words, given the choice of two time slots, one for the specialized music and one for the science offering, providing the science class at a time slot that includes a middle school student's ability to attend could guide the science period here so busing could be arranged.

Availability of the student to participate is key to generating successful differentiation opportunities. Hand scheduling the students who qualify for any and all advanced curricula ensures that the opportunity exists for all. This is much easier than it sounds if a talent coordinator gives to all district administrators two to three years of advanced warning of specific advanced talent coming up through the grades. Then a team could work together to schedule singletons prior to the other courses. This is also a place where guidance counselors could be especially helpful.

RECOGNIZES AND SUPPORTS EXCELLENCE

Recognition and support can remain "in the moment" of a particular event or they can be embedded in every fiber of the evolution of a school community. Research has identified the need to provide opportunities for talent development comparing potential ability to the potential of muscles. Both require exercise to develop.[21]

For instance, a child with linguistic abilities and no opportunity to learn multiple languages will not become multilingual. Talent development requires opportunities to actualize accomplishments. Accentuating the importance of this idea, other research specifies that some opportunities need to be provided early in a child's life, some before age six, for the most efficient and effective possible development of a talent. Recognizing this and then responding to it in every classroom are the first and second steps toward developing talents.

Although schools are not equipped to foster the development of expertise in every talent domain, they are well positioned to be, at the very least, the curators of developing expertise. Every talent domain has its gatekeepers. By interfacing with those gatekeepers, schools can be the record keepers of success to help individuals and communities optimize their potential.

NOTES

1 Lewis, 1956, *Surprised by Joy*, p. 63.
2 Hagen, 1980, p. 34.

3 Dewey, 1938; Passow, 1982.

4 This is not like earlier messages recommended to teachers for their report card comments – see McDonald 1982. Some experts clarify the difference between *measurement*, which identifies attributes or characteristics of interest, and *evaluation*, which studies those attributes considered important educational values (Wolfe, 1990). Wolfe based these comments on L. J. Cronbach's definition of evaluation

> as the "collection and use of information to make decisions about an educational program" (Cronbach, 1963). By "educational program" Cronbach meant anything ranging from a set of instructional materials and activities, distributed on a national level, to the educational experiences of a single learner. (Wolfe, 1990, p. 2)

It is this view of educational evaluation and Cronbach's interest in information relating to learner performance that lies behind this tool.

5 "Strength-based approaches employ strategies based on competencies, capabilities, and expertise" (Kanaʻiaupuni, 2005, p. 36), which would benefit any and all communities.

6 Ceci, et al. (2003), pp. 70–71.

7 Author's story

8 Kay, 1998

9 Having spent several years beginning in her third-grade year, striving to help her parents match her elementary learning environment so that she could find a friend, I knew the depth of the significance. Yet, I was surprised to see it emerge here.

10 Fraioli and Kay, 2000.

11 Of the 348 students identified as gifted/talented, 179 responses placed full names on the survey and could be identified. –Around 82 of the 179 listed academic achievements as a personal goal. Around 45 of these students were not participating in the optional gifted/talented program—held after school during athletic activities.

12 Dweck, 2007.

13 Clinkenbeard, 2012, 2014; Dweck, 1999; Hoekman, McCormick, & Gross, 1999; Hoekman, McCormick & Barnett, 2005; Lohman 2005b; Resnick, 1999; Van Tassel-Baska, 1989.

14 Csikszentmihalyi, Rathunde, & Whalen, 1993.

15 Fleming & Hollinger, 1981.

16 Feldhusen, 1991, p. 197.

17 Kay, 1999.

18 Kay & Subotnik, 1994 also see Subotnik & Calderon 2008.

19 See Kay, 1999.

20 See the work of Dr. Heidi Hayes-Jacobs (1996) for stellar work guiding instruction in interdisciplinary and multidisciplinary curriculum.

21 "Abilities are akin to potential muscles: without exercise the genetic potential will not become actualized" (Ceci, Barnett & Kanaya, 2003, p. 81).

Chapter 3

Components of the Talent Record

Chronicling the Development of Expertise

The value of a fact shrinks enormously without context.

—H. Wainer[1]

Of the 101 recommended practices found in a critical analysis of the research in gifted education, number 19 suggests, "Past and present achievements should be used" for identification and assessment of gifted children.[2] That is the purpose of the Talent Record. This chapter introduces and discusses the Talent Record as a dynamic assessment that goes beyond identification to include continual assessment for appropriate programming throughout childhood and adolescence.

POWER OF A TALENT DEVELOPMENT RECORD

The best way to see the power of this broad view of developing expertise is by example. Let's look at one that charts the information gleaned from a review of the school records of two academically able second graders, M and A. Many school districts begin standardized testing in the second grade, and this provides a measure of academic achievement for all. A typical cumulative folder on a student will house these test scores and copies of all report cards. If the district has a program for the academically gifted and the student qualifies, this would be indicated as well. This is what classroom teachers may glean from possibilities in a child's school records:

Table 3.1

Sample Talent Profiles with standard data from school records

Sample Talent Profile Record for M

Grade	Description
2	98%ile on CogAT test = placed in Academic Cluster RC far exceeds 2nd grade reading and writing"

Key: Column 2:
RC = Report Card comment from teacher

Sample Talent Profile Record for A

Grade	Description
2	98%ile on CogAT test = placed in Academic Cluster

At first glance, these students appear very similar. The only difference detected is that M had a teacher who wrote a comment on the report card. However, if achievements are listed during the same second-grade year from evidence provided by parents in other talent domains:

Table 3.2

Sample Talent Profiles including other talent domains across K-2

Sample Talent Profile Record for M

Grade	Description
2	98%ile on CogAT test = placed in Academic Cluster RC "far exceeds 2nd grade reading and writing" 1st place PTA Reflections: music Work selected for District Art Show 1st & 3rd place PTA Reflections: literature

Key: Column 2:
RC = Report Card comment from teacher

Sample Talent Profile Record for A

Grade	Description
1	1st place Tri-state Karate Tournament
2	98%ile on CogAT test = placed in Academic Cluster 1st- 4th place Tri-State Karate Tournament

A very different perspective on each of these two students begins to emerge. The perspective is altered yet again if we record observed behaviors across multiple grades:

Table 3.3

Sample of Observed Behaviors across grade levels as culled from report card comments

Sample Talent Profile Record for M

Grade	Description
K	Artwork is advanced
1	Keen/alert observer
	Acute sensory perception
2	Acute sensory perception
	Sensitive to aesthetic qualities
	Tolerance for ambiguity

Key: Column 2:
Acute Sensory Perception = extraordinary ability at perceiving information from one or more senses; may appear overly sensitive to experiences.
Sensitive to aesthetic qualities = will comment or be enthralled by the beauty of something; can be something unusual like a number or pattern or movement.
Tolerance for Ambiguity = Contemplates uncertainties; attentive to pun, irony, or double entendre; enjoys and creates jokes, metaphors, brainteasers.

Sample Talent Profile for A

Grade	Description
K	Keen/alert observer
1	Keen/alert observer
	Learns basic skills immediately
2	Unusually advanced vocabulary
	Sponge-like absorption of knowledge

Based entirely on observed behaviors, two very different types of learners begin to emerge prior to the end of second grade. When observed behaviors are added to the context of achievements, across multiple grades, each child's uniqueness regarding developing expertise is richly provided:

Table 3.4

Adding observed behaviors to 5 grades of Talent Profile achievements

Sample Talent Profile Record for M

Grade	Talent Area	Description
K	AR.v	Artwork is advanced
1	AC	Keen/alert observer
	CR	Acute sensory perception
2	AC	Unusually advanced vocabulary
		98%ile on CogAT test = Cluster group
	AC.l	RC* "far exceeds 2nd grade reading and writing"
	CR	Tolerance for ambiguity
		Sensitive to aesthetic qualities
		1st & 3rd place PTA Reflections: literature
	AR.m	1st place PTA Reflections: music
	AR.v	Work selected for District Art Show
3	AC	Asks provocative, sophisticated questions
		99%ile on State tests
	CR	Willing to risk being wrong
		Curiosity/ energized questioning
	AR.m	1st place PTA Reflections: music
4	AC	98%ile State Tests
	CR	Sees various perspectives/viewpoints
		3rd place PTA Reflections: literature
	CR.t	1st place Odyssey of the Mind Regional
		1st Odyssey of the Mind State
		12th Place Odyssey of the Mind Worlds Final
	AR.m	Started cello
		Advanced piano
		Accompanied 3rd grade chorus (piano) for winter concert (& See recital list)
		1st PTA Reflections: music
	PK.t	Soccer team, summer travel soccer

Note: The talent areas found here are from the original 1972 Federal definition for Gifted/Talented children. Each year, all Talent Profile entries for only the **active** talent areas are listed in the order provided in that definition, skipping any area not pursued. Full list of options are only found on the Summary page.

Key: Coulmn 2: In order of appearance:
AR.v = visual art, AC = general academic
CR = Creativity, AC.l = Academic.language
AR.m = music, CR.t = Creativity.team
PK.t = Psychomotor/Kinesthetic.team

Table 3.4 (continued)

Adding observed behaviors to 5 grades of Talent Profile achievements

Sample Talent Profile Record for A

Grade	Talent Area	Description
K	AC	Keen/alert observer
1	AC	Keen/alert observer
		Acute sensory perception
		Learns basic skills immediately
	PK.i	1st place Tri-state Karate Tournament
4	AC	Unusually advanced vocabulary
		Sponge-like absorption of knowledge
		98%ile on CogAT test = Cluster group
	PK.i	1st- 4th place Tri-State Karate Tournament
		Straight A's on report card
5	AC	Cluster IS* topic: Electronics
		98%ile on State tests
	PK.i	1st-4th Tri State Karate Competition
	AC	Cluster IS* topic: Solar System
		Straight A's on Report Card
		97%ile State Tests
	CR.t	1st place Odyssey of the Mind Regional
		3rd Odyssey of the Mind State
	AR.m	School orchestra
	PK.t	Local soccer league
		National Fitness Award

Note: The talent areas found here are from the original 1972 Federal definition for Gifted/Talented children. Each year, all Talent Profile entries for only the **active** talent areas are listed in the order provided in that definition, skipping any area not pursued. Full list of options are only found on the Summary page.

Key: Column 2: In order of appearance:
AC = general academic
PK.i = Psychomotor/Kinesthetic.individual
CR.t = Creativity.team
AR.m = music
PK.t = Psychomotor/Kinesthetic.team

Note that A had no records for grade level 3 due to a move from one district to another. Although appearing as a significant hole in the record, this is in fact what we currently know about all children who are without a record of observed talents: not much.

The system was designed to depict areas of talent by using a column of abbreviations that highlight areas of expertise: IA = intellectual ability[3]; AC = academic (general academics) (AC.l = specifically language, AC.m = specifically mathematics, AC.s = science, AC.h = social sciences); C = Creativity; L = Leadership; AR = visual/performing arts (AR.v = visual arts, AR.a = acting, AR.d = dance, AR.m = music); P = psychomotor/kinesthetic (PK.t = team sport, PK = individual sport or acute tactile/motor skills applied to areas other than arts).

Also notice the difference in length between the Talent Records of these two students. Where some Talent Records may reach four pages by senior year, others may reach a maximum of one and a half pages. The length of these emerging profiles may simply describe the difference between a child or the family's preference to explore a variety of choices or hone into one specific passion with the intensity of a laser. Length and number of entries are not the point of these individual records. Each record is valuable as it is, whatever is provided. (There are many possible reasons for a short or a long record, none of which can ever be accurately identified, nor are they necessarily important.)

What is most important is that both students pursued talent development that enriched each child. The second most important information gleaned from this is that they both achieved very advanced levels in several talent domains prior to leaving high school. How can one tell? There is another layer to the Talent Record system—degrees or level of developed talent (see Table 3.5 on following page).

Although varying degrees of exceptionality or levels of achievement are acknowledged in the literature,[4] no formalized method of communicating these individual differences reaches assessment in schools. Without a structure or normative system of identifying degrees of exceptionality, parents and educators are left with their own personal definitions or perceptions. This situation is problematic in a number of ways.

For one, treating a child as either talented or not in a particular area is a false dichotomy that helps no one, including the talented. The chart of Levels of Talent guides parents, teachers, and administrators toward matching appropriate curricular modifications to the child's needs in those demonstrated talent areas. Of course, this is particularly relevant to schools with regard to areas of academic achievements, but there are many useful modifications that a school can and needs to make to assist talent development in any of the defined areas.

So, the five levels of talent were designed to help with rating every accomplishment by listing the types of achievements that place a student within the top 15% to the top 1% of those who are active in a field of activity.[5] By delineating each opportunity, event, or other occasion for developing a particular talent by the five potential levels of accomplishment from novice (5) to the top 1% (1) in performance category, there is a greater view of the entire trajectory to guide decisions by all involved.

Secondly, a system of equivalencies for levels of developing expertise between talent domains is embedded in the third column of "Categories."[6] For ease of translation, understanding, and communication in the real world

Table 3.5

Levels of talent/expertise from different points of view

Levels	Rate	Academics/Arts/Other*	Sports
5 - Basic	15% of population	Classroom or about (+ 1 grade level)	Local participant
4 - Moderate	2 - 3% of population	School district or (+2 grade levels)	Local award
3 - High	1 - 2 in 1,000	County (+3 grade levels)	Regional recognition
2 - Extreme	3 - 4 in 10,000	State (+4 grade levels)	State recognition
1 - Exceptional	1 - 2 in a million	Nation (+ 5 grade levels)	National rank

Source: Adapted from Kay, S. & Gagné, F, 1997

Notes: *Levels of talent does include observed behaviors identified from the research in the talent area. As they are either noticeably remarkable or not, this is a qualitative evaluation that was added to the achievement table. These behaviors merit inclusion here because they have been associated with advanced talent in a field and could inform any current strategies for matching appropriate instruction. Behaviors receive a level 5 rating only when characteristically remarkable in the child.

1st column:
The concept of levels of talent was inspired by the work of Miraca Gross.

2nd column:
The Rate column is based on definitions for identifying gifted/talented students and appropriate quantitative assessments as originally recommended by M. Gross and quantified by F. Gagné.

3rd column:
Although the difference between best in classroom and demonstrating skill 1 grade level above expectation can be very different in degree, the classifications in identifying Academics/Arts/Other need to be wide and varied to accommodate all of the ways any child may begin to demonstrate notable behavior or achievement. Not recognizing any spark defeats the purpose here.

4th column:
Most are familiar with ratings in Sports. In fact this column was the backbone used for all the others.

of developing talents, the system mirrors athletic rankings (e.g., "We're #1!") with "1" the highest attainable level and "5" the lowest or entry level of emerging talent. Far more people understand athletic rankings than nationally ranked academic or artistic accomplishments. The chart illustrates commonalities in degree of achievement to help all to understand and respect each avenue.

The third reason: although often required of them, it is unreasonable to expect novice teachers to identify levels of talent based on their classroom experiences alone. For example, in the first year of teaching, an elementary teacher can identify the top performer in a class of approximately 25 Kinder-garten students. In this situation, without training in gifted education, it would take 5 years of comparisons for that teacher to identify a top performer out of 125 students, 15 years to identify the one in 375, and 40 years to experien-tially know the top one or two students in 1,000.

The top one or two students in 1,000 equates to a Level 3 in the five levels or degrees of observed talent identified for the Talent Profile page. Yet, cur-rently teachers are often asked for student recommendations of above grade level performance for programs or opportunities based solely on their teach-ing experience, no matter how brief. Perhaps this helps explain findings that suggest teacher recommendations for gifted programs are the least reliable measures. This is another area that needs improvement—especially with regard to early identification of the creatively gifted.

The multiple columns on this chart provide *choices* for the authority (be it school system or larger organization) overseeing the entries to properly match any local achievement encountered, as new ones will emerge forever. The purpose of the chart is to provide several categories so that the one cat-egory that best fits the accomplishment can be used. For example, any type of competition might use the sports category to assess level of accomplishment, whereas academic courses or scores (especially above grade level ones) might benefit the most from the designations in the column labeled "Academics."

Other classification systems that approximate the progressive selectiveness such as standard deviation (SD units), ratios within the general population, above grade achievement, and the familiar geographic system of levels of competition and excellence used in sports were organized to facilitate the task of assessing the degree of exceptionality in fields where standardized measures are not available as in the arts, creativity, or leadership.[7]

One of the columns provided would best describe the parameters of the specific accomplishment as defined by each outside organization. For example, the second column of the chart needed to reflect the fact that some theories of giftedness recommend identifying the top 15% of a given popula-tion while other G/T programs or opportunities for acceleration or enrichment alternatives in specific disciplines identify students scoring in the top 5% to 7% or the top 2% to 3% of the population. Again, to be useful by reflecting current practice, a revision of the percentile rate classifications to match cur-rent practice/actual opportunities led to these approximations: Level 5 = top 8% to 15% of a population; Level 4 = top 5% to 7%; Level 3 = top 2% to 4%; Level 2 = top 0.5% to 1%; and Level 1 = 1–2 students in a million.

Some accomplishments can be determined through this type of classifica-tion. Gifted program identification procedures illustrate this well: some school districts identify students in the top 15% for their gifted programs while others identify only the top 5% to 7%. Whether or not they use multiple criteria or just test scores to identify the child, a program that identifies the top 15% would rate that a Level 5 entry on the student's Talent Record. Other achievements made by the student might be much higher, but this entry would be rated at a 5, whereas a program that only identifies the top 5% to 7% would be rated at Level 4.

To those not familiar with the mobility of students from multiple states seeking school districts with the best gifted/talented program, the complexities this resolves may not be apparent. However for those who have administrated programs for the gifted, the experience of having students enter a school system having been identified as "gifted" in their former school in another state and then requiring remediation rather than enrichment or acceleration happens. Unfortunately, if students are identified for a gifted program because they are performing in the top 10% to 15% in an underperforming school, there is more than an outside chance that will not immediately carry over to a high-performing school. Again, with the purpose of providing the best match for talent development within each child, accurate classifications of measured achievements are most helpful.

There is nothing wrong with having a G/T program for any student performing in the top 15% of the population. However, thinking that participation in that G/T program translates equally to the student being able to perform in a program designed for the top 2% to 4% of the population is a disservice to all involved, especially the students. The concept of "formerly gifted" doesn't sit well with anyone. Where schools only provide programs for the top 2% to 4% of the national population, that program would be evaluated at a different level from the programs that identify the top 15%, thereby ranking achievement, not student.

Behaviors identified with each specific talent domain were cultivated from the research on behaviors identified as gifted, behavioral rating scales, and historical identification measures for gifted programs. The initial research was done between 1994 and 2008. Behaviors found in at least two sources that met the standards of the field of gifted/talented education, studies of expertise in various forms of psychology including neuropsychology, or research conducted within appropriate educational settings from individual content areas are included. It is not a comprehensive list, but what is here is research-based. The tool was designed to start a unifying conversation and be useful in every classroom. Behaviors are either observed or not observed so they are a qualitative measure and always ranked at the entry level of 5.

Outstanding behaviors and achievements are placed on the Talent Profile page and are organized according to three successive sequencing criteria: (1) chronologically, starting with the first year that a behavior or an outstanding achievement was observed (excluding any year in which no behaviors or achievements were observed); (2) according to the talent category, following the order outlined in the 1972 Marland definition; (3) according to the level of talent, starting with the least outstanding achievements within a given category. Thus, the Talent Profile can look like this:

Table 3.6

Talent Profiles with levels of talent identified

Sample Talent Profile Record for M

Grade	Talent Area	Level	Description
K	AR.v	5	Artwork is advanced
1	AC	5	Keen/alert observer
	CR	5	Acute sensory perception
2	AC	5	Unusually advanced vocabulary
		1	98%ile on CogAT test = Cluster group
	AC.l	5	RC "far exceeds 2nd grade reading and writing"
	CR	5	Tolerance for ambiguity
		5	Sensitive to aesthetic qualities
		4	1st & 3rd place PTA Reflections: literature
	AR.m	4	1st place PTA Reflections: music
	AR.v	4	Work selected for District Art Show
3	AC	5	Asks provocative, sophisticated questions
		2	99%ile on State tests
	CR	5	Willing to risk being wrong
		5	Curiosity/ energized questioning
	AR.m	4	1st place PTA Reflections: music
4	AC	2	98%ile State Tests
	CR	5	Sees various perspectives/viewpoints
		4	3rd place PTA Reflections: literature
	CR.t	3	1st place Odyssey of the Mind Regional
		2	1st place Odyssey of the Mind State
		1	12th Place Odyssey of the Mind World Finals
	AR.m	5	Started cello
		4	Advanced piano
		3	Piano for 3rd grade chorus concert + (See list of recitals)
		3	1st place district PTA Reflections: music
	PK.t	5	Soccer team, summer travel soccer

Key: Column 2: In order of appearance:
AR.v = visual art, AC = general academic
CR = Creativity, AC.l = Academic.language
AR.m = music, CR.t = Creativity.team
PK.t = Psychomotor/Kinesthetic.team
Column 3: Levels (as found on Summary page or as follows)
5 Basic (top 15%), 4 Moderate (top 2-3%),
3 (high (1/1000), Exceptional (1/30,000)
1 Extreme (1-2/million)

Table 3.6 (continued)

Talent Profiles with levels of talent identified

Sample Talent Profile Record for A

Grade	Talent Area	Level	Description
K	AC	5	Keen/alert observer
1	AC	5	Keen/alert observer
		5	Learns basic skills immediately
	PK.i	1	1st place Tri-state Karate Tournament
2	AC	5	Sponge-like absorption of knowledge
		5	Unusually advanced vocabulary
		1	98%ile on CogAT test = Cluster group
4	AC	5	Straight A's on report card
		5	Cluster Independent Study (IS) topic: Electronics
		2	98%ile on State tests
	PK.i	2	1st-4th Tri State Karate Competition
5	AC	5	Cluster Independent Study (IS) topic: Solar System
		5	Straight A's on Report Card
	CR.t	2	97%ile State Tests
		3	1st place Odyssey of the Mind Regional
	AR.m	2	3rd place Odyssey of the Mind State
	PK.t	5	School orchestra
	PK.i	5	Local soccer league
		NA	National Fitness Award

Key: Column 2: In order of appearance:
AC = general academic
PK.i = Psychomotor/Kinesthetic.individual
CR.t = Creativity.team
AR.m = music
PK.t = Psychomotor/Kinesthetic.team
NA= Awards that are received but do not qualify for a rating in terms of developing talent are recorded as such and receive a Not Applicable (NA) to position and define the accomplishment. As a communication/teaching tool the Talent Record must be inclusive to be most useful.

The Reference Set

To operationalize levels of talent in each talent field requires knowledge from experts in the specific area as well as careful examination of the criteria of each benchmark or award. A Reference Set of potential accomplishments available for each talent field at each developmental level with ratings on a 1 to 5 scale determined for each categorical achievement is essential to application of the complete system. The ranking of any entry in any field of achievement needs to be analyzed. The collection of specific details on the pool of potential information leads to a journey that opens dialogue between disciplines and areas of expertise.

This lays a foundation of support while establishing the validity of the instrument. For example, district curriculum coordinators and directors in various school systems across the United States were instrumental in ranking accomplishments pursued in music, athletics, and other areas. Also, criteria for awards were examined carefully.

Academic honors such as the Presidential Recognition Award for Academic Achievement can be deceptive. This impressively titled award merely requires an 85% average on two consecutive report cards. An award that, at first glance, appears to rank at the national level (1), actually reflects less than a level (5) achievement. If listed on a Talent Profile, it would need to state an NA for not applicable to rating scale. This would also assist with placement of "awards for participation" as well—acknowledging the completed activity as interest based. Choosing to include these NA events reflects the fact that the Talent Record system is also an important communication tool for everyone involved.

Each talent domain—intellectual ability, specific academic ability, creativity, leadership, visual/performing arts, and psychomotor ability—has behaviors and achievements associated with that particular domain. Some behaviors have been found in more than one talent domain. The Reference Set of possible entries for each of the talent domains provides a model that can and needs to be modified with additions found in particular contexts. (Ideally, a national or federally funded office could be far more comprehensive.) Each of the six fields of talent originally defined by Marland in 1972 has associated strengths and degrees of talent that may be applied to a Talent Profile record. Chapters 5 through 10 address each of the Reference Sets with supporting examples and a variety of examples of available achievements, providing a more focused introduction to the domain.

The Summary Page

The summary is a one-page grid with rows corresponding to the different talent domains and columns for the successive years from K to 12th grade. The highest level achieved that year in that particular ability domain (a number from 5 to 1) will be placed in the appropriate cell. A cell is left blank if there is no particular achievement in a given domain for a given year. This summary will allow a quick survey of (1) areas of strengths, (2) when new fields of talent become evident, (3) any gaps in talents previously present, and (4) a change in level—increase or decrease—for a given talent over the years. Realizing that talent development in children, especially young children,

Table 3.7

Summary of Talents

Name:

Academic/ Intellectual (AC)	K	1	2	3	4	5	6	7	8	9	10	11	12
Games (AC.g)													
Language (AC.l)													
Mathematics (AC.m)													
Science (AC.s)													
Social sciences (AC.h)													
Creativity (CR)	K	1	2	3	4	5	6	7	8	9	10	11	12
Individual (CR.i)													
Team (CR.t)													
Leadership (L)	K	1	2	3	4	5	6	7	8	9	10	11	12
As Individual (L.i)													
Team (L.t)													
Arts Visual/ Performing (AR)	K	1	2	3	4	5	6	7	8	9	10	11	12
Visual (AR.v)													
Acting (AR.a)													
Dance (AR.d)													
Music (AR.m)													
Psychomotor/ Kinesthetic (PK)	K	1	2	3	4	5	6	7	8	9	10	11	12
Individual (PK.i)													
Team (PK.t)													

Source: The use of these subcategories for the talent areas was either requested or most appreciated by teachers and parents in pilot studies.

Key: Levels of Talent:
5 = Basic (top 15%)
4 = Moderate (top 2–3 %)
3 = High (1/1000)
2 = Exceptional (1/30,000)
1 = Extreme (1–2/million)

Note: Chart reflects Academic/Intellectual overlap in developmental opportunities.
Only the highest level of talent attained in each year in every category cited on the Talent Profile page is noted here.

often does not grow in a linear fashion, it is a useful tool to use with students as they review accomplishments with regard to their desired next step in goal setting.

The Student's Blueprint for Learning

This is an outline for the dialogue that can occur between teacher and student, parents and child, two friends, or any other possible combination. The purpose is to help an individual take part in setting personal goals and benchmarks toward the development of the individual's chosen area of expertise or areas of exploration. The form of this step can vary tremendously depending on the student and the context. A discussion of the patterns and combinations of what is displayed on the student's personal summary sheet thus far *in combination* with the student's current interest(s) forms the foundation/basis for further possibilities, explorations, and growth.

Taking notes, sketches on graph paper, keeping a log or journal, creating a mind map, or developing a paper or electronic form are different ways to record the outcome of the dialogue. Learning to keep a journal consisting of words, drawings, and relevant mathematical formulas has additional merit as a tool of professional producers of ideas. A reflective self-assessment can also be obtained using the survey instrument as another measurement tool for a periodic review of his or her own "big picture" by the student.

THE TALENT RECORD SYSTEM AS A WHOLE

The components are designed as a system, but each component can be useful even when added progressively. There are Reference Sets of Possibilities for each talent domain and a formalized rating system for each entry, an individual's cumulative Talent Profile, and a Talent Summary Page, as well as a Blueprint for Learning form or journal.

The heart of the system is the Reference Set of Possibilities for each talent domain, which provides behaviors associated with each talent area gleaned from research and an overview of many potential achievements in each domain often available to students as gleaned from public school and private practice. The possible behaviors on the Reference List of Possibilities provide individual teachers with ideas for potential report card comments and an observation that can offer a positive start to the first parent-teacher meeting.

The completed Talent Profile provides a cumulative record of each student's behavioral strengths as observed in any context as well as accomplishments attained in all talent domains across time and situations. The chart of Degrees of Exceptionality provides a context describing the known parameters with regard to the field's demonstrated expertise and situates the student's current attained level of accomplishment within the top achievements available. The Summary page provides a synthesis and quick overview of the highest levels of accomplishments in each category for each year to mark patterns across time. The Blueprint for Learning page provides one possible way to help a student learn to design personal objectives to reach a chosen goal.

VENUES OF COMMUNICATION

The underlying purpose of the Talent Record is to provide communication and integration of pertinent data between observers, among all disciplines, and across time. The physical existence of a form that reflects information on all areas of accomplishment creates a "level playing field" literally as well as figuratively. When the field is level, there is an opportunity for academics to rise to the stature of music or sports in the minds of some, and for the arts to rise to the level of academics in the minds of others.

What a student does well may be the most important perception a teacher can share with the child and his or her family.[8] Ideally, with the Talent Record as part of formal student records, all teachers are provided with a record of student strengths, aptitudes, and talents as evidenced by their level of accomplishment in areas outside of school as well as within the academic world. This comprehensive identification of advanced talent development encourages a child to strive for continued excellence while at the same time serving as a communication tool for those seeking to provide appropriately meaningful challenges for each student.

If, in that class or any other environment, among a host of other learners, a child's characteristic behaviors consistently serve as a strength and stand out in the classroom, that qualitative judgment is useful in conjunction with other factors and observations. In the proposed system, the Reference Set of Behaviors provide possibilities for teachers to consider as they reflect on behaviors demonstrated by their students in the context of their classroom. Anecdotal evidence in the form of observations of descriptive behaviors provides all students with potential for an entry indicating a particular strength.

The six areas of gifted-level achievement identified by the U.S. government[9] helped reveal certain behavioral characteristics that were found in two or more studies. Behavioral Checklists based on these sample behaviors were then compiled for teachers, family, or community members as they seek to identify individual strengths of each child.[10] These checklists serve as a skeleton of possibilities with room for additions in behaviors or achievements related to talent development as they become available from the research.

The power of these observations increases with multiple reinforcement (i.e., many people seeing the same behavior become characteristic over time or in many contexts). The same checklist used by family, school, and/ or community members provides a common language to describe observed behaviors in a variety of contexts.

By triangulating the observed strengths and achievements of a child, the context is enlarged. Combining several perspectives from different points of view will hone the accuracy and could better identify when and what characteristic is emerging.

For instance, the behavior described as "Keen and alert observer (sees or gets more than others)" found on the Intellectual Ability Reference Set of Behaviors may look the same or similar to "acute sensory perception" found on the checklist of creativity behaviors or "advanced perceptual acuity is evident through attention to details" found within the Visual Arts context of researched behaviors. This may be a reflection of the fact that each domain does its own research and uses its own language to describe the same or similar behaviors of advanced attention and scrutiny to sensory stimuli. It also may not be the case. This requires further research.

What is important in the classroom is the context or contexts in which this kind of behavior is witnessed. There are students who will receive a check on each of the behaviors on a checklist as demonstrated on tasks reflecting each of those domains, and there are students who will demonstrate only this type of behavior in one of the contexts. None of us can accurately project what either of those observations actually indicates at this point. We can, however, record what we observed.

ADDRESSING CONCERNS

Other than kindergarten teachers who "do it all," some teachers may not feel "qualified" to rate student strengths in a particular area, such as performing arts or leadership. But the only qualification required is an ability/intention to *notice* behavior that significantly stands out in a particular setting. The purpose of this evaluation system is to provide a dialogue among as many people as possible. When the perception of each instructor is added to the efforts of a team of observers, the depth and breadth of a child's emerging record is enhanced algebraically.

This assessment is current and site- or context-specific. It is a snapshot, not a feature film. Noticing a specific behavior in a child does not predict future outcomes of any kind. Prediction can occur only if well-constructed educational research is conducted on a very large number of individuals. The idea that a child might be expected to continue as a creative writer once identified as such is as misinformed as the idea that once a child is labeled as poor in mathematics he or she owns that identity. (One could expound upon how many people leave childhood with that mistaken identity.)

Similarly, the expectation that talent will thrive with or without opportunities to do so is as invalid an assumption. While "cream may rise to the top of a container," unidentified talent has not been proven to have the same properties. In fact, some observations suggest just the opposite.[11]

Another advantage of providing a list of the known behaviors describing each of the talent domains is that it can enlighten those unfamiliar with a particular area of talent development. Just as it's important to be aware of the big ideas or underlying principles of a domain of knowledge, it is just as useful for educators to be aware of the behavioral strengths that have been found to be associated characteristics of expertise in each particular domain.

Some of these academic or creative behaviors may be apparent in a child when engaged in one particular subject area or as an approach to all learning. The descriptors are as pertinent for early childhood observations as they are for behaviors seen in high school students or adults. All students exhibit different behaviors at different times. For the purposes of this assessment system, the students for whom the behavior should be noted in their Talent Records are those who exhibit a specific behavior so intensely and frequently that they come to mind immediately when the behavior is mentioned.

The subjectivity of recording "impressions" of strengths as demonstrated solely by behaviors may raise concerns among some educators as well as some measurement specialists. However, if qualities that need improvement can be measured and recorded on a report card by trained observers (e.g., "needs to develop a more advanced vocabulary"), strengths can be defined by the same method ("often uses a very advanced vocabulary in class").

The breadth of useful observations is multiplied when all talent domains are examined and initial achievements are added to characteristic behaviors. The relevant behaviors characteristic of strengths pertinent to a specific new activity can be combined for review. To illustrate, in a problem-based science assignment a teacher may use the academic and creativity behaviors listed on both Reference Set of Possibilities to monitor exceptional observed behaviors on either list. If the activity required group interactions, leadership behaviors may become evident as well.

Reviewing relevant behaviors to write those names that stand out during or after an activity or as a weekly summary can lead to important observations by the teacher or any other observer. Many teachers have also found these lists of behaviors very helpful for writing comments on report cards. This is the most efficient way to officially document strengths for each child if a formalized system for the evaluation of talents is not yet in place.

NOTES

1   Wainer, 1997, *Visual Revelations*, p. 25.

2   Shore, Cornell, Robinson, & Ward, 1991, p. 60.

3   In most schools, test scores from standardized group ability tests are only used internally to help determine academic placement. Unless specifically requested, these scores are not shared with parents or students. Therefore a separate Aptitude Profile was used to record measurements that reach the talent levels. Also on that page of abilities are those measures like perfect pitch and speed/endurance measures evaluated in physical education assessments. This provided another "same page" categorization of innate abilities to place IQ scores in a familiar context for appropriate appreciation. Only achievements in games such as chess tournaments would be found on the Talent Profile with the IA designation.

4   Gross, 1995; Ericsson, 1996, p. 7.

5   Kay & Gagné, 1997 — For those achievements, based on standard deviations noted on the normal curve (Gross, 1995), a framework was established by altering Gagné's proposal (1995) of five levels that use the standard deviation (SD) units (+1, +2, +3, etc.) to fix the approximate cutting points for the successive levels.

6   When gathering the data about each of the domains, I interviewed many experts—starting at the local level. Department chairs, district coordinators, coaches of specific athletic opportunities, parents of children seeking Olympic-level status and pursuing specialties not offered in the school, religious figures in the community, PTA officers, and anyone and everyone with a useful perspective on these issues. Throughout the data collection, I ran into a lack of translation between measurement systems. As chance would have it, the mathematics chair was also a coach for track and field, so I went to discuss the dilemma with him. As a mathematician he immediately prescribed the percentile model used in academic ratings, but when I asked him how to translate equivalent accomplishments for his track stars, he fell into the silent surprise of insight unveiling the jarring difficulties between the two measurement systems. It was during that moment of silence that my unwavering decision to adopt the athletic model of number one being the best/most rarefied level of developing talent crystallized. The decision was carved in stone when that high school coach/ mathematician was the first to agree that it made the most sense to use the athletic system if this was to truly be used for communication of levels of achievement between disciplines.

7   Kay & Gagné, 1997.

8   An example of the importance of this communication is portrayed in the movie *Azaleh and the Spelling Bee* (2006) where teachers and administrators noticed and informed the child's parent of her exceptional ability and interest in spelling and again

in the film *Queen of Katwe* (2016) about a homeless girl in an African slum who becomes a chess master. Unfortunately, it is the extreme cases that seem to be made into films. Yet, the stories of a school person sharing a child's strength with parents happen all the time.

9 Marland, 1972. Also see the Nebraska State Department of Education's Identification Supplement to Rule 3.

10 This work was conducted by the author between 1998 and 2004.

11 Coleman & Cross, 2005; Csikszentmihalyi, Rathunde &Whalen, 1993; Ericsson & Pool, 2017; Kay & Subotnik, 1994.

Chapter 4

Recognizing Emerging Expertise

A teacher's greatest attribute is to find talents that students don't realize they have.

—Attributed to Vartan Gregorian[1]

Although much has changed in a child's world across the centuries, the effect of influential teachers has not. Outstanding teachers recognize strengths in their students and seek to nurture them with opportunities, challenges, and encouragement. The essence of a thank you from a student or the student's parents to a teacher is often gratitude for helping the student recognize a noticeable strength and develop it a bit further through appropriate challenges, exposures, and/or resources.

Some teachers hear from past students just how they influenced a life: "When I set the goal of being in the top ten in my class—you nonchalantly asked, why not first?" "You saw my talent and believed in me. So I believed you."[2]

The child-centered school administrator also cultivates a climate of appreciation and encouragement for excellence. One principal went beyond the daily announcements that celebrate and communicate to the community we call school. Whenever an individual or group effort led to an accomplishment, she would write exquisite letters for each student's cumulative file. If 50 students were recognized for an achievement in a music or academic competition, a personalized form letter did the job. This was in an elementary school with almost a 1,000 students.

Yet, in the long run and on average, when asked, "What do you do well?" the most frequent response from students of all ages is an honest "I don't know." It seems far easier for these students to list areas they have been informed are weaknesses—can't sing, dance, do sports or math. Solely focusing on what needs improvement in school grading procedures, may unintentionally embed that "can't do" attitude that severs further growth.

Some more fortunate students can provide a list of activities they like to do but quickly add that they do not know how to measure themselves at these achievements. The child who demonstrates interest and personal strength in any field needs to know where he or she stands with regard to the expectations of the field as well as what next steps to take to develop further. So do the child's parents. How else does an individual's potential and interest develop into an emerging talent?

No doubt an entire book could be written around times when this doesn't happen or why the proverbial glass is half empty, but this book is about the part of the glass that is full. Teachers that are credited for making a difference in the lives of their students do so by intuitively seeing potential in an individual, communicating the perceived strengths, and then encouraging growth in that area. This is also what occurs between athletic coaches, athletes, and parents. And it occurs between art/music instructors, students of the arts, and at least one parent or other advocate.

Athletic and art talent areas are built around a system of triangulated support between the parents/guardians and each current talent developer of a young talented person. However, not until later in the trajectory of academic talent does this personalized support exist and become the essence of a successful relationship with a mentor. Imagining a world in which these discussions between educators, students, and family members become standard and the foundation for all subsequent learning led to the Talent Profile concept.

TEACHER AS TALENT SCOUT

One of the greatest joys of teaching—at any grade level—is helping students discover their strengths and interests as new opportunities for learning are introduced. Providing teachers with an assessment tool that allows them to record and communicate observed strengths to all those involved with each child's care is a logical step toward improving cultivation of these observed strengths in all relevant domains.

A cumulative record of strengths and developing talents materializes from multiple entries from multiple perspectives and across multiple environments throughout the years. Classroom teachers also gain insights about unfamiliar talent domains by reading entries from colleagues specialized in a domain—so the Talent Record also becomes a built-in staff development tool for expanding expertise as a talent scout.

Understanding talent development directly impacts instruction. For example, differentiating instruction in the regular classroom is a popular instructional strategy. By definition, it describes a method of using several different ways to instruct different students simultaneously. Like all instructional strategies, there are various forms and degrees of success depending on how one alters the content, process, environment, and product by which the learners engage in their learning.

With a solid understanding of the elements of curriculum and instruction, the developing expertise of a teacher can involve knowledge of ways of identifying and developing individual talent as a framework for the differentiation strategies the teacher designs.[3] Providing a framework for differentiation that asks the teacher to be a talent scout is a minor shift in perception with a major impact.

TALENT SCOUT: "ACT ONE"—SEEING BEYOND CUTE: THE ELEMENTARY YEARS

When it came time to test the possibility these behaviors could help find an observed strength for every child, a Kindergarten teacher recognized as bright, very creative and dedicated was asked to track her time and see how long it would take to complete inputs for everyone on her class roster.

At the next meeting, all but one student had at least one observation recorded. In fact, this teacher felt that the behaviors would be useful in writing report card comments since she tried to make at least one positive comment about each child every quarter.

A week later at the next meeting, this teacher was quite visibly upset. Prefacing her concern, she stated that she is always at the forefront when it comes to women's rights, how she fights any type of stereotype on a daily basis, and how everyone perceives her to be a very candid, verbal proponent of all of her students all of the time. She was reminded that those qualities were precisely why she was asked to try this out in her classroom. Almost in tears, she mentioned one of her most adorable young ladies—then relayed her horror at discovering that until she was forced to focus on individual strengths, she had always thought of this child solely as the "ultimate in cute."

Once she tasked herself with recording strengths, she realized this child exhibited all of the academic *and* creative behaviors on the lists! She commented that if she could be this blinded by physical appearance, this tool was far more important than either of us had realized. This was an unforeseen contribution of the tool.

The conversation also led to the one student that remained on her list without an identified strength. He was undergoing a special education evaluation, and the Committee for Special Education (CSE) would be meeting the following week. In the interim, it was suggested that the auxiliary teachers (gym, art, music, health, computers) should be asked for their input. A week later, no strengths were found by any of the auxiliary teachers for the little boy that had just been classified by the CSE with a recommendation for education in a self-contained classroom.

With decades of classroom experience behind both the teacher and the researcher, a long discussion occurred over whether or not a child could exhibit strengths when not in the optimal learning environment. Pondering the possibility, she asked if the lack of ability to identify any strength might actually be used as a signal for a teacher to send a recommendation to the CSE. This is certainly an interesting hypothesis requiring further investigation.

Upper elementary school classrooms, by design, are not as intimate as the K-1 classrooms. However, even in a situation where a teacher sees 600 to 900 students per year (in art, music, physical education, or other subjects), individual strengths are as evident as individual weaknesses. What's more, teachers who specialize in a content area are, by definition, sufficiently expert in their subject area to identify students with talent.

Thanks to one excellent art teacher, a young man in fourth grade was chosen to submit his drawing to a state competition of student drawings depicting the 9/11 attacks. The student's drawing was selected from hundreds of entries for a show at the New York State capital. The most significant detail of this story is the fact that he had been classified as a special education student with severe learning disabilities. Once the school acknowledged this statewide artistic event, his reputation *among his peers* became that of class artist. Shortly after his persona's transformation, the family moved to another state. Because this state-level accomplishment was recorded on a Talent Profile for this boy, his reputation as an artist followed him to the new location.

These two examples of students with special needs, one having a difficult time in kindergarten and one a fifth grader who was suddenly redefined by his demonstrated talent, are worthy of further thought. Having a tool to identify strengths in all children is most valuable. The outcome for those defined by their weaknesses may be dramatically changed for the better when those weaknesses are balanced by strengths.

Most teachers find it very easy to identify student strengths when asked especially if they're provided with prompts and examples or benchmarks. They are however rarely asked to record observations other than those that seek improvements. One caveat in learning to look at strengths is that some of these behavioral characteristics can manifest themselves in negative ways. These negative perceptions can occur early in the life of a child:

> Even young gifted children can manifest positive or neutral characteristics in ways that appear negative (Clark, 1983; Kitano, 1990). For example, in young children, impatience with the regular curriculum can be manifested as disruptive behavior; persistence as stubbornness; hypersensitivity to others' feelings as vulnerability; nonconformity as lack of cooperation; perfectionism as refusal to attempt new tasks; and intensity of response and concern for injustice as overly critical behavior.[4]

A record of past behaviors and accomplishments could help focus further investigations and hone necessary differentiation strategies for successful adaptations to each new environment without annually reinventing the wheel by having to reassess what was already evident to another professional earlier.

TALENT SCOUT "ACT TWO"—CULTIVATING NATURAL RESOURCES IN THE MIDDLE YEARS

A middle school principal tells a parable to every new class of middle school parents at their first open house. It begins with their sixth-grade child entering a boat (middle school) on the lake (life) and needing to cross the lake to reach the teenage years. This lake has shallow waters and hidden rocks that can damage the boat, winds can appear out of nowhere, and weather is always a factor. He goes on to explain that what is about to happen to their child is a natural event and that developmentally we are all in for a rocky transition between fifth and sixth grades. With humor and kindness, he explains that hormonal and emotional challenges are behind many of these threats to a calm passage, promising these parents that by December they will wonder what happened to their wonderful child.

One minute they are talking to the child they know and love and the next minute a grumpy or hysterical stranger. He goes on to say that he tells this story to suggest that they, as parents are one of the oars of that boat and that the other oar is the middle school staff. Working together, they can help each of the children reach the other shore safely. It is a wonderful way to help all players see the importance of communication and working together.[5]

Reality Check

Some students have an inflated or otherwise unrealistic view of their capabilities. Perhaps inflated egos occur when the environment that surrounds a child or adolescent does not provide the challenges required for the necessary social and emotional growth needed to develop talents. This may occur most often with academic or intellectual talent when opportunities for growth are not extended. The young child might misconstrue the message from the environment as indicating he or she knows all there is to know.

A concrete example of unrealistic expectations is found in a common mismatch between the physical attributes of a child and his or her dreams regarding developed talent. Exemplifying unrealistic expectations, an eighth grader quite short for his age would eagerly share that he planned to be a basketball player. His parents, at a parent-teacher conference, described the doctor's appointments and the intense push their son was exerting on them to allow him to take growth hormones as part of a pilot study he had researched. It was a perfect segue to tell his parents about the goal he shared in class of becoming a basketball player. These parents were horrified at the possibility that his peers would tease him until they learned how gracious the students had been with each other's dreams, even those who had outgrown the magical thinking phase.

However, clearly a backup plan was needed. Discussing his varied strengths (and there were many) led to the possibility of providing him with opportunities to use his vast knowledge of basketball, his wonderful creative writing skills, and his enthusiasm to pursue several other activities. One idea was to write newspaper articles for the school paper. Another idea was to pursue an opportunity to try radio announcements during a game, and the third was to write short stories.

Although his parents refused the pilot study of the height-enhancing drug, no one said no to his dreams. Within a year he became quite renowned and enjoyed an esteemed reputation as a student sports writer for the school newspaper, a position he created. According to his parents, the desire to be a basketball player was replaced by a talent he was eager to and capable of pursuing. He went on to a successful career with a sports news organization.

Inflated egos are a bit more difficult to reform. High-achieving students may experience too few challenges as a result of the classroom environments they encounter. Building administrators often divide the academically advanced students equally among all classrooms to balance test scores for required teacher evaluations. This in turn means academically talented children are often the brightest in their class. Despite any and every teacher's attempt to promote cooperative learning groups, every student in every class knows who is most often correct or masters the material quickly and effortlessly. Regardless of any attempts at leveling the playing field by the teacher, student groups formally or informally assign a leader.

If group dynamics are not taught and continually monitored very closely (which is more difficult with more than one group), then academically advanced students may end up hating group work because they do all the work in order to meet their own sense of quality and the whole group gets the credit (a common experience described by middle school students). A far greater underlying problem is that these students really do not know how to work with others *as a team*.

Not only do they *think* they do not like to work as a team, they don't know how because they have never experienced the synergy and excitement of a team in which everyone contributes.[6] Teachers of the gifted, in their first experience teaching pullout classes for the gifted, very often observe the same phenomenon—through no fault of their own, these students really do not know the basics of working together to accomplish a goal.

In a group of intellectually similar members brought together for the first time in a pullout class, it is common to see that most of these young students do not know how to follow a good idea that is not their own. Some students are very uncomfortable with a situation in which they are not the first to know the answer or the group does not adopt their idea automatically. Sometimes this is called the "big fish, little pond" phenomena.[7] At times the response to the discomfort is so great that the students will claim boredom or disinterest in the class so that parents will allow them to quit an optional program.

These are the students that need extra help (from parents and teachers) to take the emotional leap into a situation where they are not always number one—moving into the "little fish in the big pond" prepares for new challenges that allow for further growth. The longer a child has been exposed to the unrealistic environment of always being the smartest in the class, the more difficult it is to adapt to the real world. Heightening their acute observation skills and intensive communication with parents/guardians, teachers need to join the parent support team to help students work through the discomfort of moving from one "pond" size to the other. Equipped with the additional skills of teamwork and cooperation, these students can more easily change the world.[8]

In contrast, in sports or the arts, talent development is hierarchical, and much of the time students are taught to focus on personal bests while familiarizing themselves with the next level or standard for the field. Additional support for this focus on "personal best" as the most worthy measure of growth can be found by reading biographical accounts of eminent people in a student's specific area of interest.

All that said, the number of students who have an exaggerated view of their demonstrated abilities is surprisingly small. In fact, public school teachers who have explored students' self-assessment in their classrooms find that students, if not realistic, often underrate themselves on a task or talent. This is in sharp contrast with research on adult self-perceptions of self-concept.[9]

TALENT SCOUT "ACT THREE"—
THE HIGH SCHOOL YEARS

Listening to the Salutatorian speech of a competitive gymnast talk about working hard to be successful at gymnastics was inspiring. She has known she needed to work hard to master every skill from perfecting a cartwheel to every other step of the way since she was eight years old. Nothing came easy, yet she claimed this is what kept it joyful and motivated her pursuit. She also noted in that speech that her colleagues with natural talents, often lost interest when the next step required advanced effort. Where she pushed herself to exhaustion from an early age, her gifted teammates grew tired of the sport when the more difficult moves required extensive effort. They left while she stayed. Her senior year marked the accomplishment of some of her longstanding goals enlightening her to the realization that the harder one must work at achieving a goal; the more meaningful one finds the success. Since many had watched her succeed, her pep talk for her classmates encouraged the effort to realize one's dreams in a most powerful way.

Beyond being very bright, she was always wise. Once, while in fourth grade, she came into the gifted/talented resource room to ask for an extension on a project. She explained that her classroom teacher had just assigned a long-term project that was due in three weeks—but in these next three weeks she had several qualifying gymnastics competitions at the state level that required much of her time after school. She could not work on both assignments and do them well during these three weeks. Fourth grade.

Several years later when students in that district were given a school-wide questionnaire asking what schools could do to help students develop their talents, her request was that teachers provide a yearly calendar of major assignments that required time outside of school. Requesting course outlines for fourth grade is more than reasonable for someone cultivating talent at the state, national, or international level.

Some students are as focused, motivated, and organized. Others need help. Many need help finding out what they enjoy and do well. There are also those who must choose between equally satisfying endeavors when the next level of accomplishment in each area requires a significantly greater investment of time.

Whatever the case may be regarding the cultivation of emerging talent, a cumulative record helps organize and summarize each individual's accumulated strengths and accomplishments in one place for a global review. Future options for talent development are easier to determine with a complete "portrait" viewed by all involved with the child's growth—especially the child.

It also serves students who do not have the support systems and/or financial resources necessary to pursue talent development opportunities. Some research suggests that other countries, such as Singapore, do better at providing opportunities for poor, bright, and motivated children than the United States does.[10] A record of outstanding behaviors and achievements provides potential advocates with necessary information to assist these students and their families realize a talent.

A Financially Challenged Case Study

The pathway from elementary to high school of one financially challenged student highlights some issues in a school community. Knowing that this one elementary student was enamored and very capable with computers, his teachers provided him with the opportunity to use one whenever he finished his other work. His computer skills became so advanced that he began helping his teachers. Yet he was the only one without a computer at home until a neighbor learned of his abilities and brought him a discarded one from work.

The neighbor learned of these abilities because his proud mother shared the third-grade report card comments commending him for his advanced abilities in mathematics and the computer. That neighbor responded by offering him that computer and arranging for the family to be included on her Internet account. A simple example of how sharing strengths among a community brings forth further opportunities—a small pebble with an enormous ripple in that particular lake.

There is more. As the oldest of several children of a single, working mother, he could not participate in after-school enrichment activities, as he was needed at home. But, the school was unaware of this reason. He claimed disinterest. The only clue that the school had of possible financial difficulty was a limited wardrobe (although many students choose to wear the same clothes every day). It was the cumulative record of his technical and mathematical accomplishments that helped advocate for him so future teachers would look beyond the detached and disheveled persona he conveyed to hide a more important secret.

One parent-teacher conference led to the disclosure. The boy had wanted to participate in an after-school program for a creative problem-solving competition called Odyssey of the Mind. After he qualified for a team, his mother came in to explain why he could not participate. She might be able to find someone to watch the other children, but they did not have the means to support any extra curricular activities. Proud and struggling to provide for her children, this mother was not accepting handouts or special consideration.

Throughout his school career, it took ingenuity (and generosity) on the part of administrators and teachers to provide opportunities with minor and not so minor fees for this student who would not have been able to participate otherwise. A way was also found to have his siblings and mother attend his first state competition in fourth grade by providing room and board because there "happened" to be an extra room and everyone else had already booked their motel rooms.

He continued as an active member of a different Odyssey of the Mind team each year throughout high school. His skills and talents always proved successful leading him to annually participate in state and global tournaments while having the tremendous travel costs that are typical of such participation covered by school families when the school budget prevented the full expenditure. Here again, administrators covered for this student from personal funds.

Suburban schools have some ways to provide for students in need through individual or group donations, particularly from child-centered teachers or administrators or their organizations, *when* the educational community is aware of the need. Urban schools receive and can obtain funding from a variety of different sources unavailable outside of big cities. Rural schools depend very much on their communities and the Internet.

Using the Talent Record as evidence of past performance facilitates communication with donors/scholarships or other opportunities necessary for development of an individual child's interest as well as expertise. It also helps bridge the great divide in a student's memory between who they are as a high school student and who they were earlier . . . a curious detached phenomenon an educator frequently observes when he or she is involved with students from kindergarten through 12th grades.

In that, according to autobiographies of eminent contributors to every field, many often found their defining interest between ages 8 and 12, a reminder of earlier demonstrated proclivities might assist the soul-searching and explorations of the teenage years. In fact, one might hypothesize that looking at a constellation of emerging strengths and talents across the early lifespan would facilitate better choices for post-secondary school and other life decisions that must be made in high school. Teachers and parents who used the Talent Profiles to help students identify potential directions to pursue in college thought so.

TALENT SCOUT SKILLS ADVANCE THE EXPERTISE OF TEACHERS

Teachers who understand and acknowledge the three Rs of good teaching—Recognize, Respect, and Reward individuals and their different strengths—in addition to the areas they need to strengthen will make a difference in their students' lives. These teachers will also have moved on from novice teacher toward the next level of their own expertise. It usually takes about five to seven years to master and then realize that curriculum is the easy part. The true complexities are within the interactions between students and instructional strategies that define the "instruction" part of curriculum/instruction.

An instructional strategist discerns what those experts in the field of K-12 education consider the essence of what goes on. Perhaps anyone can consider himself or herself a teacher if he or she imparts content knowledge. Instructional strategist is a more accurate 21st-century term for a concept that more precisely depicts the depth and breadth of what really happens, needs to happen, and used to happen more often to nurture potential in everyone within the highly successful classroom.

The work of an instructional strategist is to find the optimal match between each child's current position of knowledge and understanding within the content and identify the instructional scaffolding needed for each individual to successfully attain optimal growth in the subject area as predetermined by the curriculum. A talent record on every student can be a cogent tool for the efficacy of the instructional strategist (see chapter 11).

NOTES

1 President of the Carnegie Foundation, 2004, *TC Today*, p. 23.

2 Personal correspondence.

3 Gross, Sleap & Pretorius 1999; Gross, MacLeod, Drummond & Merrick 2001; Kanevsky & Kay, 1998, 2006; Passow, 1982; Treffinger, 1998; Van Tassel-Baska, 1988.

4 Kitano, 1990, p. 22. Also see Torrance, 1969.

5 Working with gifted sixth graders, I would remind them of this story and often ask whether I was talking to the teenager or the child at that particular moment. The question was always greeted with a laugh followed by an immediate answer. This gave everyone a sense of feeling secure in knowing that the tumultuous feelings where "normal." Emotional security is important as is feeling safe to explore new territories.

6 These misfires can occur often if not monitored with careful scrutiny. Just like the school librarians who, intending to encourage the depth and breadth of reading experiences, set up a competition to reward the student in each grade who had read the most books over the summer. With misplaced competitiveness, some winners read hundreds of books, four or five grade levels below expectation. If the competition rules had stated the books read must be "grade-level or above," other students would have received the acknowledgement/prizes the librarians had intended. As demonstrated by a discussion with enraged serious readers, one way to avoid this would suggest that district-wide initiatives include a student representative on the

committee who would see these loopholes. This committee work also serves as a means to provide authentic student leadership opportunities where there are few.

7 Marsh, 1987.

8 Some researchers are concerned that the social consequences of not having these skills are severe. See Coleman & Cross, 2000; Cross, Van Tassel-Baska, & Olenchak, 2009. This may be one way of encouraging healthy social development through ability peer contact (Shore, Cornell, Robinson, &Ward, 1991).

9 Dunning, Heath, & Suls, 2005.

10 Zakaria, 2006. Other issues are addressed in Lohman, Gambrell, & Lakin, 2008.

Chapter 5

A Look at Intellectual Aptitude (IA) Surfacing

My own interest in intelligence was able to evolve in large part because, in junior high school, when the head school psychologist threatened to burn my copy of *Measuring Intelligence* if I ever brought it into school again, my seventh-grade teacher, William Adams, supported my interest and encouraged me to pursue it.

—Robert J. Sternberg[1]

Introducing the "Marquis de Sade" of puzzles, an article in *The New Yorker* begins:

When Henry Hook was fourteen years old, living in East Rutherford, New Jersey, his grandmother gave him a crossword jigsaw puzzle for Christmas. Designed by Eugene T. Maleska, who became a legendary editor of the *Times* crossword, the puzzle had three parts. First, you had to solve the crossword puzzle on paper; then you had to fit the jigsaw pieces together in order to verify your answers. When you were done, if you looked carefully you could find a secret message zigzagging through the answers: "YOU HAVE JUST FINISHED THE WORLD'S MOST REMARKABLE CROSSWORD." Hook was less than impressed. Within a matter of days, he sent a rebuttal puzzle to Maleska. It contained a hidden message of its own: "WHAT MAKES YOU THINK YOUR PUZZLE IS MORE REMARKABLE THAN MINE?"[2]

As these two stories suggest, intellectual ability takes many forms. In educational practice it is most often identified in children beginning in second grade from scores on tests of intellectual abilities. However, as demonstrated by the Talent Records in chapter 3, test scores provide very little information compared to a cumulative profile of observed behaviors and demonstrated achievements.

70

This chapter focuses specifically on intellectual abilities by describing a few different ways astounding intellectual abilities have been observed in classroom behaviors and how these abilities manifest differently from those of other students identified for gifted programming as well as within the classification of "intellectual ability" itself. In providing these snippets of behaviors, the discussion of intellectual abilities can move beyond how one is identified or misidentified based on a test score, to include variations on the theme that merit consideration by every classroom teacher. In defining some of the parameters of this ability as seen without test scores, the usefulness of the Talent Record becomes ever more important as an observation tool.

One young third grader in a pullout enrichment class was enamored with a lesson on similes and metaphors. She had rarely spoken aloud in the class before, but this time she could not prevent herself from asking questions and providing sophisticated examples. After about two exchanges in the dialogue between us I remembered that I was not talking to an adult, but in fact standing in front of a third grade class. As I looked around at the baffled faces observing the discussion, the term "parallel universe" came to mind. Complimenting the child for her advanced connections and asking her to journal any other examples, the rest of the enrichment class was then geared back toward the scaffolds for instruction on metaphors needed by the other advanced students.

The context of this experience is a curriculum designed to develop critical and creative thinking skills in students identified as intellectually, academically, or creatively gifted. The introduction to metaphors took place at the beginning of the first year of the program to help instructors see the various degrees of flexibility and fluency in thinking currently evident in the class. Within a small class of students who had provided evidence of achievements three grade levels in advance of their current enrolled grade level, this child immediately stood out as thinking very differently than the other academically advanced students.

The child's student record and focused interviews with her parents and past teachers led to the fact that by third grade she always felt different. She had not yet found a friend and was quite unhappy. Children who feel different do not know or understand why. "Different" does not equate to better or worse in a child's heart. Without siblings or age-level playmates that saw things in a similar fashion, she felt alone in the world of children.

Her test records revealed she was one of a very few students whose CogAT (Cognitive Abilities Test) scores had topped the chart in its three subtests of verbal, mathematical, and figural reasoning, a phenomena known as "hitting the ceiling" of the test. When this occurs, psychologists tend to recommend using an individual IQ test to secure accurate measurement at this high end of development. However, schools do not provide this testing unless academic problems occur.

Every adult who worked with this child was most eager to address the child's social and emotional needs in order for her to prosper. Individuals suggested extra-curricular activities, summer programs, and multiple requests to uneager administrators for grade skipping to help her find an environment conducive to a friendship. When her parents and teachers finally succeeded in convincing the administration that she needed to skip a grade and scheduling was directed to put her in a class with another student with an extreme score on her IQ test, a friendship developed effortlessly. That friendship sustained her through high school, possibly longer.

Intellectual ability, due to its developmental advancement of cognitive stages, can look especially incongruous in a kindergarten classroom. The telltale sign for considering an early childhood teacher's request for grade skipping can be the reflection of behaviors by the other children in the class. Observing a child in the classroom as part of the procedure for considering grade acceleration can clearly illustrate these differences. Sitting near the child and carefully monitoring peer responses to the child's class discussions[3] as well as keeping a chart of peer interactions as either (a) making a personal connection or (b) asking this child for help can be powerful evidence in support for an appropriate affective environment. The list of *peer responses* to the child during a 45-minute observation, especially when peers have only included the child to ask for help, can double the power of watching the same child sitting alone at lunch and at recess.

The point of these two stories is one of awareness of what this might look like in a classroom to an observant teacher or administrator, and that this rarity, if found, needs to be a priority above all else. However, children with an extremely high IQ score do not necessarily encounter this difficulty of finding a friend, despite the tendency of cultural storytellers to embrace the stereotype of the intellectual outcast.[4]

No two intellectually able students are alike. Another student with an IQ score at the top of the measurement scale did not choose to demonstrate his abilities verbally. This student's spatial ability was evident in the maps and diagrams that surrounded his notebooks and the complex built environments that engaged his frequent focused attention. At the first opportunity this student delved into science projects, working models, or any other exploration that did not require verbal language. When forced to demonstrate his verbal capabilities, he was beyond able, yet remained uninterested in learning environments that focused on words.

Language challenges can also interfere. One year a teacher's aide came to see the district coordinator of gifted programs about a child she had been assigned to work with who had just come to the United States from Russia and did not speak English at all. She had spent a few days with him and noticed many of the behaviors that are currently listed in Table 5.1. As she described her interactions and his responses, she wondered if an ELL

(English language learner) student could be reviewed for inclusion in the middle school gifted/talented program.

Someone on staff was found who translated the CogAT test for this student in his native language. His scores mirrored the aide's observations providing enough evidence for him to be invited to participate in the program. Although the aide and coordinator were actually reprimanded for breaking district protocol that excused ELL students from this testing until they had been in the country a year, the assistant superintendent of curriculum and instruction defended the action.[5]

Most importantly, that student soared in the gifted program as well as in the rest of the school's offerings. He set a new bar for other students in the gifted program with regard to perseverance and gratitude for opportunities throughout high school. Thanks to a dedicated and observant teacher's aide, no time was lost in finding an optimal match. There is much discussion and debate among researchers surrounding the use of IQ or ability tests with regard to diverse populations including ELL students because of cultural and linguistic biases inherent in any assessment. Teachers' observations and continual assessment of learning behaviors are valuable constructs that are not yet systematically mined for future use.

INNATE DIFFICULTIES OF THINKING DIFFERENTLY

Unfortunately, high levels of abstract reasoning that allow gifted learners to "see the whole picture" immediately can actually backfire. For example, when students are asked to demonstrate the mathematical steps taken to arrive at an answer that seems as apparent to them as the color blue in the sky, these children can fail tests designed to assess content knowledge.

This true story illustrates the issue. When elementary students identified as intellectually able were failing or doing poorly on some new state-level tests, the district coordinator of gifted programs was asked to investigate why that was the case. The classroom teachers of these students, as well as the students, were interviewed. The new test required every step of a math problem be indicated accurately (as predetermined by test designers) as well as a correct answer provided. The teachers reported that these students went right to the answer without any steps after the translation from a word problem to a mathematical statement.

When the students were asked, they said they did show every one of *their steps*. In short, the solution was to teach the high-IQ students that they had to simply memorize the steps that others use so those who corrected the achievement test could follow along and check for accuracy. With a half-hour demonstration of what was being asked of them for that particular test and classroom teachers prompting them to "remember to show each step you learned" rather than "show all your steps," their perfect scores on subsequent state tests satisfied the district administration. This is a cogent example of how important it is to help intellectually able children adapt to a world that cannot seem to adapt to them. Knowing how others think is helpful to their understanding of their social environment and outside expectations as well.

Classroom experience suggests that students of all ages with a high degree of abstract reasoning as measured by aptitude tests also tend to make connections others don't see easily. These unusual, often interdisciplinary connections are more evident in young children who have not yet learned how unusual their thinking is compared to peers of the same age and so don't hesitate to talk about what they see. Nor do these children, who appear to automatically demonstrate this aptitude of transferring skills and knowledge to new situations, understand why it is also not obvious to others.

This is most notable when book learning is transferred to real-life situations or attempts are made to use knowledge learned in one domain for another. The natural tendency to make connections between two seemingly disparate entities or ideas is a skill necessary to boundary-breaking interdisciplinary thought as well as the understanding or creation of metaphors or analogies.

On the brighter side as well, the relationship between intellectual aptitude and its manifestations in games of strategy is relevant. Children and young adults with very high intellectual aptitude often approach thinking as a form of play. Many individuals with high verbal reasoning love to argue, debate, or look at multiple perspectives of an issue as if it is a sport. Reasoning with numbers and/or images/figures is just as important to notice in a child's games of choice. All of these pursuits could be listed on the Talent Profile. Some, like chess, are rated achievements with state, national, and international standards.

INTELLECTUAL APTITUDE PLACED WITHIN THE CONTEXT OF OTHER APTITUDES

Aptitude has been cogently described as "readiness" to provide a better general understanding of what intellectual aptitude tests actually measure.[6] There are other types of aptitude, and nesting this general reasoning aptitude within the context of the others that are measured in schools has provided much needed refocusing toward meaningful application of the information by all, especially school personnel. When the Talent Profile was piloted in a school system, an Aptitude Profile was included as well. As a separate page, it listed all aptitude measures, reinforcing translations between these aptitude domains.[7]

The type of aptitudes measured in schools vary: music teachers tend to identify perfect pitch when found, and physical education teachers assess endurance, speed, and flexibility often on an annual basis. Many schools continue to provide a measure of intellectual aptitude (IQ or ability test). There are also some measures of creative aptitude such as the three Structure Of Intellect (SOI) Divergent thinking subtests or the Torrance Tests of Divergent Thinking that are used in some districts. The SOI and Torrance tests measure divergent thinking using words, numbers, or images. Any scores in the gifted range would merit inclusion on an Aptitude Profile under creativity.

When intellectual, creative, and physical aptitudes are on the same page, a better understanding of the results of the intellectual aptitude measure often occurs among educators. And often this first-time realization of what the test score actually means eliminates the misunderstanding some teachers have that a high IQ score means the child does not have to be present when any new material is presented to the class. Nothing seems to work as well to eliminate this illogical behavior.

There were two reasons for continuing to separate the Aptitude Record from the Talent Profile page despite Ericsson's belief, as noted in the "Introduction" chapter, that any aptitude can be developed in everyone. First, pragmatically, and for all the right reasons, intellectual aptitude scores are kept as confidential school records unless requested by parents. These tests provide information to administrators mostly for purposes of special education placement. Knowing a child is in the average, below, or above-average range is sufficient information for most circumstances. Unless you have a background in educational measurement and will be altering instruction based on the level of scaffolding or steps needed as indicated on the measure, the test score is not properly understood anyway. These aptitude results help to explain to trained educators what needs to be done and as importantly, what does not need attention.

For example, a child with perfect pitch requires quite different instruction in vocal music from those who appear tone deaf. Identifying untrained abilities or "levels of readiness" provides useful knowledge for those designing the training or learning opportunities of those with a particular aptitude.

Secondly, the presence of a high score in any of the ability domains might lead to a reduced amount of effort as individuals and parents misunderstand and think effort to improve is unnecessary. On the other hand, the observed strengths and level of expertise achieved thus far as recorded on each child's Talent Profile page of the Talent Record are useful to everyone, especially the student seeking a next step.

Table 5.1

Sample of Reference Set of Possibilities: Intellectual Ability (IA)

Observed Behaviors

5	Has unusually advanced vocabulary/large amount of information
	Keen and alert observer (sees or gets more than others)
	Demonstrates a sponge-like absorption of knowledge
	Looks for similarities (compare) & differences (contrast) in events, people, things
	Often demonstrates insight into cause-effect relationships
	Understands underlying principles/makes valid generalizations (= quickly learns from errors)
	Asks many provocative (not just factual) questions
	Becomes intensely absorbed in certain topics/problems/ideas
	Transfers skills/knowledge to new situations (applies book learning to real-life situations or from one field of study to another)
	Displays highly abstract reasoning in a symbol system (words, numbers, images)
	Learns basic skills immediately, almost intuitively
	Exhibits fast, accurate recall of information
	Seeks complexity, challenge
	Likes to organize people or things, often through complex methods, games
	Exceptional memory is evident
	Makes connections between seemingly unrelated topics, sees bigger picture
	Shows an exceptional ability to solve problems
	Demonstrates an advanced sense of humor
	Prefers being with older children

Source: These *sample* behaviors were found in more than one research study. The descriptors listed here resonated with classroom teachers when piloted.

Note: Best strategy for choosing a match: Read the behavior and see which student(s) comes to mind immediately. If there is no immediate response, skip it and move to next behavior. You do not need to use any of these at all unless it is extremely accurate. A 'maybe' is not useful.

Table 5.1 (continued)

Sample of Reference Set of Possibilities: Intellectual Ability (IA)

Sample of emerging intellectual acievements (outside of academics)

5	Enjoys games of strategy (chess, GO), plays chess regularly with peers/club, chooses to do puzzles for fun, subscribes to puzzle magazines, reputation as a 'Jeopardy wiz', prefers adult crossword puzzles as elementary student, outsmarts computer games, exceptional memory for retelling stories, creates puzzles enjoyed by peers
4	Plays in local chess tournaments and/or often wins against adults, member US Chess Association, member Debate team, creates adult-level puzzles
3	County level award in competitions, ranked by US Chess Federation
2	State level awards, enters national competitions
1	National awards or International awards

Source: Author's research of relevant literature and pilot studies.

TRANSLATION PROBLEMS IN THE CLASSROOM

The purpose of this section is to explain the usefulness of including test scores on the aptitude part of a Talent Record. Scientific research in several fields continues to broaden knowledge and understanding of intellectual abilities, yet these findings rarely seem to be part of staff development updates. This lack of knowledge as well as lack of any training in understanding test scores may be the main reasons many educators claim to have no use for the scores and never look at them.

In order for teachers to use an intellectual aptitude test score correctly, one must realize that it is not an absolute score like a math test where one may get an 80 out of 100 of the answers correct.[8] In fact, each aptitude score marks the middle range or "ballpark" score, so that, given the parameters defined by the specific test, one can locate the range of ability. For example, on the CogAT test, the instructions for interpretation of Form 5 state that there is a standard deviation of 16 points. This means that with 100 as the middle point of the distribution of scores, a score of 120 can be interpreted as ranging between 112 and 128. Most students will fall around the 100-point score on the distribution, which is considered average ability (between 92 and 108). The 120 score marks the beginning of one standard deviation above average, and 80 (one standard deviation below average) indicates a range of limited ability.

The CogAT test[9] is administered and designed as a group aptitude test. Each report provides a verbal subscore, a quantitative subscore, a nonverbal subscore, and a composite score. In other words, if a child has a 120 verbal subscore, a 101 quantitative subscore, and a 105 nonverbal subscore the child may be slightly more capable and comfortable reasoning with words than with numbers or images. The likelihood that this child could be appropriately challenged within regular instruction in mathematics may be good because most teaching is so verbal that it is less of a problem in the early years of mathematics curriculum. However, knowing that extra scaffolding may be necessary in mathematics or scientific diagrams is critical.

The most important information for teachers that is provided by a group aptitude test like this one, it seems, is the understanding of the relationship between the three subscores for a particular individual. Solid evidence of learning difficulties is reflected in subscores that have a 15-point spread. Children with the most difficulty in school have a much lower verbal score than their quantitative or nonverbal score. This makes sense since most teaching and learning is set up to involve mostly words. Children with individual subscores that differ by 15 points with below-average or average scores have been classified as having a learning difficulty that requires mild special education services.

It is also possible (and happens more often than one would think) for students with a score of 150 on nonverbal and quantitative subtests of a CogAT to have a score of 120 or 112 in verbal reasoning, demonstrating over 30 points between subtests with their weakest area of reasoning in the area that is most frequently used to teach new concepts in school—words. But they are rarely, if ever, considered for special services. Noting a high score in nonverbal or quantitative subscores without a verbal score on the record might provide a useful clue if not a key for the informed teacher.

Because their school achievement meets minimum standards, these students do not qualify for special education services under the current definition. A child with a high nonverbal score will benefit from visuals depicting the content normally only delivered in verbal form, but there is far more at stake here. The need to define and address twice-exceptional or "2E" learners has come into better focus in special education research.[10]

Can a test result be wrong? Yes. Especially at a young age, there is the possibility that an individual child will perform uncharacteristically low or high on this measure. Every once in a while (maybe one year out of five), a second-grade teacher among the 15 or so in a medium-sized district will be outraged by the discrepancy between the test score of a child and the advanced behavior that child demonstrated in the classroom. Fueled by the discrepancy, the teacher could gather the anecdotal evidence to dispute the score. But, in the long run and on average, the test results will provide the best gauge for the *pace of learning appropriate to the person.*

Tracking the biannual results of an individual from second grade through seventh or eighth grade on a Talent Profile record provides a very clear set of snapshots of the individual's ability to reason. If a child has a bad year, it will stand out from the individual pattern. The consistency across time for most students is a powerful support for correctly interpreting scores on the instrument rather than eliminating it from the educator's toolbox.

Research has shown that the best predictors of increases in academic learning in a field are the ability to reason in the symbol systems of that domain, interest, persistence for excellence, and current achievement in that domain.[11] It has been said that "general reasoning abilities in the symbol systems of the domain are more important for novices whereas prior achievement becomes more important as students acquire expertise."[12] This developmental perspective of expertise is quite informative to educators as it demonstrates the interactions between ability, talent development, and expertise as they progress over time, especially when depicted on the Talent Profile page(s) of the Talent Record.

Other misunderstandings by teachers regarding the use and interpretation of these test results, especially at the high end of the scores, are also a significant problem. One simple problem to fix is the belief that a child with a very high score is expected to be able to know something without ever having been taught it. Teachers who present a new lesson while gifted/talented students are involved outside the classroom and do not make provisions to address that absence need remediation with regard to their own understanding of intellectual ability. In-service training in understanding and translating the scores of the tests used by the particular school can address these gaps in knowledge.[13] Incorporating the information from the tests within the context of a student's talent record would help reduce the gap in addition to focused professional development for teachers.

There are many group intellectual ability tests on the market. School districts choose which, if any, of these they will use. Interestingly, in searching for ways to provide a level playing field of equivalent accomplishments for this Talent Record system, no studies were found where all of these group IQ tests were compared so that instructional practice could benefit from a deeper understanding of the differences between the measures and the ranking of individual scores. A comprehensive chart of the various instruments, with how and what they measure would greatly benefit educational practice.

In addition to group ability tests, psychologists administer individual intelligence tests that are considered to be more accurate than group measures of abstract reasoning. The American Psychological Association is a major professional organization in the United States, and their website can be helpful in locating information as well as resources: http://www.apa.org/science/programs/testing/find-tests.aspx. An active organization for learning more about intellectual ability is the Mensa Association (http://www.mensa.org).

Intellectual aptitude can be applied to any talent domain or set of achievements. Just as individuals with perfect pitch may find this capability useful in developing their musical talent; they may experience the world differently than others because of the aptitude or may pursue a scientific career that utilizes this condition,[14] the same situation is true for intellectual aptitude. In fact, there are examples of high-IQ performers in many fields of study including and especially in the entertainment industry.

Most of the behaviors associated with intellectual aptitude are often entwined with academic achievements or games of strategy such as chess, both in the research literature and observations of developing expertise in practice. Because of this, many of the behaviors listed under intellectual ability are also listed under academic ability. However, there are observable differences in the classroom. The telltale signs are often the first three behaviors listed on the chart of behaviors provided: making connections that many adults would not see; making attempts to transfer skills/knowledge to new situations whether or not that transfer was successful; and/or displaying highly abstract reasoning in a symbol system and enjoying translating between symbol systems (e.g., word to mathematical symbols, images for mathematical concepts). So much more will be discovered, but there is much that can be immediately put to better use.

A GENERAL "WORD" ABOUT COMPETITIONS

One way of extending learning opportunities in the educational milieu of all high-achieving students, not just those with high intellectual ability, is through competitions and contests. Some competitions can assist high school students pursuing the development of academic, artistic, or athletic talent in moving to a very high level of expertise (e.g., Intel Science Talent Search, Guggenheim Fellowship, Scholastic Art and Writing Awards, Olympic Team tryouts).

Yet, competitions and external evaluations have been identified as contributors to underachievement,[15] rewards perceived as punishments,[16] and extrinsic motivation a negative influence on creativity.[17] Competitions have been viewed by some as immoral or unhealthy activities for everyone, although the samples used in those studies focused on student populations defined as having difficulty[18] or perceptions solicited from adults.[19]

This may be too simplistic especially in light of the fact that competition with oneself to do one's personal best appears to be a very grounded and noncompetitive strategy. In fact this strategy is used by many people working at the beginning or the high end of talent development—as an emerging talent or professionally at the top of a talent domain.

Despite the fact that competitions are often frowned upon by some educational researchers, experts including scientists and entrepreneurs have and continue to pursue financial awards offered via contests and grants by private and government agencies such as NASA's annual Centennial Challenges[20] and the Goldcorp Inc.'s Red Lake mine online challenge to geologists.[21]

In the *2010 Writer's Market*,[22] a resource for professional writers, there are 36 pages of contests and awards; the *2017 Writer's Market* has 86 pages listing them.[23] Historical examples of cash prizes inspiring innovations include Charles Lindbergh's flight across the Atlantic to win the $25,000 Orteig Prize.[24] Perhaps the problem is not with competitions but is the lack of formal training in healthy competition strategies. Or, perhaps, it is a more appropriate option when one has reached the highest level of expertise. The role of competition in outstanding performance continues to receive much needed attention.[25]

While educational researchers debate whether or when competition can have negative effects on intrinsic motivation,[26] students throughout the world are engaged in a variety of competitions beyond sports and arts auditions, as individuals or in teams. Some of the joys of competition that students describe are the ability to meet kindred spirits, the tacit knowledge that travel opportunities provide, an opportunity to delve into something that captivates their interest, a chance to learn about oneself, and to learn how to handle victory and defeat gracefully, and admire others' abilities/solutions.[27]

For those interested in helping students engage in a productive experience with competitions or contests, the NASSP—National Association of Secondary School Principals—has provided an important service by annually reviewing competitions submitted to them for evaluation. The five criteria they use to evaluate student opportunities are educational value; financial support; organizational structure; promotional accuracy; and fair, appropriate adjudication.

Since 1941, they seek to ensure that the experience is educational and the student's best interests have been kept in mind. As such, most building and district-level administrators encountered use this as a reference for their decisions regarding approval of a new contest or competition requested by faculty or parents. Their National Advisory List of Student Contests and Activities provides approved competitions and is available at a link on their website: https://www.nassp.org/news-and-resources/nassp-approved-student-programs?SSO=true.

There are also several useful books listing opportunities (see especially those by F. Karnes 1985; 1997; 2005 and issues of *Imagine* magazine, a resource for teens published by CTY at Johns Hopkins). The next chapters provide examples of specific opportunities.

FOR FURTHER CONSIDERATION

Using a few examples, this brief look identifies some of the complex issues surrounding identification of demonstrated intellectual ability in school settings. So much more could be useful, beginning with a chart of equivalent scores for the group IQ tests that different schools use. For example, what sets of scores on the Raven test used in some states are roughly similar to those on the CogAT that is used in many districts elsewhere?[28] How might individual IQ tests be charted in relation to scores on these tests designed for groups?

The issue and concentration on competitive opportunities come honestly from the requests of students and their parents seeking something more. So does the focus on positioning intellectual abilities among aptitudes regularly measured in schools where physical (endurance, speed, charisma) and auditory (perfect pitch) are the most commonly reported and understood. This map provides an enormous repositioning of tacit beliefs by most teachers and parents with incomplete information and places it in a more familiar context to invite understanding. No doubt more would be better, but this is a large step from what exists.

NOTES

1   Sternberg, 2000, p. 64. And he went on to develop a well-regarded theory of intelligence, see Sternberg, 1985.

2   Bilger, 2002, p. 64. Also see Davidson & Sternberg 1984 for more on the role of insight.

3   Watching others *not* respond to or piggyback on what the child said as if nothing was said or observing moments of awkward silence before someone else presents an unrelated comment without any acknowledgment of what the bright child had offered. My 'go to' reference on early childhood expertise on highly intellectual giftedness in the US is the work of N. Robinson, starting with Robinson & Robinson 1982. M. Gross's work is also stellar.

4   Of all the extremely high-IQ students I have worked with over 30 years, there were only several students whose environments needed adjusting to address friendship.

5   In fact, knowing that every student had the opportunity to demonstrate potential through learning behaviors followed by further substantiation was pivotal to the success of the identification process for the g/t program.

6   Lohman, 2005a.

7   Cropley, 2000; Kay, 1999; 2001a.

8   For an interesting brief history of psychology's early efforts to measure intelligence, see A. Kaufman's history of IQ at https://www.youtube.com/watch?v=hZxXaLZILBg.

9   R. L Thorndike and E. Hagen designed the original Cognitive Abilities Test. The author for Form 7 is David Lohman. For more information visit http://www.hmhco.com/hmh-assessments/ability/cogat-7#overview-program-author. I used CogAT 6 by Lohman & Hagen 2001.

10   Baldwin, Omdal, & Pereles, 2015.

11   Hagen, 1980.

12 Lohman, 2005a, p. 10. Other voices on this issue are Sternberg, 1999; Subotnik, 2003.

13 In the spirit of full disclosure and to highlight some of the more complex problems that occur over what these test scores might mean with regard to instructional strategies, I sought advice from one of my mentors, Dr. Elizabeth Hagen (coauthor of the CogAT test my school district happened to be using!). Years of discussions followed regarding the translation of what these score patterns mean with regard to instruction which were pivotal in my helping teachers understand how to use the scores to benefit learning in the classroom. The CogAT test is now supported with a chart of profiles designed to help translate scoring into practical information for teachers and parents. The website containing the Abilities Profile System is now found under Ability Assessments: http://www.hmhco.com/classroom/classroom-solutions/assessment/assessment-type.

14 At least one research study refutes this definition of perfect pitch as an aptitude (Ericsson & Pool, 2017) claiming early deliberate practice can develop perfect pitch.

15 Whitmore, 1980,

16 Kohn, 1993.

17 Amabile, 1993.

18 Kohn, 1993; Whitmore, 1980.

19 Amabile, 1993.

20 Hitt, 2007.

21 Friedman, 2007.

22 Brewer, 2009.

23 Brewer, 2016.

24 Hitt, 2007, p. 45.

25 Worrell, et al. 2016.

26 Ceci, Koestner, & Ryan, 2001; Cameron, 2001; Davis, 2001. See Ruenzel 2000 for another take on this issue.

27 *Imagine* Editor, 1999, pp. 4–5. Also see Ozturk & Debelak, 2008.

28 See, for example, Lohman, Korb, & Lakin (2008) for a comparison of the Raven, NNAT, and CogAT when identifying gifted English language learners.

Chapter 6

A Look at Emerging Specific Academic (AC) Ability

Childhood and genius have the same master-organ in common—
inquisitiveness.

—E. G. Bulwer-Lytton[1]

Cultivating the natural resources of curiosity and wonder as they emerge, whenever and wherever the sighting occurs is at the core of this Talent Record system. The journey from that first spark of interest to the first investigation, although often observed is rarely recorded and communicated to others.

What begins as informal guidance can and does occur naturally in the home, community, and schools by anyone interested in the child. Autobiographical accounts, research on talent development, and research on expertise, at its highest levels, often point to an individual's early childhood discovery accompanied by a knowledgeable support system that ideally works as a team to ensure a long trajectory of serious joy in the pursuit.

Despite this information, educational practice has no system of monitoring and recording the cultivation of each child's curiosity and wonder. Enrichment is ad hoc, talent development left mostly to chance.

This is especially evident in journeys of academic talent. Two stories illustrate the fact that talent alone, even in the most encouraging of circumstances, has a complex journey to actualization.

Janet Conrad, a female physicist known for her experiments to detect elusive sterile neutrinos, pinpoints her moment of wonder and awe in discovering the universe to be "at 3 a.m. on a cold autumn night"[2] as a teenager helping her father, a scientist farmer, with an experiment. The article on her continues to credit the local 4H club as providing early training in requisite practical skills, her parents for the adult conversations about how the world works, and being challenged by puzzles that her Nobel laureate (chemistry) uncle provided. The uncle also offered his undergraduate niece summer housing and suggested names for her to contact to pursue summer employment, which is how she began her career at Fermilab. Few talented teenagers have this many of the pieces to her chosen future's map at hand.

An article in a local newspaper sums up the trajectory of a less supported but also gifted female scientist.[3] The article cites age eight as the moment when Dr. Margaret Johns found wonder and awe in the act of discovering. Accordingly, she began school at age 4, graduating from high school at age 16. In spite of her precocity, she was advised (as a woman) to marry a doctor since she was interested and capable in science and to pursue her talent and interest in art as a homemaker.

Although she married and started a family, she needed more: " 'I wanted to be,' Johns says, 'I didn't want to sit on the sidelines.' "[4] She took a biology course at night because she was "fascinated by questions."[5] Her instructor strongly encouraged her to go on for a doctoral degree. Stealing chunks of time from motherhood and family life, she followed her calling and eventually enrolled in a doctoral program at Rutgers University because their stipend made it possible.

Her research proposal (environmental control of ovulation in mammals) was well received by the head of the Institute of Animal Behavior who supported and encouraged her. Unfortunately, he died a year later, taking her support system with him. However her doctoral research (discovery of the function of the vomeronasal system as the pheromone-sensing organ) was quickly published in *Nature*, with the editors predicting that her discovery "to become known as The Johns Effect, would lead to an important new field in reproductive physiology."[6]

Possibly due to the fact that there is tremendous concern for the lack of females in science and mathematics fields, the mystery behind the change in direction from her fame in science as a young adult fueled the impetus for the local newspaper article. Apparently a then-recent *Wall Street Journal* article on the renowned David L. Berliner cited Dr. Johns's contribution to the field. The local article caught more of the details:

> Even nicer than the article was the letter from Berliner to Johns: "There can be only one discoverer," he wrote. That is you. Without Margaret Johns, there would be no field." (Abramo, 1996, p. 13)

This is not a story complicated by economic, racial, or cultural factors. The important point here is that, although Margaret Johns made significant valuable scientific contributions at the beginning of her career (actually two, one in another scientific area during her post doc), talent and expertise were not sufficient to fuel her continued success. She also needed the encouragement of teachers and a mentor to navigate the cultural waters of her chosen field.[7]

REFERENCE SET OF POSSIBILITIES FOR K-12
SPECIFIC ACADEMIC

The set of behaviors and some of the achievements found on the following chart for noting specific academic ability are of a general nature. These general characteristics may be found throughout all of a student's academic endeavors, and as such, should remain in the general category (AC). However, if some or all of the behaviors appear in only one or two academic disciplines, they should be listed under the specific academic discipline in which they have been observed (e.g., AC.l for language and AC.m for mathematics).

This sampling of possible achievements is designed to provide an idea of the abbreviation that would be found when talents are profiled with the degree or level of achievement each would receive (5 = lowest, 1 = highest), as well as a description of some of the variety of accomplishments that have been available.

Developing academic knowledge in all children is a core purpose of schools. General content and skills in each of the subject areas are a reflection of local, state, and federal standards for all children. Current society's values as determined by government standards influence the given curriculum. So, for example, the current focus on STEM (science, technology, engineering, and mathematics) follows several decades that focused on acceptable test scores on English and Mathematics state tests to the detriment of science and social studies instruction in elementary schools during the last part of the 20th century and first part of the 21st century.

This top-down approach merely provides guidelines for a basic curriculum for all. It does not suggest ways of cultivating a student's natural interest and proclivity in any of these academic areas. Note how few entries of academic coursework, not test scores, are listed on the Reference list beyond high school opportunities for Advanced Placement (AP) or International Baccalaureate (IB) courses. Talent development in an academic area requires significant modifications to the general academic plan.[8]

Table 6.1

Sample of Reference Set of Possibilities: Specific Academic (AC)

Observed Behaviors

5	Has unusually advanced vocabulary/large amount of information
	Demonstrates a sponge-like absorption of knowledge
	Often demonstrates insight into cause-effect relationships
	Looks for similarities (compare) & differences (contrast) in events, people, things
	Keen and alert observer (sees or gets more than others)
	Understands underlying principles/makes valid generalizations (= quickly learns from errors)
	Asks many provocative (not just factual) questions
	Becomes intensely absorbed in certain topics/problems/ideas

Source: These *sample* behaviors were found in more than one research study.
The descriptors listed here resonated with classroom teachers when piloted.

Note: Best strategy for choosing a match: Read the behavior and see which student(s) comes to mind immediately. If there is no immediate response, skip it and move to next behavior. You do not need to use any of these at all unless it is extremely accurate. A 'maybe' is not useful.

Sample of emerging general academic achievements (followed by samples from each discipline)

5	Straight A's on report card, A Honor Roll, Extra credit/independent study, pursued optional enrichment offered in class
4	Member honor society or Academic League, selected for Knowledge Masters Open competition, Quiz Bowl, Future Problem Solving team, Honors course, G/T program, Distance learning course, content of independent study investigation is beyond grade level expectation, subscribes to adult or professional journals in field
3	County level award in competitions, exemplary performance in G/T program, advanced 1 grade level in subject area, enrolled in International Baccalaureate (IB) or Advanced placement (AP) courses
2	State level awards, advanced 2 grade levels in a subject, receives college credit for on-line or correspondence courses, excels in IB course, enters national competitions
1	National awards, advanced 3 or more grade levels in a subject, skipped a grade, early entrance to college, Simultaneous enrollment in two grade levels (like freshman in college while senior in high school); International awards

USEFUL INSTRUCTIONAL MODIFICATIONS

Prior to any academic curricular accommodations there exists each child's personal land of curiosity and wonder that can be fleetingly spotted anywhere, anytime, and by anyone. For those students with a budding interest in almost any academic field or area of endeavor, beyond other reference books and biographical stories, there are published directories of youth organizations[9] that include national honor societies as well as professional organizations that reach out to beginners by publishing junior newsletters or journals (e.g., American Numismatic Association for the coin lover) and offering scholarships. If these older hard-copy resources can be found, they offer children, especially those with undefined interests, a world of possibilities to explore further online.

Table 6.1 (continued)

Sample of Reference Set of Possibilities: Specific Academic

Sample of possible achievements in language (AC.I)

5	Savors Scrabble, puns, rhyming activities, top of grade level in reading bands; 90-95%ile on DRP (Degrees of Reading Power) or reading or vocabulary subtests (IOWA); top 3 in classroom spelling bee; writing for school publications; school reporter; announcer; subscribes to age-appropriate journals in field. Member Debate team; school newspaper, literary journal, poetry club; Studies a language other than English (LOTE); participation in community-based extracurricular courses open to all (local library, and so on)
4	End of grade 2 reading level band as 1st grader; 96-99%ile on DRP or IOWA subtests; top in grade level/school for spelling bee or other language based contests; accelerated courses; subscribes to adult or professional journals; advanced in language other than English (LOTE); participation in language-focused correspondence courses from identified talent search or university Saturday/ summer program courses. Maintains a blog or other writing source with followers.
3	End of grade 3 reading level band as 1st grader; > national median in Regional Talent Search language score (gr.5-7); County level award in regional competitions, exemplary performance in language-based G/T program, Advanced placement (AP) courses, internship/volunteer/paid writer for local newspaper
2	State level awards including Regional Talent Search certificate (like Johns Hopkins CTY in the Northeast, Duke in the South, Northwestern in Midwest and Stanford in the West) awarded at State Ceremony; advanced 2 grade levels in a subject, receives college credit for on-line or correspondence courses, excels in AP course, enters national competitions
1	Johns Hopkins CTY (Northeast) or other regional Talent Search award or other National awards, advanced 3 or more grade levels in a subject, nationally published article, book, poem; International awards

Table 6.1 (continued)

Sample of Reference Set of Possibilities: Specific Academic (AC)

Sample of possible achievements in mathematics (AC.m)

5	Straight A's in mathematics on report card, 90-96%ile on IOWA subtests in math & advanced math; Math Club member; subscribes to age-level math puzzle magazines, participates in math circles, blogs, free math sites on a regular basis
4	97-99%ile on IOWA or other achievement test for math; top 5 scores for grade level on NYS math test; subscribes to adult or professional journals in field; helps older sibling with their math homework
3	County level award in grade level math competitions; > national median on CTY math test; ranked as top 3 in state for NYS Math League Contest; Participant in USA Math Talent Search; advanced 1 grade level in subject area, enrolled in Advanced Placement (AP) math courses
2	Talent Search Certificate awarded at State Ceremony; Advances beyond round 1 in USA Math Talent Search; Participant in MAAAMC8 as 5th-7th grader; other State level awards in math, advanced 2 grade levels in a subject, receives college credit for on-line or correspondence courses, excels in AP course, enters national competitions
1	National awards such as Talent Search Regional Award or further recognition in Mathematical Association of America's American Mathematics Contests or USA Math Talent Search, advanced 3 or more grade levels in a subject; International awards

Sample of possible achievements in science (AC.s)

5	Science Fair participant; reads age-appropriate science journals on a regular basis; active member 4HClub; member natural history museum; maintains a collection of scientific "artifacts"
4	Participates in summer/Saturday community courses/lectures on archeology/geology or other scientific discipline; Science Fair award; subscribes to adult or professional journals in field; honors courses;
3	Advanced 1 grade level in any topic area, Advanced placement (AP) courses; participates in mentorship or internships with expert
2	State level awards, advanced 2 grade levels in a subject, receives college credit for on-line or correspondence courses, excels in AP course, enters national competitions such as the Regeneron/Intel/Westinghouse Competition (high school courses & multi-year program are offered to prepare students for this competition with help from scientists)
1	Receives any Intel/Westinghouse national recognition or award, advanced 3 or more grade levels in a subject, International awards

Table 6.1   (continued)

Sample of Reference Set of Possibilities: Specific Academic (AC)

Sample of possible achievements in social sciences (AC.h)

5	Subscribes to age-appropriate journal in any social science field; National Geographic contest; history, forensics, sociology, psychology, civic/government; politics; environmental studies club member; interest in maps, member of Student Council
4	Model UN active member; Class officers in student government; Honors course; Distance learning course; subscribes to adult or professional journals in field
3	County level award in competitions; college enrichment courses for high ability students; enrolled in Advanced placement (AP) courses including art history
2	State level awards, advanced 2 grade levels in a subject, receives college credit for local college, on-line or correspondence courses for adults, excels in AP course, enters national competitions
1	National awards, advanced 3 or more grade levels in a subject, early entrance to college, Mainstreamed in college course while in HS; Selected as Presidential Scholar (Kennedy Foundation); International awards

Source: Author's research of relevant literature and pilot studies

Not-for-profit organizations are helpful when their purpose includes educating the novice in a field of inquiry. These organizations will provide the essential questions that guide the field, the activities that are currently of interest to the field, names of important people, and what is worth knowing and learning about. With the help of a knowledgeable teacher or reference librarian in a public library, potential interest in any topic can be directed toward a useful organization.[10]

When the gleam of curiosity is spotted in a child's eye then proper instruction and guidance for an independent inquiry can make the magic occur, leading the child's curiosity first to wonder and then on to talent development. For instance, when third graders were asked about their passions, one girl said she loved collecting shells. When asked if there was anything she would like to find out about her shells, she made her list of what she knew and what she wanted to know.

The responses on that chart unveiled to the teacher that there seemed to be a scientific bent to the child's curiosity. Not to interfere by jumping to conclusions too early, the teacher asked that the child write three questions she might want to investigate. She could do some more reading on the subject beforehand if she liked, but she needed questions that she could not find the answers to easily by just looking them up. With instruction on different types of questions based on the half-written questions typical of a beginning investigator, she was led by open-ended questioning to clarify and choose her three specific discovery questions.

One of those questions asked, "Why do shells come in many colors?" This, along with the other two scientific questions, was shared in an inquiry letter that the child learned how to effectively write (as instructed by the independent inquiry teacher) to the curator of the appropriate department (which she had to figure out with help from the teacher) at the Museum of Natural History (whose address a school librarian helped her find by showing her the resources to look it up herself).

In a response that arrived on official museum letterhead, she learned that experts do not yet know what causes shells to have different colors! Most kindly, she was also invited to share any leads from her research should she discover something she thought was important. The response from the director of the museum was the "highlight of her life" (according to her and her mother). Witnesses say the gleam in her eye intensified and continued in the following years.

Many more of these examples surface in classrooms where children are encouraged to engage in and learn the authentic skills required for independent inquiries. A fourth grader had a subscription to *Discover* magazine, a magazine that highlights new discoveries in all science fields for those *adults* who are "curious." Hidden among his stack of textbooks, the current issue was never far from reach. In fact, it was the corner of that periodical protruding from the pile of notebooks that offered the first clue that this new student needed to be quickly screened for the gifted/talented program.

His independent inquiries demonstrated scientific sophistication beyond his years, leading him to find more opportunities for growth thanks to the witnesses to his work. The desire for adult-level information in a field can occur very early. Having access to opportunity to investigate first-hand in the field is irreplaceable. So is finding a like-minded community. These examples occurred before the current citizen-scientist efforts that invite, for example, amateur astronomers to assist experts in specific data collection.

Once an interest has become focused based upon the types of questions posed, students can be directed to helpful sites such as the Association for Library Service for Children: http://www.ala.org/alsc/externalrelationships/organizations. When a specific interest is evident, the question to be asked of the librarian is for help finding a youth organization or adult group that addresses the identified focus. As interests continue to develop, other resources will be needed to fuel curiosity and the acquisition of advanced skills, but now with a few "guidance counselors" from the field, the success of that next step is more likely.

ACADEMIC CURRICULAR MODIFICATIONS

There are two basic types of curricular modifications in academic course work—enrichment and acceleration. Every school district has its own formal and informal policies and opinions regarding the efficacy of each of these modifications.

Enrichment can take many forms but all seek to offer opportunities for depth and breadth in the current topic being studied by all. Generally speaking, enrichment options such as differentiated instruction, academic contests, gifted pullout programs, and independent study options are the most common choices available in elementary through to middle school classrooms.

As evidenced earlier, independent study conducted in the classroom or at home is a form of advancement that could include both enrichment and acceleration, depending on the child's interest. Acceleration opportunities typically begin at the secondary levels.

There are times when enrichment is just not enough. One student—much like the young man who inspired Dr. Julian Stanley to create the Johns Hopkins Talent Search for children precociously talented in mathematics[11]—was an outlier with regard to his degree of mathematical talent.[12] Dubbed by his elementary teachers as the "absent-minded professor," he was so advanced in mathematics that these teachers requested mentors for him throughout elementary school. By sixth grade this student was enrolled in high school math classes while support was provided for the social, physical, and organizational skills that remained underdeveloped.

Students advanced in a subject area can require a very different set of academic opportunities to continually realize their potential depending on the degree of advanced achievements. Sometimes the student just needs to have the trajectory of learning accelerated a grade level (which may be as simple as providing the cost of transportation or as complex as scheduling advanced courses at a time that also works for the outlying grade-level student).

Having a record of all the student's past achievements can provide concrete evidence of a lineage of specific enrichment activities that demonstrate the need for acceleration in a subject area. A Talent Profile can also indicate the need for radical acceleration such as skipping one or more grades because it provides solid evidence of prior accomplishments to add to the complexities of choosing the best fit for a child who is developing in a manner unlike his or her peers. Psychologists call this "asynchronous development," a term often used to describe the developing constellation found in a gifted individual.

This uneven development often fuels the research and practice regarding acceleration. To close the very large gap between educational practice and the extensive research on acceleration, a comprehensive study of all the research studies done on acceleration was conducted and published in 2004 as *A Nation Deceived* and followed in 2015 by *A Nation Empowered: Evidence Trumps the Excuses Holding Back America's Brightest:* http://www. accelerationinstitute.org/Nation_Deceived/.

These can be downloaded for free and provide indisputable evidence that acceleration is an important tool in the education toolbox. Despite this strongly supportive research, school districts and sometimes parents, rarely consider the option of acceleration of any kind, especially radical acceleration.

Some of this reluctance seems to be caused by stories in school systems of "so & so" whose acceleration was approved by an administrator only to crash and burn. Perhaps these events occur because research on best practices with all of the variables effecting gifted and talented education are not taught to general educators including those who become administrators. Many districts do not have a coordinator of gifted/talented services who is well versed in the research, and some that do also have an administrator or two who don't realize that the complexity of the decision requires expertise they have not yet developed.

An excellent resource to help administrators make well-informed decisions about if and how to accelerate is the questionnaire designed by the Belin-Blank Center experts at the University of Iowa. Family, teaching staff, and student input provide a comprehensive guide to all of the physical, social, and intellectual issues surrounding any acceleration. For example, the most critical intellectual issue often left unaddressed in acceleration is the need to identify any scaffolds to teach the child any possible gaps in the content that is being skipped over. Although sometimes it may seem as such to a casual observer, osmosis of knowledge does not occur if the child was not at least exposed to it.

This tool has been very useful to many administrators in helping all involved form a team to objectively seek what is best for each child. It is designed to guide the decision process and outline important considerations for school administrators and other decision makers to keep in mind: http://www.accelerationinstitute.org/resources/ias.aspx. This process has helped all parties (parents, administrators, and teachers) understand the complex dynamics of acceleration and assist with successful interventions.

Although described as a grade-level acceleration tool, it is most often useful for considering subject area acceleration needs. The document also defines reasons and times when subject area acceleration is not the best option for a particular child and when enrichment is suggested. The way it helps all of the child's advocates, both at school and home, begin on the same page and work together toward research-based best practice in a team approach is an elegant solution that channels efforts to secure a child's continued success.

DIFFERENT FORMS OF OPPORTUNITIES FOR
TALENT DEVELOPMENT

Professional organizations for gifted/talented education list different options for academically talented students from various resources (see Council for Exceptional Children's TAG and National Association for Gifted Children for two examples). There are directories of programs for the gifted (e.g., *Educational Opportunity Guide: A Directory of Programs for the Gifted*, Duke University Talent Identification Program, 1997, 2005) that provide a reference tool for students advanced in their level of achievement.

Duke University's *Opportunity Guide* is now online and invites those who are not affiliated with Duke to submit the opportunities they offer for these students for online inclusion on the list for parents and students: https://blogs.tip.duke.edu/giftedtoday/category/tog/. However excellent and current the online version might be, it is unlikely to be thoroughly complete, suggesting that an investigator use multiple resources for student resources. To help categorize some popular examples of types of opportunities for academic students, the following examples are provided.

Professional and leadership development opportunities often begin in high school with Honor Societies in most of the disciplines. For example, some schools have an English Honor Society that will sponsor local Writing Festivals to celebrate students' writing achievements at their annual Induction ceremony (CHSN English Department, 1994). These organizations help develop the necessary standards and intellectual traits[13] as well as social rules and procedures to follow, plus the landmines to avoid—all necessary to be successful.

At the other extreme, like the specialized schools designed to develop elite athletic skills in a particular sport or exceptional talent in the arts, specialized schools for academic talents exist as well. Despite the fact that many children or their parents do not want or cannot send their child away to a special school or uproot the rest of their family, this remains an excellent option for some.

Simon's Rock in Massachusetts has been a well-respected private school alternative for students who are self-motivated and need instructors well versed in these students' productive needs. So is the Illinois Mathematics and Science Academy, which is a free, public residential high school for 250 of the top STEM students in the state.

For the extremely talented and tech-motivated child with a healthy social network of peers outside of school and the desire to stay at home rather than relocate to a school servicing extreme levels of talent, Stanford has introduced a highly selective independent virtual school providing courses for students in grades 7–12 "where dedicated teachers help students worldwide pursue their passions in real time online, seminar classes."[14]

Many colleges and universities offer summer experiences. In fact, there is a network of Talent Search programs affiliated with universities to provide services for extreme talent, especially in mathematics, where students who qualify in the regional talent development screening can attend summer programs. See Johns Hopkins University's Center for Talent Development, Duke University, Northeastern University, or Stanford University for their specific offerings. The Belin-Blank Center at the University of Iowa has been a major leader in research and programs for the gifted with a stellar summer program as well.

The College of William and Mary has a nationally and internationally renowned Center for Gifted Education publishing outstanding curriculum units for K-12 classrooms. The material presented to teachers for their students provide worthwhile and relevant issues at a level that includes the needs of high-end learners.[15] These units were ingeniously created by teams of experts in content in combination with expertise in teaching to provide significant exemplars in language arts, science, social studies, and mathematics for classrooms. This multidimensional collaboration of expertise raises the bar regarding content as well as instruction.

Some State Education Departments provide summer programs at a university for students (usually high school) with demonstrated talent where high-level instruction takes place, while expanding the student's pool of colleagues with similar interests who they might befriend or encounter again in college. North Carolina, for example, provides summer programs for advanced talent development at Governor's Schools. Illinois Mathematics and Science Academy offers summer experiences as well.

Internships and mentorships are another set of opportunities. Johns Hopkins Center for Talented Youth (CTY) has listed summer science internships across the country on its website: http://cty.jhu.edu/imagine/resources/internships/science.html.

In addition, the Jack Kent Cooke Foundation Young Scholars Program: www.cty.jhu.edu/gifted/jkc.html is administered through the previously mentioned talent search organizations to provide funding as well as ongoing advising and guidance to students in financial need. A bridge remains to be built to help these students and their families find the information they need as well as assistance in completing the application forms. This could be an important contribution from school personnel. Having a record of measured talents could also assist in connecting young scholars in need of financial assistance and businesses interested in sponsoring them.

Some opportunities offered are in the form of competitions with or without a mentoring component. Many professional organizations in academic fields promote furthering the field by encouraging young talent by way of contests and competitions. For instance, the Art of Problem Solving Foundation, a 501(c)(3) nonprofit, sponsors the USA Mathematics Talent Search, whose goal "is to help all students develop their problem solving skills, improve their technical writing abilities, and mature mathematically while having fun."[16]

Established mathematicians volunteer to grade problems that have been posed to interested middle school and high school students and provide comments on their work. Designed for middle and high school students, participation is free, and earlier competition problems are offered to all students, although only those with mathematical talent would enjoy the challenges. An impressive feature of this organization is that the authors of the problems as well as the authors of the solutions are credited.

Another mentoring opportunity in mathematics worth investigating is within Math Circles, a program sponsored by the Mathematical Sciences Research Institute's organization: the National Association of Math Circles: http://www.mathcircles.org/what-is-a-math-circle/. What was once a series of contests provided to any interested students is now described as "Math Circles combine significant content with settings that encourage a sense of discovery and excitement about mathematics through problem-solving and interactive exploration. Ideal problems are low-threshold, high-ceiling; they offer a variety of entry points and can be approached with a minimal mathematical background, but lead to deep mathematical concepts and can be connected to advanced mathematics."[17] They now have circles for students (MSCs) and circles for K-12 teachers of mathematics (MTCs). These seem to have replaced the contests that were offered for advanced talent and those contests that were a healthy challenge for students working at the top of their grade level.

One example of math contests that have, for decades, been fairly easy to administer while providing excitement for those students who enjoy testing themselves are the Math League contests http://mathleague.com. Historically, there was a small cost to cover a nominal fee for registration, copies of the tests, answer forms and answer keys to the 40-minute multiple-choice exam, and a review of the top ten scores from each school and ranking of the top performers by school and individually in state and national populations. Offering the opportunity to anyone interested within each grade level from fourth to eighth, each grade level took the exam on a designated day in the fall. The top ten scores and student names for each grade in each elementary school were submitted to receive state ranking.

Many academically talented students loved this challenge as much as others love competing with other schools in sports. In fact, some students immediately asked to take the next grade level test as well. With classroom teacher and parents' permissions, self-selected fourth graders would unofficially take the fifth- and sixth-grade quizzes.

Administrators loved it too. Top students received recognition from the organization as well as the Board of Education. Most importantly, classroom teachers at the elementary level who did not have a mathematics department coordinator to assist with enrichment resources could see the students who enjoyed challenges in mathematics and would ask for more challenging resources. When the district memo reporting these test results and state rankings to elementary principals was also copied to the middle school and high school math department chairs, a vertical watch list for mathematical talent was informally registered and appreciated by secondary colleagues.

There are other useful contests: the American Mathematics Contest and the USA Mathematical Olympiad are two of them.[18] The contests are designed to promote problem-solving skills and enthusiasm toward the variety of topics in mathematics. Once again, cross-checking with the National Association of Secondary School Principal's ratings on a program or contest provides an independent review of the benefits of any program or provision they have been asked to screen. Checking with the current contest website provides updated information, as the content or procedures can change at any time.

Science is one field that cultivates at least one direct route toward advanced expertise. The Regeneron Science and Engineering Fair (formerly Intel and very early on a Westinghouse contest) is often considered the pinnacle of national competition. According to the website the Regeneron scholars are chosen from all entries:

> Three hundred semifinalists are awarded $2,000; with an additional $2,000 going to their high schools to support STEM education. All 40 finalists win an all-expenses-paid trip to Washington, DC for the Regeneron Science Talent Institute where they explain their research to some of the country's top scientists and compete for the top 10 awards. The top award is $250,000. (Retrieved January 21, 2017; https://student.societyforscience.org/regeneron-sts)

Further acknowledgments within this series of events include choosing the Gordon E. Moore (as in Moore's law) Award, which is given to the top Best in Category Project for each area. From there, two national winners are chosen to receive the top prize of that Fair—the Intel Foundation Young Scientist Award. Those two students then compete in the Intel International Science and Engineering Fair, where nations send their best to compete for the top research awards in 14 categories of scientific topics. In the past, several of these elite awardees of the international-level fair would win a trip to the Stockholm Youth International Science Seminar that ends with attendance at the Nobel Prize ceremonies (Sohn, 2005). This is the finest built-in mentoring by the field's finest for the future finest.

A few high schools offer a specific research course that prepares students for this competition by having them conduct research with assigned mentor scientists over their summers. This offering is in addition to AP or IB high school coursework. But the path to getting to qualify for that course, even if known to be on the map of opportunities, is not direct or easily found. Children in elementary schools without a faculty member with a love for science might best seek opportunities outside of school and directly from the field.

ROLE OF THE GATEKEEPERS OF A FIELD

Each academic discipline has its gatekeepers—the leadership of a national organization and editorial boards of the major journals of that profession are two examples. Gatekeepers are often considered screeners who keep out those they feel do not qualify for elite status, but they can also be an excellent resource for encouragement. Effective gatekeepers know how to swing the gate both ways, helping newcomers of all ages contribute to the profession as the novices discover the potential requirements and opportunities ahead. Significant gatekeepers in K-12 education are building administrators as well as the department chairs or district coordinators of academic subject areas.

It is likely that every school district or principal or high school department chair knows of and offers *some* enrichment opportunities in *some* academic areas of interest at *some* grade levels. And, no doubt, math teachers will know of a contest or two to suggest to the eager and able student, but having a bird's-eye view of *all* the enrichment and acceleration opportunities available in a subject area (like geometry) or domain (all mathematics) is beyond the capability of any individual or school.

RECOMMENDATIONS

With only a few examples in math and science described here, the charting of all available accomplishments for students is a useful but extremely comprehensive task. A central clearinghouse with sufficient technological and human resources could work with teacher organizations specializing in each subject area to locate and evaluate all opportunities using the standardized rubric of assessment categories provided in chapter 3. Monitoring these opportunities and maintaining accurate updates would best be served by an entity capable of acting as a national or international clearinghouse, unifying the important efforts of organizations such as the Association of Secondary School Principals who annually publish a list of programs they have been invited to evaluate that year for assurance of a student-centered organization.

Garnering the resources of the professional education and educational research organizations in each subject area with other knowledge of useful student opportunities in the field from community resources (programs and businesses) could provide comprehensive attention to listing what we know and what is available in each talent domain. The creation of a think tank or research center specifically designed for this goal could unify the multiple perspectives on talent development research and practice.

Some believe that unifying the focus on developing talents in all children is a national responsibility leading to a nod toward appointing this responsibility to an entity such as a redefined U.S. Department of Education that is fed by a consortium of all State Education Departments. Others see the government agencies as capable of maintaining and implementing but leaving the research arm of knowledge on developing expertise a separate scientific entity.

NOTES

1 Nelson & Psaltis, 1967, Preface to part II.

2 Cole, 2003, p. 48.

3 Abramo, 1996.

4 Ibid., p. 2.

5 Ibid., p. 2.

6 Ibid., p. 13.

7 Up until that article, Dr. Margaret Johns was known as a well-respected community leader and a skilled, successful watercolor painter. Her life was full and rich but not involved in the science she once loved enough to contribute two important discoveries. These stories about two female scientists suggest challenges without economic, social, or cultural differences that would magnify only the importance of early guidance and then continual mentoring of experts in any academic field. The role of gender is undeterminable here but may have been a factor too.

8 Van Tassel-Baska, 1998.

9 Erickson, 1994; 1998.

10 The public library is an excellent source of information for these students. Note the coverage on the story of what a boy and a book can achieve—as he built electric windmills for his rural community out of junk (Sheerin, 2009).

11 See Assouline & Lupkowski-Shoplik (2011), Benbow (1991), Stanley (1998) for a lineage of this comprehensive research on mathematical talent.

12 With over two decades of administrating gifted and talented programs and provisions, there was only one child who surfaced with this extreme talent in the district. Fortunately for him, he had a mathematician in his home environment who also mentored him.

13 See especially the intellectual traits proposed by Dr. Richard Paul and Dr. Linda Elder at www.criticalthinking.org

14 https://onlinehighschool.stanford.edu/; Retrieved October 25, 2018.

15 See J. Van Tassel-Baska's (1994) work.

16 www.usamts.org; Retrieved January 21, 2017.

17 Retrieved from website August 27, 2017.

18 For a comprehensive list of resources for mathematical talent, also see Assouline & Lupkowski-Shoplik's (2011) section.

Chapter 7

Early Sightings of Creative/Productive (C) Ability

Students who fail to acquire a flexible and creative attitude toward life are at risk for obsolescence, not only in their knowledge, but also in their skills for coping with life.

—R. J. Sternberg[1]

There is the doubt we stand to sacrifice if we can't embrace error—the doubt of curiosity, possibility, and wonder.

—K. Schulz[2]

Creativity is often described as the phoenix that emerges from the ashes of failure.[3] This is as true for Silicon Valley[4] as it is for individuals such as N. Tesla or T. Edison. Trial and error is an important strategy that escapes the experiences of many academically talented students who do exceptionally well at knowledge and comprehension activities that seek one correct answer (like most standardized tests).

Creative thinking requires being comfortable with the possibility that there can be more than one answer and it can be intimidating to the point of panic for some academically exceptional students. It's a sobering experience to watch "total meltdowns" in children from grades 3 through 8 when a game of "Spontaneous" is introduced to close or open a class.

The game is simple enough to play. A verbal challenge such as "Name things that are red" is presented to the group. They have one minute to think of all of the possibilities they can come up with before they're called upon to share answers in a fast-paced, round-robin format that lasts between two and five minutes depending on the size of the group.

Creative, defined as unusual responses, get two points while any relevant answer that has not yet been given receives a point. A creative answer for this challenge would be newspaper because the term "red" was also perceived as "read." Another creative answer might be symbolic like "anger."

There have been times when the game elicited so much discomfort that parent-teacher conferences were held and peer tutors arranged for a specific child. In fact, it was the meltdown of the valedictorian during a seminar on creative problem-solving that became the impetus for directing a gifted/talented program to focus on developing creative thought. Watching his distraught reaction as well as the assistance he required to continue with the new experience kept a cohort of multidisciplinary high school teachers in deep discussion and research for a long time.[5]

Curriculum units on invention help to scaffold some of the creative thinking skills for these successful, convergent academic learners. Based heavily on the history of former inventions and inventors, most units provide a comfortable, focused excursion into the realm of imaginative or at least innovative, problem-solving. Learning to identify an observed need found within their daily lives, they could follow the steps of invention to solutions. Some solutions were more elegant than others. In fact, it became immediately apparent that U.S. copyright procedures could be made available to parents of these students prior to the annual public display of the products they had designed http://www.loc.gov/teachers/copyrightmystery/text/steps/. It is always exciting to see the invention of a fifth grader come on the market years later.

However, it is the longitudinal evidence about the process that matters most:

> *My favorite story of this success came from a teaching colleague. Her son, a former student, went on to work at a major computer company after college. As a proud mother, this colleague stopped by to share that he had obtained his first patent within a year or so of working for the company. Almost whispering, she said that he would not let her brag to the family at Thanksgiving dinner! But she had to tell me because as an educator, she knew how important it was for us to know. When she asked him why she couldn't share the achievement, he said something along the lines of "it was no big deal—he had used the exact same process that he learned in his enrichment class in 4th grade for his invention. This is just the way everyone is supposed to think." How do you measure that success?*

The students described thus far were initially identified for either academic or intellectual ability. Creative ability was developed by introducing the skills and encouraging the behaviors associated with this talent domain as depicted in the research literature:

Table 7.1

Sample of Reference Set of Behaviors: Creativity (CR)

Observed Behaviors

5   Curiosity = energized questioning

Good imagination

Resourceful, can improvise with ease

Task commitment, persistence, & determination = pursues in-depth investigations despite obstacles

Adventurous = eager to play with ideas, discover

Alert to gaps in knowledge and novelty

Tolerance for ambiguity = contemplates uncertainties; attentive to pun, irony, or double entendre; enjoys and create jokes, metaphors, brainteasers

Independence/nonconformity = not affected by others; interprets uniquely; original

Self-confidence/willingness to risk being wrong or fail

Drive to experiment & willingness to try difficult tasks = seeks out or is willing for a challenge

Acute sensory perception = extremely keen observation skills, notices any minute changes

Ability to escape perceptual sets and find order in chaos (like perceptual puzzles as well as in real life)

Attentive to gathering information through his/her senses, sees patterns or relationships.

Often sees a variety of perspectives (points of view) including unusual perspectives like a bird's eye view, demonstrates flexibility

Is sensitive to aesthetic qualities = will comment on the beauty of something (sometimes unusual items like the beauty of a number or a pattern.

Demonstrates keen sense of humor

Will do anything to avoid boredom

Source: These *sample* behaviors were found in more than one research study. The descriptors listed here resonated with classroom teachers when piloted.

Note: Best strategy for choosing a match: Read the behavior and see which student(s) comes to mind immediately. If there is no immediate response, skip it and move to next behavior. You do not need to use any of these at all unless it is extremely accurate. A 'maybe' is not useful.

Table 7.1 (continued)

Sample of Reference Set of Behaviors: Creativity (CR)

Sample of emerging creative achievements

5	Writes poetry, or prose in spare time; enjoys playing with numbers, designing mathematical puzzles; makes up jokes; composes & performs plays; uses descriptive language often peppered with simile or metaphor; enjoys Improv theater; creates computer games, unusual blog or web pages, original art or inventions in spare time; Engages in self-directed or independent investigations; business ventures
4	Seeks out creative problem-solving teams such as FPS, Odyssey of the Mind/Destination ImagiNation; Participates in Invention Conventions; Submits creations to professional group for feedback;
3	Regional award for Odyssey of the Mind/DestiNation Imagination teams Publishes stories, cartoons or poems in school paper/magazine; Designs inventions that receive attention from professional groups
2	State level team or individual award; Publishes creative writing in state-level magazine
1	National team or individual awards, Receives patent, copyright; Publishes book, story, or poem in nationally circulated publication or article in refereed journal

Source: Author's research of relevant literature and pilot studies

Without help navigating these perceptions, thinkers who are naturally creative can find some school tasks unreasonable. The inventor Dean Kamen remembers having difficulty in school taking tests or identifying a correct answer:

> For instance, when asked to select a word that didn't belong to the set "add, subtract, multiply, increase," Kamen might choose "add" because all the others had seven letters. (Levy, 2002, p. 56)

Kamen found himself often at odds with his teachers because he would argue that his answers were not wrong. Also not wrong would be the answer "subtract," which might not belong because all the others refer to a gain. There are those students who cannot help but think like this.

Concern for these creative students fuels further investigation. The fact that they entertain multiple possibilities that are all correct adds much time to the timed tests that are used to measure intelligence or academic ability. These students are of particular concern because they do not know they are "thinking outside the box" or that there is a box. The creatively gifted student just thinks differently and feels different. Many need help finding a way to belong and flourish in school.

One young man was a sophomore who qualified for the new program for the gifted based on identification procedures for creativity. His grades were far from stellar, yet he was quite interested in archeology. Years earlier a local archeologist had come to his fourth-grade classroom as a guest speaker. Immediately following this talk, the young man contacted the local scientist and found ways to be mentored for years—unbeknownst to the school.

By high school he was hoping to conduct his own archeological dig at a local mine he had discovered. Needing resources, he applied to the program for the gifted with a self-nomination. After qualifying he applied for an NSF (National Science Foundation) student grant and was awarded the funds to hire some classmates and conduct the dig. He was one of the first recipients of these student awards.

At the completion of the dig, the study was published in a professional archeology journal. [Yes, his other grades improved dramatically, and yes, he is currently an archeologist.] In fact years later he wrote, " I have a photo of me as an 11-year-old with the co-discoverer of the Paleo-Indian point and caribou bones from Dutchess Quarry cave. The occasion was a class fieldtrip when I enrolled, precociously, in a non-credit adult education course at OCCC in 1973 or 1974. I have the photo on my desk at work."[6]

There are two reasons for mentioning this particular student. First, his creative ability led to the realization of his academic talents, a connection worthy of noting. Second, he would be the first to tell you (and did at various invitations to speak as an alum) that he was floundering in high school to almost the point of no return before this opportunity provided what he needed to develop his potential.

"Nan" (not her real name) in fourth grade also demonstrated how difficult it could be for a creative thinker to navigate through school. Although her second-grade teacher had commented on her report card about her creative interpretation of stories, she was otherwise floundering in school. Her fourth-grade CogAT (Cognitive Abilities Test) test scores were 121 verbal (baseline for determining gifted in more generous procedures) and 150 quantitative (the highest mathematical reasoning score possible on this test). Yet, according to her teachers, she was not comfortable in classes and lacked a sense of belonging in school.

Fortuitously she tried out and made the team for a creative problem-solving program called Odyssey of the Mind (OotM). As one of seven team members, Nan found her place and her passion. The coach provided them with the open-ended, theatrical problem they were required to interpret; taught them strategies for creative problem-solving and teamwork; and monitored the team as a facilitator. Charged with having to write an original script that solved the presented problem in an eight-minute skit, teams needed to be extremely creative, inventive, and work well together. Nan volunteered to write the script and came in the following afternoon with a draft. The team loved it, and they all worked well together to complete the final touches. Her team competed in the regional competition against teams from other school districts, placing first to qualify for the state competition.[7]

Nan continued with the OotM program off and on for years, but notably, immediately following this accomplishment, her list of achievements multiplied to include Select Chorus, work selected for District Art Show, and participation in the district's gifted and talented program. The G/T program she participated in was a pullout program where students were taught creative thinking strategies and were given assistance to complete an independent inquiry of their choice. Nan soared, finding like-minded friends and a better understanding of her "sense of being different." By early high school she was reading Alex Osborne's book *Applied Imagination* (a text designed for adult designers) and looking at an engineering career where she could combine her ability in mathematics and creativity.

The difference between the students who need to harness their creative thinking toward fruitful results when introduced to beneficial structures and those students who need to loosen the reigns of their experiences to include creative thinking strategies begs further research. Although much of the research on creativity in adults favors a domain-specific theory of creativity where creativity occurs only within a specific domain after becoming an advanced expert, developmentally this may not be the case.

Decades of observations of a K-12 population within the framework of identified creative behaviors found in the research literature suggest the possibility that a general creativity theory may be a useful predecessor to the acquisition of subject area expertise. Certainly the hypothesis that there is a need for both general and domain-specific creative thinking strategies is anecdotally supported.[8]

In either case, opportunities to demonstrate creative achievements at an early age are few and fragile in school settings. Recognizing and responding to any glimpse in the classroom usually opens the floodgates of pertinent information.

CREATIVE PROBLEM-SOLVING WITH TEAMS

The greatest need of a creatively gifted child, like any other child, seems to be finding a friend who understands him or her and provides a sense of belonging. For schools, the easiest way to facilitate that possibility is to provide team-based opportunities to be creative. Perhaps the longest running team-based creative problem-solving competition was designed and created by Paul Torrance to foster creative problem-solving through the study of futures. Aptly named Future Problem Solving, this international competition is academically focused on future scenarios and current real-world problems. Participation in the program can begin in upper elementary school and continue through high school. In addition to advanced research skills, teamwork, and creative problem-solving processes, students engage in fore-casting skills.

The topics are real, chosen from a variety of disciplines that are currently being addressed by experts. For example, the 2016–2017 topics included: Problem #1: Educational Disparities; Problem #2: It's All in the Genes: A Qualifying Problem; 3D Printing; and an Affiliate Competition: Identity Theft. The description of the genetic problem as found on the organization's website (http://www.fpspi.org/topics.html) is an indication of the sophistica-tion the competition seeks to attain:

> The genes of organisms can be altered using biotechnology techniques. New genes can be inserted into plants and animals to create new varieties and breeds or to lessen certain genetic activity such as susceptibility to disease. Since 1970 GM has helped produce greater numbers of crops with higher nutritional value and has been prominent in animal agriculture. Critics claim there are serious ethical, ecological, and economic issues with GM techniques. For example, GM crops can cross-pollinate with non-GM crops creating unpredictable character-istics in plants. Bioherbicides and bioinsecticides can be added to crop seeds, but are not always effective. Resistant weeds now infest 75 million acres of land across the world. Domesticated animals are being genetically modified to pro-duce proteins that have applications for human medicine—proteins to control blood clotting or kill cancer cells, for example.
>
> What will be the long-term impact of genetic modification of plants and ani-mals? If plants and animals are genetically modified to resist current pathogens, will new, more resistant pathogens develop? Already, GM has led to interna-tional controversy and trade disputes, protests, and restrictive regulations on commercial products containing genetically modified organisms.[9]

There is also a designation titled "Community Problem" that can be identified and defined by a team once they are comfortable with the problem-solving procedures and how to choose research readings on their own.

Scenario writing is another advanced aspect of the program for those inter-ested in scientific creative writing. A coach must be identified to assist in the process, not the product of the investigation. This in-depth investigation does not require every team to participate in the organization's formal competition. For example, schools can have everyone participate and then select one or two teams to be sponsored for the regional competition.[10]

Past research problems and the accompanying resource book of research readings can be used as curriculum materials for teaching students advanced teamwork skills. Resources from past competitions are available for minimal costs. A full set of former problems can serve as enrichment curriculum

exemplars for any interested subject area high school teacher seeking pertinent enrichment for advanced learners in his or her classrooms.

This program identifies Elegant Problems[11] that by definition invite fluency, flexibility, originality, and elaboration of solutions; encourage elegant
solutions; and most important, are meaningful to the learner as well as the
field. Together these make the endeavor a worthwhile problem.[12] It also
means that the challenge is complex, requiring in-depth commitments from
all involved, just like real-world creative problem-solving. And like creative
thought, it is as exhilarating as it is complex. For more information, including
instruction books and past competition problems, visit the website at www.
fpspi.org.

Odyssey of the Mind is a very different type of creative problem-solving
program. Introduced for the first time at a presentation at a state conference
for the gifted/talented community in the early 1980s, the New Jersey State
G/T director and the industrial arts teacher employing these problem-based
challenges presented the new program for school children that they had
adapted from a college course. Newspaper stories at the time showed photos
of college students dropping an encased egg off the roof of a building to try
out their solutions to the now classic challenge of creating better protection
for an egg.

Translating some wonderful problem-based challenges designed by professor Sam Micklus for his Industrial Design classes at Glassboro State College
(now Rowan University), the two presenters outlined a new competition
(formed much like the Future Problem Solving Competition) that encouraged
creative thinking and rewarded the process over the product for elementary to
high school children. Developing creative thinking has always been at the forefront of gifted education, so this idea took off in this field and spread quickly.[13]

The seed of this idea has blossomed into an extravaganza of performances in response to specific kinds of challenges. Many of the 20 to 26
team coaches that the author supervised each year would choose one of
the five types of problems, such as the "classics" or the "vehicle" or the
"balsa" challenge and stick with it throughout their years of coaching as the
requirements were so complex for each type of problem it took a very long
time to learn how to help students through the process. For example, once
Industrial Arts became Technology and then disappeared from the curriculum in public schools, teachers would agree to coach the balsa challenge
in elementary or middle school divisions if they knew a structural engineer
who could come in and provide students with lessons on tensile strength.

An example of the 2016 Vehicle Problem Synopses is quoted here to provide the flavor of the problem as presented. It is followed by the noncompetitive K-2 problem.

Problem 1: Catch Us If You Can

Divisions I, II, III & IV

This is your Odyssey, should you choose to accept it . . . your team will design, build, and run vehicles from a multi-level Parking Garage to a secret meeting place without being stopped. Vehicles will travel different routes to reach the same destination. During their Odyssey, the vehicles will do something that prevents them from being followed. The performance will include the reason for the meeting, someone that wants to prevent the meeting, a simulation of a scene taking place inside a vehicle as it travels, and a soundtrack to accompany the vehicles' travel.

Primary: Movin' Out!

Grades K-2

Teams will create and present a performance about a group that is moving out of one place and into another. In one scene, team-created props and scenery will make up the first setting. To transform into a new setting, team-made devices will move the scenery and props to a new location. Everything in the setting for the next scene must be made from the transported items. The performance will also include a humorous Moving Character, a reason for the move, and a lost item that is rediscovered in an unusual place.[14]

The primary problem (K-2) is a noncompetitive exercise that is performed at the regional competition to develop performance skills. The challenge for the presented problems is far more difficult as each problem comes with a booklet of given specifications for the required parameters set by the problem designers that all must be met to avoid receiving penalty points.

Destination ImagiNation (www.IDODI.org), recognized by the NASSP and most State Education departments, is another team creative problem-solving competition (similar in organization to the OotM Competitions). This group was formed by educators seeking to provide an optimal match between K-12 children and the type of team challenges (as well as the written description of parameters of the problem) that these students would spend months working on.

For over 25 years, student teams have been immersed in creatively solving one of the presented challenges, including "side trips" that encourage demonstration of individual talents (e.g., art or music specialization) and preparing for the instant challenge given to teams on the day of competition. Books of both types of challenges are available for training purposes and some free resources are available to teachers who sign up on the organization's website.

Commonly abbreviated to the title "DI," the five problem challenges also highlight different disciplines. The first one listed on the website provides a flavor of the way the problems are presented:

The Technical Challenge prompts students to complete tasks by using engineering, research, strategic planning and related skills.

Points of Interest

- Present a show that includes an opening act and a headlining act.
- Design and build a stage on which the acts will take place and that will move a team member from one location to another.
- Enhance each act with a technical effect to amaze the audience.
- Create and present two Team Choice Elements that show off the team's interest, skills, areas of strength, and talents.[15]

The skills of Improvisation are highly valued in the DI organization and reflected in the level of improvisational expertise students acquire over multiple years. There are five competitive challenges that focus on a specialty and are often sponsored by a company whose values and requisite skills match the challenge's focus. Each year there is a Technical Challenge like the one described before that usually requires some object to move on its own and do certain tasks along the way; a Scientific Challenge; a Fine Arts Challenge; the Structural Challenge; and a Service-Learning Challenge. There is also a noncompetitive challenge designed for very young children to begin to learn teamwork and problem-solving in a supportive, fun way. They too perform and are recognized on competition day.

Of the seven challenges provided, the Improvisational challenge is the most open-ended, and therefore most difficult.[16]

Our Improvisational Challenge is all about spontaneity and storytelling. Teams receive topics and produce skits right on the spot.

Points of Interest

- Create three improvisational skits from the same story prompt.
- Present each skit in a different performance genre.
- Portray a different stock character in each skit.
- Enhance each skit with props.

Improvisation skills are also required to solve the Instant Challenges presented to all students during the competition. Under very tight time constraints (a matter of minutes), they must demonstrate teamwork, creative use of materials, performance skills, and creative problem-solving techniques.

The flexibility, fluency, and originality of the responses are celebrated. Many coaches find these, or the Spontaneous problems posed in OotM, to be wonderful class starters for the first three minutes in any classroom, providing an engaging student challenge while the teacher takes attendance. Instructional strategists have found that these challenges also significantly reduce the number of late arrivals to middle school classes.

The DI organization provides classroom curricula designed to enhance teacher and student skills in facilitating teams and the thinking skills needed for problem-solving.[17] Evidence of the transfer of these skills from an extracurricular activity to the classroom instructional environment has not been found.[18] The difficulty, time, and focused attention required to assist just one team of five to seven students develop the requisite skills—skills demanded by the call for 21st-century learning[19]—appears to be too much of a challenge at this time for creative teachers to incorporate successfully when their job description/expectation has a very different focus/purpose. Until that changes, sharing worthy resources outside of the classroom with students and their parents/legal guardians can enrich and expand opportunities. Here are a few more:

CREATIVITY IN SCIENCE

The U.S. Patent and Trademark Office has supported several activities for students across the years. For some time the National Inventive Thinking Association sponsored a Young Inventors & Creators Competition with rules and categories for inventions and for copyrights.[20] Currently, the U.S. Patent Office, in partnership with the National Inventors Hall of Fame Foundation, seeks to inspire children, especially 8- to 11-year-olds, through an ad campaign and internet site: www.InventNow.org.[21] The not-for-profit National Inventors Hall of Fame administers several national programs for students including Camp Invention, Club Invention, and the Collegiate Inventors Competition. For more information see www.invent.org. There are also well-researched curriculum guides for classrooms such as *Invent Iowa*.[22]

The Smithsonian National Museum of American History's Lemelson Center is another national resource for invention materials and research. Materials are available to help foster the qualities of invention in adults and children and address the purpose of the center.[23] The material includes a series entitled "Innovative Lives," which can be accessed at http://invention.si.edu/tags/innovative-lives-program. Biographical resources are significant catalysts in any field of interest.

Foundations and companies often sponsor competitions to promote inno-vation in science sometimes with the help of federal funds. Once again, checking with the NASSP (National Association of Secondary School Prin-cipals) list of approved contests and activities will provide an indication that the activity is primarily educational. (Administrators will often check this list before approving a program for a classroom.)

The Christopher Columbus Awards, an endorsed competition that often receives local newspaper coverage, challenges teams of three to four middle school students to apply the scientific method to a community problem. Solu-tions are submitted and judged on: creativity (20 points), innovation (20), scientific accuracy (24), feasibility (18), and clarity of communication (18). Thirty teams are selected as semifinalists and go to the next level. But each submission receives feedback from three individual judges. A new team of judges evaluates the entries to pick the final eight teams to compete at the National Championship Week competition. However, this powerful, well-designed program lost its federal funding mid-challenge in the 2014–2015 school year and was forced to abandon the competition.

The fragility of funding required for these competitions is portrayed here to illustrate a caution as well as another important reason for establishing a cen-tralized location and assessment of opportunities for use in Talent Records for students. Once an opportunity is abolished, it is difficult to know the degree of expertise it commanded without an objective evaluation of the parameters of the challenge. Talent Records profiling accomplishments and experiences for over 12 years could easily have "phantom entries" regarding a significant opportunity that no longer exists for whatever reason.

Also, one central list of programs might provide a direct link for businesses and other organizations to match interests or create new options to sponsor or provide financial support for developing talents. This would be a significant contribution by businesses and philanthropists interested in supporting talent development opportunities. With the latest neuroscience research on cogni-tive development pointing to the physical growth monitored in early learning that supports the biographical accounts of eminent contributors, providing financial resources carefully crafted by educational experts knowledgeable in developing expertise through elementary school would make an especially significant contribution to cultivating talent in the population of this country. This is not a new idea. It occurs now in ad hoc fashion but most often only in secondary schools, especially at the high school level.

SAMPLE OF CREATIVITY IN WRITING

The Scholastic Art and Writing Awards administered by the Alliance for Young Artists & Writers may be the oldest not-for-profit organization that honors creative excellence in writing for secondary students. There are two categories for the Writing Awards: Group I for grades 7, 8, and 9 and Group II for grades 10, 11, and 12. The organization also publishes books with samples such as *The Best Teen Writing of 2016*. Students gain inspiration and skill from this annual publication. Long before a student is ready to apply, valuable insights and information can be found on the website: www.artandwriting.org.

Another national organization that seeks to recognize exceptional talent in writing (creative nonfiction, novel, play/script, poetry, and short story categories) as well as visual (visual arts, photography, film, and video) and performing arts (dance, jazz, music, theater, and voice) is the National Foundation for Advancement in the Arts' Arts Recognition and Talent Search. Although there is a cost for registration, entry in this search is required for selection in the prestigious Presidential Scholars in the Arts program. For more information: https://www.scholarships4school.com/scholarships/arts-arts-recognition-and-talent-search.html.

CREATIVITY IN LEADERSHIP: ENTREPRENEURS

This category is described in the next chapter on leadership. It is worth acknowledging here that there are several leadership behaviors that overlap in the research literature with behaviors identified with creativity. The ability to tolerate ambiguity, ability to solve problems creatively, flexibility in thought and action, and ability to see new relationships have been found to be characteristic of leadership ability as well by some researchers.[24]

NOTES

1   Sternberg, 2000, p. 60.

2   Schulz, 2010, p. 319.

3   Kelly, 2012; Tharp, 2006. For a scientific perspective on creative expertise, see Simonton, 1996.

4   Saffo, 2002.

5   It became my life's work (Kay, 2013).

6   Personal correspondence, April 9, 2006.

7   These carefully orchestrated problems have many rules that the students must learn to overcome or translate in unique ways.

8   Gruber & Richard, 1990. Also see M. Root-Bernstein 2014 for another developmental perspective on imaginary play leading to adult creativity and Seivert, 2001 also on play.

9   Retrieved January 21, 2017.

10   Our state's champions came with their coach and introduced the process to some of our district's high school students in a workshop to help us consider formally participating in the competition.

11   Kay in Simpson, J., et. al, 1998.

12   Kay, 1998, 2013, 2016.

13   Gourley & Micklus, 1982.

14   Current site for problems is now https://www.odysseyofthemind.com/our-problems/.

15   https://www.destinationimagination.org/challengeprogram/challenge-pre views/. Retrieved January 21, 2017.

16   One of the highlights of chaperoning so many of these out-of-state tournaments for both OotM and DI was the moment I witnessed a team of high school students achieve a position in the top ten spots (I don't recall what number) at the DI Global Tournament on a regular challenge one year. On the bus home from that competition, they decided to challenge themselves the following year to improve more by accepting this more difficult improvisational challenge next time.

17   Cadle & Selby, 2010.

18   With over a decade of experience with all of these after-school programs as a coordinator helping 25+ coaches per year develop the necessary skills of a facilitator/ coach, no evidence of a teacher/coach incorporating these creative problem-solving methods or skills into their classroom activities can be reported.

19   Named Engage, 2007, when first located, now Partnership for 21st Century Learning (2007). For a thorough introduction into research and recommendations for creative teaching and learning see Torrance & Myers 1974 book.

20   NITA, 1998.

21   USP&TO, 2009, p. 2.

22   Baldus, Blando, Croft, & Hirsch, 2005.

23   Small, 2005.

24   Feldhusen & Pleiss, 1992; Karnes & Bean 1997; Karnes & Chauvin, 2005; Roets, 1992.

Chapter 8

On Materializing Leadership (L)

Without a more comprehensive look at leadership over the lifespan, leader development practices will not meet their full potential.

—Murphy & Johnson[1]

Paul Orfalea's successful leadership style for Kinko's was based on a philosophy best described by his wife: "The goal of management is to remove obstacles."[2] Yet, Kinko's was the brainchild of a person who had flunked second grade and coped with dyslexia throughout school.[3]

Perhaps that's where he learned to remove his own obstacles so well. Or it could have been modeled at home, as responsibility for others can be and often is modeled early at home.[4] Wherever this leadership ability was fostered, it did flourish into a significant success. Leaders in diverse fields and with different leadership styles often describe a sense of belonging to or being responsible for something bigger than themselves as a guiding force.[5]

When given the opportunity to investigate an interest, the students who emerge as leaders often design assignments or independent inquiry projects that are service oriented. As a seventh grader, one young man created a program where academically capable students could volunteer to provide extra academic help to students in need. He worked with the guidance department of a middle school to design the entire program. Long after his departure, the program continues as a function of that department. In high school he continued to blossom in every talent domain (academics, sports, arts) including leadership. His Talent Profile was probably one of the longest on record. The group's needs always came before his.[6]

Other examples abound. Almost a decade later and despite more bureaucratic obstacles than an educator would care to admit, another middle school student designed a club for girls to help them develop self-esteem and self-efficacy skills through leadership. As a seventh grader she did the research and wrote and submitted a proposal to the Board of Education for her independent inquiry project. As an eighth grader she designed and, with the help of appropriate staff volunteers, implemented a pilot study that included bringing in female community members and motivational speakers to discuss exciting pursuits. The club met after school and had a very diverse (in every sense of the word except gender) membership.

In ninth grade after her curriculum and club were officially approved and in full force, she discovered she could no longer be co-advisor of the club because of a district rule that high school students were not allowed to be physically in the middle school. Working with administrators and a persistence that knew no bounds, she prevailed *and* developed a method for selecting another high school candidate to take over when she graduated. She too has made her world a better place.

There is another side to this area of strength that merits discussion as well. With an incredibly supportive principal, a high school gifted program was developed for students identified as gifted/talented in any federally defined talent domain.[7] In fact, this principal often nominated students for the program. Sometimes his nomination came from an encounter with a student who was close to being expelled. When he recognized leadership qualities gone astray, he suggested that the student be screened (tests, past accomplishments, and any relevant activities). If the student qualified, he or she had the option of participating in the program or being expelled. Every student nominated by this principal demonstrated strength in leadership within the program and succeeded in school because of that man's wisdom and insight into leadership potential.

When given a chance, leadership skills can be clearly exhibited in elementary-age students, although the context of these abilities would likely be lost without a cumulative record. One example will demonstrate the cumulative effect of recording long-term patterns:

Her first grade teacher noted in the first quarter "Always capably ready." By October she received the Citizen of the Month Award in her class. Third quarter comment was: "Displays many leadership qualities." There were two entries on the profile that highlighted academic strengths as well. In the first quarter of second grade, the teacher focused her comments on the outstanding academic strengths exhibited in behaviors and substantiated on achievement tests with one comment indicating leadership: "Adept at clarifying concepts for those in need of assistance." The last teacher comment on the report card that year was "Displays many leadership qualities." Third grade listing on the record included high academic scores and participation in a gifted program. In fourth grade, when many opportunities are offered for the first time, she added participation in orchestra, chorus, a creative-problem-solving team (OM or OotM) and Girl Scouts. Other than continuing in Girl Scouts, the only other entry under leadership at the elementary level was "Tour guide for incoming 5th graders" as a 6th grader.

Well rounded and multiply talented, this child had a long Talent Profile, yet the leadership strengths that were evident as she engaged in her world were not identified as often as they were witnessed. Had there been a list of behaviors to review, all of her teachers would have been able to easily identify at least a few behaviors each semester.

Table 8.1

Reference Set K-12 Leadership (L)

Observed Behaviors

5   Sets personal goals and benchmarks/objectives = has a plan

         Responsible, reliable = can count on to get task done well

         Listens well. Recognizes/cultivates/channels individuals' strengths toward group goal

         Keen sense of justice, fairness

         Exhibits empathy and understanding of others and their problems

         Sees multiple perspectives

         Willing to do more than expected, enthusiastic

         Demonstrates self-control, courage, conviction of decision or plans, loyalty

         Careful attention to detail, hard worker

         Knows own strengths, weaknesses; acknowledges mistakes, shows interest in self-improvement

         Often is asked (peers or others) to direct activities

         Employs a creative imagination toward group efforts (generates ideas/solutions)

         Understands and applies the principle of cooperative effort (has the ability to organize, get others to perform)

         Uses social skills/sensitive to social etiquette

         High level of verbal expression

         Exhibits 'wisdom of spontaneity' (sizes up situation & moves are made for the group's benefit)

Source: These *sample* behaviors were found in more than one research study. The descriptors listed here resonated with classroom teachers when piloted.

Note: Best strategy for choosing a match: Read the behavior and see which student(s) comes to mind immediately. If there is no immediate response, skip it and move to next behavior. You do not need to use any of these at all unless it is extremely accurate. A 'maybe' is not useful.

Table 8.1 (continued)

Reference Set K-12 Leadership (L)

Sample of emerging achievements

5	Often seen as leader of playground activities or in cooperative group projects; often selected by peers as group spokesperson; teaching assistant (school, scouts, religion); peer tutor; peer mediator; asst. coach; volunteers in hospitals, nursing homes; involved in student government; member of FBLA (Future Business Leaders of America); asst. coach; volunteers in hospitals, nursing home; scout badge for leadership
4	Started own business in spare time (lemonade stand, community library, toy exchange); holds elected office in student government or clubs (editor of school newspaper); member of community youth organization for multiple years; project team leader or PI for research; Captain or co-captain of athletic team
3	Begins a new club or program; create service or not-for-profit opportunities for others; student member on official school/district/town committees; Eagle Scout = Girl Scout equivalent; MIP on sports team; selected to attend regional leadership institute
2	State level recognition (Future Business Leaders of America, for coaching, for teaching); selected to attend state leadership institute; state conference presentation (solo or group of adults)
1	National level recognition; National Young Leaders Conference member

Source: Author's research of relevant literature and pilot studies

INTRODUCTION TO THE FIELD

Potential leadership needs much more research.[8] However some research on leadership skills suggests that students must have talent or expertise in another area prior to cultivating leadership talent.[9] Other research on leadership potential indicates an overlap of characteristics with the domain of creativity,[10] such as the aforementioned ability to tolerate ambiguity, solve problems creatively, be flexible in thought and action, and see new relationships. [These four behaviors are located on the "Reference Set of Possibilities" in the creativity list in this system, so are not repeated here.]

Students who exhibit leadership characteristics may do so in conjunction with creative ones. Reflecting this dichotomy, the *Encyclopedia of Giftedness, Creativity, and Talent*[11] has two entries, one on "'creative leadership" and one on "leadership."[12] Young entrepreneurs exemplify this overlap. In fact, there may be an equal number of creative and leadership characteristics observed in the profile of an individual entrepreneur. There also could be none. In at least one study, no correlation was found between creativity and leadership.[13]

Most students' first recognition of interest in leadership happens through informal encounters with family, friends, and community organizations. Working toward a common goal while encountering the challenges and rewards of a group effort can provide all group members with opportunities to learn leadership skills while developing personal strengths. Collaborative situations may identify promising leadership behaviors not evident elsewhere.[14]

For example, a 10-year study across the United States of youth-based organizations in at-risk environments identified an emerging leadership skill that may or may not be found in adult leadership.[15] Labeled "wisdom in spontaneity," this behavior was defined by these researchers as "the ability to assess situations quickly and step forward or backward in taking direction for the benefit of the group."[16] This ability to spontaneously "know" whether to have the group retreat or advance toward a sudden and unexpected change in the environment may be an adaptation of survival skills in leaders involved in transitional or dangerous environments.

A SAMPLE OF RESOURCES

The Academy of Achievement celebrates developed and developing leadership expertise. This organization inspires young leaders of tomorrow annually by honoring them and distinguished guests of honor—adults with exceptional accomplishment "from every facet of American life . . . the sciences, business, the professions, sports, literature, entertainment, the military, the arts, and public service."[17] This not-for-profit has existed since 1961 and was founded to inspire and educate young people to realize dreams that serve others and may be difficult or look impossible.

Toward that goal, this website (like the Lemelson Center's mentioned in the "Creativity in Science" section in chapter 7) now offers the opportunity to "Explore the Achiever Universe" by including interviews, biographies, and more on current and historic leaders who have been recognized for making a difference in their field. It is an informative site for students and educators alike: www.achievement.org. In the past, young leaders were identified as high school honor students[18] but are now selected from university Fellow or Scholars programs. For planning purposes, it is useful for students to know the program requirements for being recognized early on in order to choose to be prepared to work toward meeting all the qualifications. The website also includes a "Search for an Achiever" section for those with a known direction who are seeking exemplars.

A number of leadership training programs developed for high-ability students have been designed.[19] These formal leadership programs tend to include study of leaders, leadership styles, problem-solving experiences, and a self-evaluation of leadership potential. However, these programs are rarely found in schools. Some classrooms do use biographies written for students, including those on entrepreneurs, to offer an introduction to leaders in a field.[20] The Internet has exponentially increased wonderful opportunities to hear/see current leaders in diverse fields (see especially: www.ted.com/talks).

With respect to the K-12 population, leadership tends to be most often recognized within business achievements. Newspapers love to publish stories about enterprising (younger-the-better) youngsters at their lemonade stands. Business leaders provide scholarships to recognize young leaders each year in high schools across the country.

Young entrepreneurs can apply for national scholarships such as the NFIB/Visa Free Enterprise Scholars Awards.[21] A nonprofit organization that promotes business education for K-12 students is Junior Achievement, Inc.: http://www.ja.org. The U.S. Small Business Administration offers a teen web guide for starting a business: https://www.sba.gov/tools/sba-learning-center/ training/young-entrepreneurs. There is also a National Foundation for Teaching Entrepreneurship offering two- to three-week summer programs for interested 13- to 18-year-olds called BizCamp: https://www.nfte.com/bizcamps.[22]

The Boys and Girls Club of America has a curriculum designed by the same financial content developers responsible for designing curriculum content for the websites of major banks and other financial institutions that offer financial learning centers for their clients, sometimes with a section specifically designed for the clients' children. All of these curricula include a unit on entrepreneurship. *Money Matters: Make It Count*, the curriculum designed by Lightbulb Press for the Boys and Girls Club, provides the same quality of content to many through this community-run organization and is an excellent example of collaboration between business and a national club to meet a perceived need in a larger population.

High-level instruction in problem-solving designed specifically for student leaders by experts in leadership service can alter the recipients' state of being, with even a single short exposure. For an exemplar, West Point offers an annual one-day workshop on leadership and character development for local high school juniors. Space is limited to one or two students per school who are selected by the principal or designee.[23] The aftermath of enthusiasm, excitement, and empowerment that this experience embedded in participants each year is awe-inspiring.

According to students' comments as well as their actions and accomplishments within quite varied leadership roles for the next few years, the impact was authentic. Evidence of the impact of the one-day program designed for them lies in the fact that those qualities they discussed as pivotal to their understanding of the role of leadership did not dissipate in any of these students for the remaining two years of high school.

Triangulating these observations were comments by teachers and facilitators working with these students. Although sample size might be too small to conduct a quantitative study, something must be said about the qualitative factors such as consistency of certain leadership behaviors seen by all following the exposure. Requests to just replicate the curriculum content might be ineffective as the choreographed *instruction* by cadets and leaders demonstrating the tenets taught significantly contributes to the empowerment.

No doubt there are leadership opportunities designed for children in most, if not all, local community organizations or religious groups. Many organizations such as the Board of Education, Mayor's offices, Village Planning Boards, and PTA groups could have a position for a high school representative on their Board or for pertinent committees that benefit from a young person's perspective or the role played in collecting opinions. High school students are selected to participate as teaching aides for Sunday school in many Christian denominations. Rabbinical scholars begin their journey in high school or earlier within the Jewish tradition. A full list of all the possibilities for developing leadership skills in each sector would be enlightening for all. So would the opportunities to highlight teaching as leadership in other capacities.

Like any of the achievements listed, leadership opportunities can carry the same name yet change over time. As stated earlier about any opportunity listed in this book, checking with the approved programs reported each year by the National Association of Secondary School Principals is recommended as they review programs submitted to them and list only those programs that demonstrate that their offerings are in the best interest of the children they wish to serve. Until a central clearinghouse on all accomplishments that model these values and concern makes one continually updated list available, it would be useful to match the review of the achievement by the NASSP with the year that the accomplishment took place in the child's life.

This is because an activity can maintain the same name yet change its character or alter the level of demonstrated expertise in either direction. In line with this recommendation, asking parents to include a formal description or published materials of the actual context of the activity would also help delineate the level of talent development with precision.

For example, an international conference for youth seeking enrichment opportunities in leadership outside of business has historically been The Congressional Youth Leadership Council. Their conferences brought many leaders in government and politics to student populations. As of 2007 or so, however, it moved from a government-sponsored program to a private, for-profit company with differing opportunities and exposures.[24] These transitions from public funding to private funding typically alter the offerings in some way, often to a degree that needs reevaluation to determine if or where to place the level of achievement on the Talent Record.

Any "achievements" that merely require tuition payment are not achievements but enrichment. Paid lessons or exposures certainly belong as level 5
candidates for the Talent Profile as they indicate initial interest. On the other
hand, earning a placement through measured service, with that being the only
route, suggests at least a level 4 talent development achievement.

Furthering the Thought

One of the benefits of looking at all of the talent domains together as a
system is the advantage of seeing what opportunities are missing in each
environment.[25] Other than teaching classmates, limited positions in student
government, or offices held in extra-curricular clubs such as the Future
Business Leaders of America, most accomplishments found in K-12 leadership are derived from sources outside of schools. Obviously this is another
reason for combining community and school records for a holistic portrait of
accomplishments.

NOTES

1 Murphy & Johnson, 2011, p. 459.

2 Orfalea, 2005, p. 94.

3 Orfalea, 2005.

4 Lawson, 2004.

5 Harari, 2002; Lawson, 2004; Orfalea, 2005; Passow, 1977.

6 In third grade he knew he wanted to have a leadership role in federal law.

7 Dembo, et al., 1981.

8 Mumford, Friedrich, Caughron, & Antes, 2009; Passow, 1977; Riggio &
Mumford, 2011, Sisk, 1993.

9 Feldhusen & Kennedy, 1988; Roach, et al., 1999.

10 Feldhusen & Pleiss, 1992; Karnes & Chauvin, 2005; Roets, 1992.

11 Kerr, 2009.

12 If ever there is the opportunity for research, a statistical analysis may shed
some light on this question.

13 Feldhusen & Pleiss, 1992.

14 Jolly & Kettler, 2004; Roach, et al., 1999.

15 Roach, et al., 1999.

16 Roach, et al, 1999, p. 17.

17 37th Annual Salute to Excellence, p. 6.

18 37th Annual Salute to Excellence, also p. 6.

19 Feldhusen & Kennedy 1988; Karnes & Bean, 1995; Karnes & Chauvin, 2005;
Manning, 2005; Roets, 1992, Van Tassel-Baska, 1988.

20 Bisland, Karnes, & Cobb, 2004; National Foundation for Teaching Entrepreneurship, 2000; Karnes & Bean, 1997.

21 *My Business*, 2004.

22 It is important to know organizations such as this exist, but again, it is a sample and further research is always recommended.

23 Contrary to assumptions, the program was not specifically about military leadership or about becoming interested in applying for West Point, although many guidance counselors used it as such. Because we held an annual essay contest for a spot in the program, a variety of students qualified and participated over the years. Regardless of what side one is on in any debate about the role of government in schools, I think anyone observing this program would see that their ecumenical curriculum about leadership and character would be a service to our schools.

24 The Congressional Youth Leadership Council (http://nylfmed.org/sitecore/content/envisionexperience-website/envisionexperience-homepage/about/our-history-of-experiential-learning/congressional-youth-leadership-council) and the National Young Leadership Forum (http://www.nassp.org/activity/junior-national-young-leaders-conference/) are both now run by Envision EMI. Retrieved Wikipedia, January 16, 2017.

25 One gap that becomes apparent in many circumstances is the fact that the notion of "helping or being a part of others" used to be introduced in civics instruction and humanities curricula.

Chapter 9

A Closer Look at Visual/Performing Arts (AR) Abilities

To speak in metaphors, the work of art is another human mind incarnate: not in flesh and blood but in sounds, words, or colors.

—Dutton[1]

If you listen to artists talk about their craft, this concept of "negative capability"—the ability to live comfortably in the presence of mystery and the absence of certainty—comes up with remarkable frequency. "Whatever inspiration is," the Polish poet Wislawa Szymborska said in her 1996 Nobel Prize acceptance speech, "its born from a continuous 'I don't know'.

—K. Schultz[2]

At its core, the arts remind all of us (and provide the necessary practice) to obtain information through our senses. Sensory-based ways of knowing cultivate the primal method of obtaining knowledge—through perception.[3] Observational skills (through all senses) remain core not only to our physical survival[4] but also to our emotional and intellectual well-being.

The arts also serve as universal communication systems across cultures and time. Beyond the fact that those familiar with producing an art form are the most serious appreciators/connoisseurs of world-class art, cultivating and appreciating aesthetic sensibilities in various cultures is as expanding as experiencing a culture by speaking its language. Thus, the skills and behaviors developed in these talent domains have been linked to developing skills of empathy.[5]

Experts in science often give credit to their advanced artistic skills for enabling breakthroughs in their scientific field, whether the scientist studies performing arts[6] or visual art.[7] This pattern of astute observation skills and aesthetic proclivities is found throughout history, cultures, and fields of inquiry. Noticing these behaviors is not to be aimed solely on the class thespian or artist.

Reflecting the research, the sections on the visual arts and the performing arts are separated here. Essentially, the Reference Set of behaviors found in the research on visual arts highlights visual perception, and the performing arts studies address sound and movement as key perceptual factors.

VISUAL ARTS (AR.v)

Art washes away from the soul the dust of everyday life.

—Pablo Picasso

Talent in the visual arts often makes newspaper headlines when a child prodigy is discovered. Picasso, Michelangelo, Raphael, and many more have demonstrated intense interest and ability, if not graphic mastery, by age 10 or 11.[8] In describing the life of caricature artist Al Hirschfeld, an author noted, "The artistic prodigy arrived in New York city at the age of 11 so that he could get the proper training for his talent."[9] The pioneer of abstract expressionism Willem de Kooning was a full-fledged member of the Academy of Holland at 12 years of age.[10]

A more contemporary prodigy, the young female painter Wang Yani made newspaper headlines around the world as a five-year-old with amazing brush strokes. A special exhibit at the Smithsonian heralded her accomplishments. Her work was compared to a composer whereas other child artists "are more like instrumentalists interpreting someone else's compositions."[11] Wang Yani's father was an artist and art educator who nurtured her observations and art skills from infancy. She was a year old when the strict limitations on art subjects and styles were lifted in China. Both are significant, as environment provides the sustenance that talent needs to grow. Although her fame as a young prodigy went international, the trajectory of her developed talent, like other identified prodigies, remains unknown.

Precocity is only one of many potential characteristics of visual art talent and one found only sometimes in a few of the very talented who have all the necessary supports to succeed. Yet, it does not automatically ensure success. Al Hurwitz described four levels of visual art talent: "There are those with an aptitude for art; those of minimal talent who nevertheless enjoy making art; those whose attitudes and skills set them above their classmates; and those who combine skill, intellect, imagination, and drive on a high level."[12]

Hurwitz has also described the essence of an artistically gifted child: "A child gifted in art observes acutely and has a vivid memory, is adept at handling problems requiring imagination, and although open to new experiences, prefers to delve deeply into a limited area. The child takes art seriously and derives great personal satisfaction from the work, is persistent, and spends much time making and learning about art."[13] Two other behaviors identified with professional artists are also found in the artistically gifted: the ability and desire to define a problem to solve and the need to satisfy personal aesthetic preferences.[14]

Drawing or sculpting from life develops observational skills like no other task. The ability to draw has been a recognized talent of many in their youth who move on to other accomplishments, marking it as an ability that goes beyond artistic competence. For example, filmmaker James Cameron attributes his early childhood drawing efforts to his intense observation skills. Some architects and sculptors describe their very early interests with building blocks (Froebel, Wright, or Legos) and then drawing their creations.

There are also those, like the sculptors interviewed by Bloom,[15] who did not demonstrate their artistic talent in two-dimensional school activities and found art in school distasteful. There are those who pursue photography, video, collage, and crafts that all require specific exposure to ignite interest. The visual arts also include design fields such as architecture, or graphic, fashion, industrial, and product design.

Every young artist develops differently. It is in studying many sources over time that one sees patterns. One interview with a six-year-old who had presented a full portfolio of about 30 drawings demonstrates one example of the indisputable evidence of specific behaviors:

> When I asked this 6-year-old if he remembered when he started drawing, he answered, "I was very young. I think 4 or 5. No, I must have been 3 [mother nodded confirmation]. I wasn't as good as now. I get better." Asked why he needed to draw so much (20 to 50 drawings a week), the response was "Because I love it! I just love it!"

The rest of the interview went as follows:

> "How do you choose what to draw?"
> "Oh, I pick which picture would look good as a drawing."
> "What do you mean? Where are these pictures you pick from?"
> "In my head. I pick which one I would like to see as a drawing."
> "Are there many to choose from?
> "Oh, yes!"[16]

That portfolio of work was submitted to several art teachers to review asking what grade level they thought the child was who had completed this work. Without exception, art teachers around the country thought this work by a five-year-old was done by a seventh or eighth grader. This led to filming the child as he prepared for and completed a drawing in the presence of an unbiased researcher to eliminate speculation that this was an impossible feat.

It also provided documentation for future issues surrounding difficulties in school, as this extreme level of asynchronous development is rare and difficult to comprehend. Videotaping a child immersed in an activity for several hours without breaks can also eliminate discussions surrounding lack of ability to focus.

Public schools rarely include artistically gifted students in the pool of identified gifted/talented programs unless the school is specialized to address that talent. One successful exception was designed with developing expertise in mind.[17] When art teachers have an understanding of child development as often mirrored in drawings, they bring a specific expertise to portfolio reviews that include artists and other art professionals (gallery owners, art advisors, and other gatekeepers in the field) looking to identify artistic talent based on demonstrated achievements.

This was the impetus behind an identification process that required five to seven reviews of a portfolio that had been submitted by a student after a nomination had been made by any one of the following: teacher, parent, peer, or self. The matrix for objective decision-making had multiple weighted criteria, including the group IQ score used for everyone else in every talent domain. But because other criteria such as screening forms describing behaviors, past accomplishments, and audition/portfolios were incorporated in the matrix, the weight of any one evaluation was reduced as it added to the sum.

The portfolio evaluations were conducted individually so the scores were not collaboratively attained but rather applied to create a group score. Two reasons influenced this decision: first of all any student submitting the portfolio requirements deserved some specific, constructive feedback from each of these assessors as good evaluation instructs. Evaluators agreeing to the portfolio review task knew they were to provide some feedback to the child that would help advance the process the child seemed to be seeking. This was usually shared with the student in the form of a personal note unattached to the ratings. Students reported this to be the most profoundly helpful aspect of the process whether or not they were admitted to the program. Often those who lacked what was necessary were told the specifics that were missing and encouraged to reapply when they were mastered if they remain interested in pursuing the goal.

Secondly, where discrepancies of scores between judges were large, seven reviews were sought with the top and bottom score eliminated. The criteria for the judging was based on *seeking potential*, leaving the past accomplishment form for rating current expertise. In the identification process, the average score for all the portfolio evaluations was then recorded on the primary matrix[18] as one score that was to be combined with the other diverse criteria. The four criteria for just that portfolio evaluation (technical ability such as composition, line quality, and control; problem-solving ability; communication of ideas or ability to make a strong statement; and inventiveness/imaginative ability) were also successfully used in committee work choosing art awards for senior art majors.

SAMPLE RESOURCES IN ART

The Internet has opened up the world of art to many. Museums across the globe have virtual tours of their collections. There are interviews with artists and others interested in the visual arts (see www.ted.com/talks for some inspirational examples).

The National Arts Honor Society and the National Junior Art Honor Society recognize students in grades 7 to 12 who have been nominated by their teachers for their outstanding ability in art. For more information: https://www.arteducators.org/audiences/nahs-njahs.

The Alliance for Young Artists & Writers, which administers the Scholastic Art and Writing Awards, may be the oldest not-for-profit organization that honors the creative excellence of secondary students in visual arts. They offer a large number of visual art awards in a broad range of categories that include fine arts (painting, drawing, mixed media, printmaking, sculpture, photography, computer graphics, and video, film, and animation), design

Table 9.1

Reference Set of Possibilities: Visual Arts

Observed Behaviors

5   Passionate need to draw and/or sculpt which results in intense joy is stated by child or observed

Often describes seeing many vivid images in mind's eye (visual memory, visual fluency)

Artwork advances beyond developmental age (precocity, rapid development)

Self-directedness (high level of self-motivation, independence)

Demonstrates extended concentration

Themes may emerge as possibilities are explored in large volumes of work

Advanced perceptual acuity is evident through attention to details

Creative imagination is idiosyncratic in its originality

Demonstrates personal aesthetic preferences (strong sense of what is beautiful, elegant, or personally correct

High technical proficiency (includes verisimilitude, being true to life)

Has problem-defining skills = prefers personal interests rather than class assignment

Source: These *sample* behaviors were found in more than one research study. The descriptors listed here resonated with classroom teachers when piloted.

Note: Best strategy for choosing a match: Read the behavior and see which student(s) comes to mind immediately. If there is no immediate response, skip it and move to next behavior. You do not need to use any of these at all unless it is extremely accurate. A 'maybe' is not useful.

Table 9.1 (continued)

Reference Set of Possibilities: Visual Arts

Small sample of Achievements in visual arts (AR.v)

5	Draws a lot; makes movies with camcorder; often makes sculptures; reputation as artist with peers; does extra credit art assignments; asks for/takes art classes, subject matter is advanced
4	Selected "artist of month" by art teacher; award recipient PTA Reflection contest; places in County art shows; competitions; member art club; Olympics of the Visual Arts team member; illustrator for school publications, posters; work selected for District art show
3	Award from countywide art shows; local, non-juried, gallery exhibition; Honors courses
2	Award recipient state-level competitions; juried gallery exhibition (group show); AP courses
1	Award recipient national level; juried, one-person gallery exhibition; work selected for Binney & Smith Dream-makers exhibit; Kennedy Center Fellowship

Source: Author's research of relevant literature and pilot studies

(environment, graphic, and product), and crafts (ceramics, jewelry and metalsmithing, and textile and fabric design). In addition there are numerous awards for portfolios and Best of Show. Long before students are ready to apply, they can gain valuable insights and information from the website: www.artandwriting.org. Viewing the work of prior winners often inspires!

National and regional visual arts opportunities appear plentiful on the Internet as well. As mentioned in the creativity chapter, the renowned Arts Recognition and Talent Search offers cash prizes and scholarships as well as the nomination of finalists to be Presidential Scholars in the arts: http://www.house.gov/content/educate/art competition/. There is a Congressional Art Competition for two-dimensional work by 9th to 12th graders from Congressional Districts that participate: https://www.house.gov/educators-and-students/congressional-art-competition and an annual Reflections program for all grade levels through the local PTA: www.pta.org/Reflections. More opportunities can be found in Johns Hopkins CTY 2003 issue of Imagine: Focus on the Arts.

Most summer programs are pre-college programs for high school students, but there are a few that cater to young students as well (Idyllwild Arts Summer Program for ages 5 to 18: www.idyllwildarts.org; Interlochen Arts Camp for students in grades 3 through 12: www.interlochen.org; and Massart's Summer Art Programs include a commuter program called Creative Vacation for students in grades 3–9: https://www.massart.edu/Continuing_Education/Youth_Programs.html. Governor schools for the arts and high schools for art and design can be found in a few states and some large cities.

THE PERFORMING ARTS

The performing arts included in the Talent Record are those found in the federal definition: acting, dance, and music. No doubt a case could be made for other categories or descriptors. Comedians and Improvisational Theater fall under this same "acting" category as Sawyer's research on Improv provided support.[19] Although timing and many of the other anecdotal behaviors found here would be found in a performing comedian, there would necessarily be creative behaviors observed as well. The term "performing" is the operative word. Juggling, modeling, or magic could be added or combined within the acting section if research on developmental levels of expertise are either found or conducted.

Table 9.2

Reference Set of Possibilities: Performing Arts

Observed Behaviors

---

5   Learns basic skills immediately, almost intuitively (words, melodies, movement)

         Demonstrates a good memory for movement, patterns or sounds (rhythm and pitch)

         Displays advanced motor skills (gross and/or fine motor)

         Perceives very fine differences in voice, musical tone, dance movements, and/or theater skills

         Seeks out opportunities to participate or observe music, dance, or dramatics

         Is sensitive to "background" noises, movements, stage settings

         Can accurately mimic the way people: speak, walk, gesture, sing, or play instruments

         Others enjoy the storytelling/improvisations/role-playing/music; commands audience

         Effectively uses sounds, or facial expressions and gestures to communicate feelings

         Uses descriptive words to add color, emotion, and beauty or sensitive to the aesthetic qualities of sounds or movement seeking aesthetic expression/response

---

Source: These *sample* behaviors were found in more than one research study. The descriptors listed here resonated with classroom teachers when piloted.

Note: Best strategy for choosing a match: Read the behavior and see which student(s) comes to mind immediately. If there is no immediate response, skip it and move to next behavior. You do not need to use any of these at all unless it is extremely accurate. A 'maybe' is not useful.

Table 9.2 (continued)

Reference Set of Possibilities: Performing Arts

Small sample of Achievements in acting (AR.a)

5	Participates in recitals, talent shows; frequently rehearses routines (comedy, magic); member of cast in school plays; storyteller; Drama Club member, takes music, dance, or acting lessons; performs at expected standard or top 15%ile
4	Member of community acting assoc.; lead role in local plays (school or community); attends enrichment/training classes in professional theater (music) (dance) school (Sat or summer repertory); Odyssey of the Mind /Destination Imagination State Competitions; performance rated (by experts in field) as top 2-3%ile
3	Member profession Member professional actors or magician's guild; auditions for professional roles in TV, theater, movies, or advertising; participates in summer repertory theater
2	Member professional acting company
1	Any national recognition for performances

Small sample of Achievements in dance (AR.d)

5	Always dancing or moving to sounds; student in dance school
4	Selected for local (community) dance recitals; soloist in dance recital
3	County-level recitals; contests; Pre-professional summer/Saturday program at dance school
2	State-level performances; Professional division summer/Saturday program at professional dance school; internship/mentorship with professional school or performing group
1	National level recognition; internship/mentorship with nationally recognized person or organization

This talent domain is one that is rarely addressed in public schools after kindergarten—except for those communities that may still maintain a music program or put on a grade-level play. In these instances, most opportunities to advance one's expertise more likely will come from family, friends, community, and religious or neighborhood organizations.

Performing Arts.acting (AR.a)

Based on the 1972 U.S. Federal Marland definition of gifted/talented education, one high school program for gifted/talented students identified students in all six areas—including visual/performing arts.[20] In determining the

Table 9.2 (continued)

Reference Set of Possibilities: Performing Arts

Small sample of Achievements in music (AR.m)

5	Member band, orchestra, chorus, plays piano, selected member for religious organization's music group, private lessons
4	Select band, orchestra, chorus; award recipient for school-level PTA Reflections contest; selected for soloist part or accompanies conductor during school concerts; NYSSMA level at grade expectation [Level 1: gr.5-6 (percussion gr. 6-7); Level II: gr. 6-7 percussion gr. 7-8); Level III: gr. 7-8 (percussion gr. 8-9); Level IV: gr. 8-9 (percussion gr. 9-10); Level V: gr. 9-10 (percussion 9-10); Level VI: gr. 11-12] OR any other standard from field that assesses performance at top 2 to3%ile of population
3	All-County orchestra, band, chorus member; strolling strings; Jazz ensemble; Voice ensemble; District Orchestra II & III; NYSSMA rating -2 grade levels above expectation; composes music; solo performances; Area All-State
2	NYSSMA rating 3-4 levels above expectation; Julliard early-entrance sat program; All-State Chorus, band, orchestra; Youth Symphony
1	All-Eastern (Regional), National Competitions, internship at Metropolitan Opera

Source: Author's research of relevant literature and pilot studies

identification process they would follow, an English teacher who was also an active member of the professional Screen Actors Guild provided guidance. By using the standards of experts in the field, identification of advanced performance was far more accurate and meaningful.

Auditions based on the standards of the professional acting world provided opportunities for every applicant's growth and encouragement—a desirable outcome of any worthwhile evaluation. Task commitment was demonstrated as students signed up for a date to perform and prepared for their auditions. Without this level of expertise from in-house resources, school officials could ask community members with the proper credentials to assess the level of talent or, less ideally, decide to base the assessment purely on past accomplishments.

One way for schools to accommodate a lack of knowledge in a field is to list on the student's record the specifics for each accomplishment. For example, rather than state "lead in 6th grade play" one would state "lead in 6th grade play: Music Man." This information is more useful to the experts who do know the standards of a field.

Looking at the pinnacle of this talent domain, the issue of school for professional child actors and performers deserves some attention. "Home schooling" and tutoring appear to be the most likely solution to years of working in the TV studio or film business. A thoroughly child-centered approach to schooling took place behind the scenes of the television show "The Wonder Years."[21] Teachers were employed to work with the children on their schoolwork any minute that any child was not required on the set. These teachers not only taught their charges, they maintained constant contact with all the teachers in each child's home school district on a daily basis so that any one of those students could fly home to attend their own school on any day and be literally on the same page.

This attention to the synthesis of all of the elements of a child's life is found in other successful situations involving the development of exceptional talent. An administrator of Cirque du Soleil also described a need to provide more than a career to the young members who agree to a seven-year commitment on the road.[22]

They have identified four factors that are favorable to the natural social development of young artists: (1) The young members do not feel isolation, as there are many age mates with the same artistic objectives; (2) the troupe recreates a family style of living with the degree of intimacy where everyone "has a place to cry," and they encourage regular family visits; (3) a sense of balance between work and personal time is choreographed to counter the tendencies toward perfectionism or being consumed by the art form; and (4) they monitor the psychological profiles of potential participants regardless of talent, looking at youth, circumstance, and anorexia. In training of performance skills or life skills, the process is one of cultivating a lifestyle, not just a career in a production company.

Performing Arts.dance (AR.d)

The Alvin Ailey American Dance Center, the official school of the Alvin Ailey American Dance Theater, accepts students to their Junior Division as early as three years of age (Junior Division Program Brochure, n.d. https://www.theaileyschool.edu/sites/default/files/TheAileySchool_JrDivision-brochure.pdf) and offers classes for beginners and novice dancers up to age 15. Offering diverse programs in both the Junior Division (ages 3 to 15) and the Professional Division (ages 15 and older), a match between interest and expertise is carefully channeled toward appropriate opportunities for growth. Like most professional arts schools, there are levels and benchmarks that clearly state the standards/expectations of each step along the way.

In the Netherlands, a ballet dancer in the making would have moved from a local dance school to a professional school that incorporates academics with dance instruction by the age of 10.[23] In the United States, large cities are more likely to offer world-class, professional dance schools with these endless opportunities. Other geographic locations will range from not having any private dance instructors available to having a wide assortment of opportunities featuring various degrees of expertise. Local opportunities for study can be found with the help of the research librarian, college or university faculty, or Internet search. In the arts there are usually people who want to help connect interest with opportunities, so local groups can provide leads as well.

Performing Arts.music (AR.m)

The development of musical talent is a heavily researched area.[24] Like all other talent areas, musical talent can take form in or outside of school. Of the three case studies described in an article on the subject,[25] one student began conservatory piano training at age four, another began piano at age five and later played clarinet in school band, and the third began with the guitar at age eight and continued composing and playing jazz music outside of school. As the author indicates, only the second of these three students would have been recognized as musically talented in school as the other two studied and performed outside of that context. Yet the one that would be recognized at school was the least professionally accomplished.[26] These scenarios are more common than one would think.

On First Steps of an Emerging Talent in Music

There are many students who pursue their talent domain outside of the school context, yet they would benefit from sharing their personal talents with school personnel. A few other music talents come to mind: one female student wanted to study opera, an area not addressed in an exceptional public school music department. However, there was an English teacher at the high school with a passion for opera and professional training who performed for local groups. She would have been the perfect match for the student's English classes so that sharing their interest and perhaps some informal mentoring could have taken place over time. This simple, cost-free accommodation of matching student interests with those of an instructor can take place only with prior knowledge of developing talents.

"The earlier the musical ability of a child is discovered the better will be his or her chances of developing that talent."[27] One example begins to unfold with the material collected from the mother of a girl who qualified for Juilliard's Saturday program while in middle school. Collected for a Talent Profile, the following provides a glimpse of the trajectory of talent and opportunities that preceded the achievement:

Birth to 2 years—much stimulation was provided at home. Many Fisher-Price instruments & an upright piano were always available for L to experiment with, I had music tapes playing much of the time: Ex. Red Grammar, Linda Arnold. By 2 yrs. of age L was able to independently operate our stereo system. She would chose music on her own, & dance and sing constantly.

Age 2—used her piano as a "rattle." Would climb on piano bench & "make music" with 2 hands and sing along.

Age 3- L listened to Disney songs & played melody of many on piano at home. She was reading and writing @ 3 yrs. old. I had nothing to do with it. She was truly a "self-directed learner."

Age 4—pre-K—I chose this pre school because music was emphasized. L. sang songs in school and at home. Was able to play music on piano (both melody and chords). Class play (Peter Rabbit) was acted out. L was able to play all the songs for the play (by ear). Family friend invited L to her house regularly as she was aware that a music talent was evident. This person was also a pianist. L was asked to play for . . . an accomplished pianist. Pianist decided that L should begin to take piano lessons as she felt L would rely on her ear vs. written music. (This would be a habit very hard to break.)

K (age 5) [Author note: formal schooling begins] piano lessons were 2x/ month. Teacher focused on board games to teach musical notes + signs. She also assigned written music from books for L to practice. L would also play familiar songs during music class [at school]. Music teacher recognized L's talent & provided opportunities to share music with peers in school.

[Grade] 1 - Piano lessons continued 2x/month. L continued to have opportunity to share music w peers in school. L would play all new songs that were sung in music class at school.

[Grade] 2 - Piano lessons continued 2x/month. [Music teacher] was aware of L's talent from [K-1 music teacher] L was always encouraged to play at school. Won 1st place PTA Reflections contest (music) at school, then 1st place district-wide (original composition).

[Grade] 3 - Piano lessons continued now 1 hour/week. Won 1st place PTA Reflections contest (original composition) at school, piano medley performance at school talent show, accompanied teacher for grade 3 chorus performances, state-level music guild for piano (judged performance).

[Grade] 4 - Piano lessons continued 1 hour/week. Won 1st place PTA Reflections contest (original composition) at school, piano medley performance at school talent show, accompanied teacher for grade 3 and grade 4 chorus performances, state-level music guild for piano (judged performance), L decided to also study "violin" with school music teacher.

[Grade] 5 - switched piano teachers - focus is mostly on classical music. #1 Reflections winner (original composition - notation done w/out adult assistance, lyrics written and sung by L.) continued to study violin, joined Allegro Chamber orchestra, NYSSMA violin - 4 pieces (2 duets, 1 quartet, 1 solo) scored in superior range, plays violin in school orchestra, accompanied 4/5 grade, chorus with school music teacher, chosen to sing in select chorus

[Grade] 6 - Piano lessons continued 1 hour/week. Won 1st place PTA Reflections contest (original composition with notations) at school, continues violin, school orchestra (first chair) and Allegro Chamber Orchestra, select chorus. Accompanied 5/6th grade chorus with school music teacher, chosen to sing in All-County chorus, District-wide chorus.

Also, L excels in all academic/art areas. (Received from mother, 1995. Used with permission)

The successful try-out for the Saturday Program at Juilliard began her career climb toward an elite-level musician in an entirely new milieu, one where everyone is extremely talented in music. All that preceded that successful audition provided just the preliminary step in the journey toward elite-level talent. Once the context of the journey of a developing talent goes beyond national-level accomplishments, the teaching experts seek additional qualifying criteria for further advancement. This major environmental change is captured in the reflections of the studio teachers studied at The Julliard School:

> According to our interviewees, the audition process works well at unveiling "God given talent" developed by way of intensive focus and hard work. One studio teacher summarized this perspective by saying, "I think the biggest most important part of it is innate. You can recognize it, squelch it, encourage it, develop it, but you can't put it in." (Subotnik, 2004, p. 5)

In addition to auditions, prospective candidates for entrance in the school may be subjected to an interview or a sample lesson to determine the candidate's physical memory, musicianship, and "teachability." There are also many subjective qualities that are critical to formal success as well. Research has found that "in the final stages of the talent development process, personality factors clearly outweigh all other variables."[28]

Fostering Talent Development

Following the musical trajectory of one child from her infant beginning to the doorway of opportunity to further development in an elite professional music school may provide a glimpse of the depth and complexity required to realize potential. Unspoken is the time and effort on the part of a supportive parent(s) with the means to provide the path without obstacles. Renting a studio apartment in New York City for weekly trips on Friday nights so that the Saturday morning lessons were as productive as possible; organizing the family's life around this pursuit; and providing the endless emotional and physical support to ensure a balanced, well-adjusted teenager throughout this journey is not a small task. And each individual's journey is a unique constellation of many factors.

NOTES

1 Dutton, 2009, p. 235.
2 Schulz, 2010, p. 329.
3 Kay, 1990. See examples in Kogan 2003.
4 Dutton, 2009.
5 Burton, 2017; Greene, 1995.

6 Root-Bernstein, 1989.

7 Root-Bernstein, 2000, 2011.

8 Ho, 1989.

9 Plagens, 2003.

10 Scrivani, 1988.

11 Ho, 1989, p. 55.

12 Hurwitz, 1983, p. 95; Karnes, 1978b.

13 Hurwitz & Day, 2007, p. 89.

14 Kay, 1989, 2000, 2001c, 2008.

15 Bloom, 1985.

16 Kay, 2003, p. 126.

17 Dembo, et al., 1981.

18 Although the author developed the secondary matrix for the visual arts, the idea of uniting the various criteria from different talent areas by using a secondary matrix designed specifically to each area, which was then applied, to the universal criteria on the primary matrix was the brilliant work of Ana Dembo. See Dembo, et al., 1981.

19 Sawyer, 2012.

20 Dembo, et al., 1981.

21 The director Ken Topolsky allowed me to visit their bus-like vehicle that was permanently set up behind the studio.

22 NAGC, 1997, Montreal, Quebec.

23 Van Rossum, 2001.

24 Bamberger, 1986; Bloom, 1985; Csikszentmihalyi, Rathunde, & Whalen, 1993; Davidson & Scripp; 1994; Haroutounian, 2000; Howe & Sloboda, 1992; Richardson, 1990; Sloboda, 1996; Subotnik, 2004.

25 Haroutounian, 2000; Karnes, 1978a; Meeker, 1977; Subotnik & Jarvin, 2005.

26 Ibid., p. 4.

27 Kough & DeHaan, p. 43.

28 Subotnik, 2004, p. 6.

Chapter 10

Early Sightings of Psychomotor/ Kinesthetic (PK) Abilities

When I'm scratching I'm improvising. Like a jazz musician jamming for an hour to find a few interesting notes, a choreographer looks for interesting movement. I didn't start out knowing this; it came to me over time, as I realized I would never get to the essential core of movement and dance through a cerebral process. I could prepare, order, organize, structure, and edit my creativity in my head, but I couldn't think my way into a dance. To generate ideas, I had to *move*. It's the same if you're a painter: You can't imagine the work, you can only generate ideas when you put pencil to paper, brush to canvas—when you actually do something physical.

—Twyla Tharp[1]

An amazing choreographer, Twyla Tharp's description captures the way many students first enter into their talent field.[2] As she clearly states, the generating of ideas in her artistic domain is done through doing a physical, not cognitive, act that leads to a new idea. She is not alone in stating that many painters claim the same process. So do many others.

The term "kinesthetic" describes the sensory experience provided by sensory organs called proprioceptors found in the muscles and joints of our bodies that form an awareness of the position and movement of parts of the body. Information gleaned from this experience guides thought. For those unfamiliar with the idea of learning by doing rather than learning by thinking, perhaps this may be seen as a more concentrated form of what occurs during the ritual of walking and thinking often mentioned by other brilliant minds describing their preferred method of generating ideas or solutions.[3]

Watching young minds investigate their worlds in particular ways, this ability is clearly evident in some, even though the method eventually may lead to accomplishment in another domain, especially, it seems, STEM-related work.

Like the chapter on emerging expertise in the arts, these psychomotor abilities lead to a forked road: (1) a hard-to-classify "What do I need to do or undo on this object to figure out how it works?" approach to the world, and (2) the easily recognized "How do I have my body do this?" approach needed for athletics. Each is powered by the need to figure out how things work physically first in order to learn to do the activity properly.

PSYCHOMOTOR/KINESTHETIC ABILITIES

Scenario 1: A five-year-old plays by himself during his kindergarten recess. His teacher watches as he pretends to be a Delorean (car), changing gears, turning on the eight-track tape player (obsolete at the time), putting himself in reverse, with extremely accurate sound effects. Back in the classroom, he has so much trouble sitting still his teacher wisely places him in the back of the room with the computer. Immediately she notices that his concentration *on her lessons* has improved significantly when he is allowed to listen and "play" on the unplugged keyboard simultaneously.

Scenario 2: A child in an upper elementary classroom sits in back of the room quietly catching a fly and tying a note to a back leg creating a miniature, low-tech banner. If this task was one assigned to an entire grade level, I suspect all but this child would fail.

Scenario 3: "But there were also lessons from my Dad, serious lessons that got me an incredibly early start in engineering. These lessons would always start because I'd ask a question. And I had a lot of questions. I remember we actually spent weeks and weeks talking about different types of atoms and then I learned how electrons can actually flow through things—like wires. Then, finally, he explained to me how the resistors work—not by calculations, because who can do calculations when you're a second grader, but by real commonsense pictures and explanations. You see, he gave me classical electronics training from the beginning."[4]

One point of these scenarios is that ability does not always emerge and find its way to an acceptable path without help. Each of these children needed a perceptive mentor who recognized a special talent and was able to encourage it.

In short, psychomotor/kinesthetic ability is where the students who learn best "by doing" begin to shine first. Whether it is an athletic activity, mechanical savvy or a technological advancement, there is a sensory and physical quality or "physicality" that guides the learning process and subsequent achievements. This physicality is first observed in those children who want to know how to build, construct or fix. It has also been noted by some as critical to developing advanced expertise in diverse areas such as brain surgery, music, and sports.[5]

Another way to demonstrate abilities is to describe their absence. The following true story provides an illustration:

Sixth graders participating in a G/T program who were mostly identified under academic or intellectual talent areas were informally complaining to each other about how long it takes most of the students in their regular classroom to understand anything new. After watching the G/T students unsuccessfully cut paper for simple puzzle pieces, the instructor introduced a unit on building paper models—a skill all producers of ideas would find useful. The unit included multiple tasks for building three-dimensional models that moved from paper that ended with the construction of a well-designed advanced kit for a moving toy that everyone was excited to make.

But the students' frustration and need for remediation for basic physical skills such as measuring, cutting with scissors and especially gluing were shocking. In each class, when the frustration became too much, the students were told to put their tools down and asked to notice how they were feeling and describe it in words in their journal. Some shared out loud. Then, they were gently told that this unfamiliar emotion was called "frustration". The instructor explained that it is an important emotion to conquer, and that their classmates most likely feel this level of frustration when they cannot do schoolwork as easily and quickly as they see some of their classmates do. Beyond a newfound empathy, learning to muster the commitment to rebuild until the moving toy was right came slightly easier to them after that. The value of the lesson led to it becoming a significant mainstay of the curriculum.

TECHNOLOGY

Technological and/or mechanical abilities come under psychomotor/kinesthetic abilities, and it is this area that does not receive much attention in schools or elsewhere. In our postmodern world we have moved from applied arts and sciences and industrial arts to the term technology. The change in terminology heralds the tremendous alteration of our world due to computer science and the advancements witnessed because of this technology. Some children embraced the movement long before our schools did:

Roy Niederhoffer's dad thought his son should play outside more. In 1979, then-13-year-old Niederhoffer spent lots of his time in his room, playing on one of the first computers, a TRS80. When he developed a clone of the popular "Space Invaders" game, he sent it to a company that advertised for such games in a magazine he read. "At first my dad said, 'what are you doing upstairs in your room like a Gollum; play outside like the other boys and quit wasting your life,' Niederhoffer recalls. But that attitude changed when the royalties to the game started amounting to a few hundred dollars a month. (Mullich, 2004, p. 37)

Of course there is more to this success story than just technical abilities—leadership and creativity are entwined here—but the hours of deliberate practice with computer programming are at the foundation of this story. How many young minds are or want to be engaged in developing computer games? Schools that have programs that encourage self-directed investigations[6] see this interest early and often. And games are not the only programs students challenge themselves to create.

Before leaving for MIT, one high school student developed an entire program that would allow the school district to create student photo IDs that incorporated each student's current class schedule on the back of the ID. This was his senior independent inquiry project when typing on computers had just entered the curriculum in schools. No one understood how advanced it was and how well it worked until a member of the community who worked for IBM and *happened* to attend the end-of-year celebration event for parents and community members, *happened* upon his work and acknowledged him for his outstanding work in the field. The irony lies in the fact that the school program had spent two years seeking a mentor for this young man's talents. The incident fueled a magnificent outreach by parents and community members to include their names on a list of potential mentors listing their areas of interests.

Interest in fixing or building computers is another area that captivates many young minds. Finding local, live mentors for this important field has always been most difficult. This huge gap in the expertise of school personnel could be addressed through internet-based mentoring by the experts in companies who will be seeking more computer engineers in the future. With careful planning for protections of all involved, an online mentorship option would be ideal for many students; especially those students who don't live near a technology hub or have a family member in the field.

Major companies could provide an online help desk for students through Skype-like environments and mentorship opportunities for advanced students that would fuel interest by developing needed skills. The same could be done for all types of engineers. If interested employees could use a fraction of a percentage of their work time cultivating the interest and expertise of those ready and willing for some help with online mentoring, there might not be any shortage of engineers.

Fortunately, some leaders in the technology field such as Alan Kay of Viewpoints Research Institute are concerned with fostering talent and interest. He has spearheaded the design of freeware for children (e.g., SqueakEToys and Croquet) and sees computers as developing from the social phenomena they currently are to learning environments that mentor children in deep thinking skills, especially in mathematical thinking.

Some Other Related Opportunities

In fact, businesses have recently provided an introduction to programming for all students through annual Hour of Code events: https://hourofcode. com/files/hoc-one-pager.pdf. Computer programming has had a national and international platform for developing expertise through the USA Computing Olympiad: www.usaco.org. Students can prepare for the grueling five-hour competitions with guidelines, practice problems and a level set for beginners.[7]

Intense interest in building models from building blocks or Legos can also begin before school age. The same interest in three-dimensional model building can occur using paper (origami, cardboard architecture, pop-up mechanisms for books or cards). At some point in the journey of some learners, the interest in following patterns gives way to an interest in creating environments and unique pieces that contribute to a private microcosm. Photos of basements transformed by these complex "other worlds" occur more often than one would expect.

Marketing experts at Lego realized the need to cultivate this interest by offering awards or competitions for new designs, developing kits for schools to teach the basics, and offering a robotics challenge to 9- to 14-year-old students. The *F.I.R.S.T. Lego League* provides an annual challenge to teams of students who can then compete at a local and state level (see www.first-lego-league.org/en/2016.html).

The *First* Robotics Competition began in 1989 as an idea of the inventor of the Segway scooter, Dean Kamen, who states, "Societies get what they celebrate."[8] See http://www.firstinspires.org/robotics/frc/kickoff. An excellent review of selected opportunities in robotics/engineering was highlighted in the May/June 2017 issue of *Imagine*, an outstanding journal for academically talented youth published by Johns Hopkins Center for Talent Development: https://cty.jhu.edu/imagine/about/back_issues.html. Other team competitions that include elementary-age students are *RoboCupJr* (see http://robo cupjunior.squarespace.com) and *RoboFest* (grades 5 to 12; see https:// www.robofest.net). There are quite a few more robotics competitions available to middle and high school students. Competitions geared for older students may require the team to work with a professional engineer (see *F.I.R.S.T. Robotics Competition* mentioned before). Some of the competitions require the purchase of a standard kit to be used in solving the challenge.

Many of the competitions are international and can lead to travel abroad. The Maker's Movement has taken off full steam with organizations and World competitions as well as local events available for those who would have liked the Popular Mechanics/Woodworking magazines of the past and live in a place that fosters these sub-communities where resources are repurposed: https://makerfaire.com. Cost, availability of expertise, and coordination of these experiences seem to limit opportunities to develop this talent within a school or university context.

However, the two international creative problem-solving programs that were designed with schools in mind, Odyssey of the Mind and Destination Imagination include a technical component as a significant part of the problem posed to each team of seven students. Without a technically savvy student member, teams have far fewer chances of reaching an award-worthy solution to the problem (See section on creative ability for details.) Unfortunately, some states and many districts have recently ended or reduced financial support for these programs in schools due to tightened budgets.

SPORTS

Most people equate physical abilities with athletics. Because athletics are integral to most schools and because coaches tend to be superb at fostering talent development, this category may seem to require little discussion beyond asking coaches to list potential achievements on the Reference Set of Possibilities. Leaning on many sports enthusiasts' understanding of this category, the inherent rating system of #1 as the best was used to anchor the rating system of the achievements listed in the Talent Record which provided a basis for extending this understanding to the needs of the other domains, furthering discussions of the equal treatment of unequals. However, there are several other important reasons for reinstating the authentic inclusion of this psychomotor/kinesthetic category of abilities, beyond the premise that the Talent Record is foremost a communication tool that needs to be inclusive.

First among these reasons is that this talent domain behaves in similar fashion to the others. Athletic expertise is expected to develop early at some point during the K-12 continuum, sometimes as early as seven years of age.[9] Although developmental issues regarding physical growth can limit participation in some team sports such as football to secondary school age, core athletic skills develop earlier. Looking beyond the carefully monitored, talented elite football player in high school who is strongly encouraged to attend summer camp at personal financial cost, if a position on the team is desired, opportunities to cultivate exceptional talent in other athletic areas are sometimes funded by outside organizations (e.g., basketball clinics or Arthur Ashe tennis programs). Individual sports, including those that may not be fostered in schools (i.e., gymnastics, tennis, competitive skiing or horseback riding) can begin quite early in the life of a child.

The story of a young lady who was pursuing a position on an Olympic team for ski racing exemplifies the trajectory of individual sports that begin early. In her own teenage words:

> I raced Nastar for the 1st time, at Sterling Forest. KB showed me how to go around the gates. Their (sic) I stood at 4 years of age in this big starting box. The man at the start counted backwards 321 go! Before I knew it I was through the finish with a time of 30 sec. with a handicap of 74, which gave me my 1st nastar gold pin. That year I made 1st place in the Coca-Cola Nastar State Rankings. This was the start of my ski racing career. (No date, student correspondence)

The journey from regional competitions to qualifying races (United States Ski Association—USSA Points List, Trophy Series, Empire Winter Games Invitational) to state (Alpine team), regional (Eastern Championship, 5 State Discretionary Selections) and national championships (U.S. Alpine Championships) are part of the journey this individual pursued throughout her school years. Her training involved one or two days after school and two days every weekend for her entire childhood and adolescence.

All of this was unknown to most of her classmates, teachers and administrators. It was really not until she needed to enroll in a specialized high school to continue her athletic development that her advanced accomplishments were generally acknowledged. Her desire to remain enrolled in the gifted program at her local high school while attending an out-of-state school (via correspondence) led to a rare dual enrollment.

Here lies another crucial reason for including all psychomotor/kinesthetic abilities back into the federal definition of Talent. Research across all disciplines has found that meeting the unique needs of an individual developing his/her expertise requires a concerted effort from more than the family. School systems could easily facilitate the cultivation of academic growth and opportunities during this focus on athletic expertise. Knowing the complexity of daily life outside of school invites the possibility of providing a course outline of the year's at-home expectations like due dates of major projects, and/or designing time for homework or remediation during the school day, perhaps a study hall in lieu of one period of physical education.

Again, these are not trivial accommodations for these students and their families juggling multiple requirements to pursue talent development. And they are not difficult or costly accommodations to foster talent development. A guidance counselor can mitigate most of the needs, and a building administrator in charge of scheduling could fix anything else required given focused intent.

There are also many common skills that anyone developing advanced talent in any area needs to master. One of the greatest advantages of a meager two-hour per week program for gifted students is the opportunity (if designed as such) for meeting others with similar needs. Some of these skills include advanced organizational techniques, metacognitive strategies, managing intrinsic motivation, coping with failure, focusing on personal best in competitions, resourcefulness, mindset, the character and mental strength needed to pursue elite talent, and exploring the map of the territories of one's talent field including choosing a mentor or evaluating a potential program/opportunity, as well as appreciation of the efforts, successes and failures involved in other talent domains.

The combination of students talented in various domains within a G/T program provides opportunities for all students to see the similarities and differences in cultivating expertise in those various domains while cultivating appreciation for other talents.

Additionally, the organizational skills required to seriously pursue a talent domain outside of and/or unrecognized by the school, like gymnastics, skiing, or robotics events while accomplishing all that is required within the school, leaves little or no time for anything else including clubs or other social activities that are school-based. This severely limits the opportunities to make friends and find others with similar interests outside of the sport/competition. Every child needs to have opportunities to find a friend who likes them for all they are, not just what they do well. This broadened view of a program

Table 10.1

Reference Set of Possibilities: Psychomotor/Kinesthetic

Observed Behaviors

5	Learns basic skills immediately, almost intuitively
	Demonstrates a good memory for movement, patterns (muscle memory - easily translates motion into separate movements then translates movement into action)
	Displays advanced motor skills (gross and/or fine motor)
	Enjoys taking things apart and rebuilding them
	Demonstrates persistence, concentration, self-confidence with physical activities
	Sensitive/alert to movement of people/things
	Notices precise details, mechanics of things
	Eager to do well/win at activities that require strength, speed and/or endurance
	Strives to develop physical fitness
	Replicates complicated process with accurate detail

Source: These *sample* behaviors were found in more than one research study. The descriptors listed here resonated with classroom teachers when piloted.

Note: Best strategy for choosing a match: Read the behavior and see which student(s) comes to mind immediately. If there is no immediate response, skip it and move to next behavior. You do not need to use any of these at all unless it is extremely accurate. A 'maybe' is not useful.

Table 10.1 (continued)

Reference Set of Possibilities: Psychomotor/Kinesthetic

Small sample of achievements

5	Sports individual or a team member; Varsity Athletic team member; karate belts, enters local competitions (tennis, gymnastics) Invention Convention participant, Computer Fair, Maker Faire, Hour of Code, student member of Woodworking guild, reputation as computer fanatic/expert, 4H or AV (audio-visual) or Garden Club member, culinary pursuits, fixes a variety of tools or machines; designs patterns, sews; enters robotics contests; subscribes to journals; constantly builds with Legos or building sets, Robotics
4	Top score in class on Athletic Fitness test; black belt karate; attends specialty camp; Starter on Varsity team; local awards, exhibits; "Pinball wizard" reputation; participant in USACO National Championship training/qualifying competitions; apprentice to carpenter, plumber, mechanic, printmaker, electrician
3	Scores in League/Sectional championship; varsity member as underclassman; School record holder individual event; county-level Robotics Contest; OM/DI regional award; technical assistant; consultant, troubleshooter, hired as a computer program designer; ICT (Internet Communications Technology) Interfacer
2	Scores in State championship in specific sport; partial college/special high school athletic scholarship; junior ranking by professional organization (tennis); invitation for further testing (USA Gymnastics Federations' Regional Talent Opportunity Program); OM/DI State competition award; state exhibits, awards; Robotics and other team awards placing at state level
1	Scores in National Invitational tournament in particular sport; full college athletic scholarship to a Division I school; selected for Junior Olympics; OM/DI World/Global award; Origami U.S.A. contest winner; national exhibition; All America status in particular sport as judged by a national publication; full college athletic scholarship to a Division I school, awards (HS All-American @ National Scholastic Track & Field Championships); OM/DI World/Global competition award; places in USACO (USA Computing Olympiad)

Source: Author's research of relevant literature and pilot studies

for talent development alters social and cultural dimensions for the students. The skier acknowledged almost immediately that she was relieved to meet others as driven as she had always been. Belonging to a group who saw this as normal relieved some of her shell of shyness immediately. Getting to know a gymnast with similar challenges fortified them both.

Ideally, a multidisciplinary team of coaches, educators, and physicians (physical and psychological) could outline recommendations for interested students and their parents who seek talent development in an athletic specialty. By devising a trajectory of known ways for developing expertise for each of the sports available to children (soccer, basketball, field hockey, lacrosse, and others), the highest level of experts would provide their perspective and expert guidance to parents and children.[10]

Knowing what traits, proclivities, behaviors, and skills are required for success in that domain, along every step of the way all the way to the top of the sport, as found in the research in that talent domain, provides a more comprehensive path. Rather than leaving "soccer moms" and "little league dads" struggling to figure out what is the next best move for their child regarding options and opportunities as well as all of the physical, mental, and spiritual strengths it will take to pursue furthering a talent toward the elite level, there would be built-in guidance toward the known behaviors and achievements needed for advanced success.

FURTHER WORK

The area of psychomotor abilities may be the least understood of Marland's original 1972 definition, which might explain its subsequently being dropped from the federal definition of gifted/talented education. Much more research needs to be done, but this chapter highlights some places to begin. Hopefully this chapter has provided the evidence needed to see the need for the research as a worthwhile pursuit. Although there is talk and some movement to bringing back the trade school model through community college degrees, opportunities to learn by doing currently remain limited. Perhaps the interest in STEM opportunities in schools and the popularity of the Maker movement that is fueling some desires to build or construct will merge with sustainability concerns which could lead to the return of respect and interest in this type of formal "hands-on" (or kinesthetic) instruction.

NOTES

1 Tharp, 2006, p. 99.

2 This is one of several reasons I find it necessary to retain Marland's sixth category in the original federal definition.

3 I have not found scientific evidence to suggest the same method is used to gain deeper thought or insights. This is merely an analogy to help understanding.

4 Wozniak with Smith, 2006, p. 14.

5 Research reported in Gladwell, 1999. See Robinson, Kidd & Adelson 2017. Robinson, Adelson, Kidd, & Cunningham 2018 for age appropriate assessments in engineering and talents for tinkering; also see what is included in the Qualifications and Curriculum Authority's National Curriculum for the UK for an interesting perspective.

6 Dembo, et al. 1981; Kay, 1994.

7 Mathews, 2000.

8 Lemley, 2005, p. 56.

9 Note the seven-year-olds training for soccer at the academy in Amsterdam in Sokolove, 2010.

10 Van Rossum, 1996, 1997, 2000.

Chapter 11

So What?—The Synergy of Collaboration

Two overarching purposes of education and schooling in a democracy are the fullest development of individual potential and the nurturance of specialized talents to fill society's need for creative, imaginative, productive individuals.

—A. H. Passow[1]

There are no known limits to the kinds of talent [the human psyche] can demonstrate and to the heights to which it can climb in any domain. But the mind is not motivated to achieve every possible form of excellence. The cultural milieu makes that decision in the broadest possible sense.

—A. J. Tannenbaum[2]

This book outlines the call for a new synergy: the interaction of discrete institutions and/or conditions so that the whole of a child's potential for emerging expertise becomes much greater than the sum of its parts. Parents, legal guardians, relatives, teachers, and school institutions along with community members of the "whole village" surrounding each child may have perceptions that can offer insights into a child's talents. Those qualities and achievements that are required to become an Eagle Scout, or a ranked, junior tennis player, or a long-term member of a 4H club are major contributions to a comprehensive Talent Profile of a student's interests and efforts toward developing talent.

With a common language and platform for recording talents, contributions from all aspects of every child's life could provide meaningful entries to a child's Talent Record. Including all local, state, and national government institutions or programs sponsored by government monies as well as privately funded opportunities to record observed strengths increases the synergistic energy. This includes leadership qualities exhibited throughout the community that go unnoticed, especially leadership roles in alternative "communities" such as the leader on the local basketball court or in a group of troublemakers who exhibit some of the behaviors in an objective list of leadership characteristics. As talent scouts, educated adults can recognize and address leadership potential in all its forms. This is equally true for potential in all the talent domains.

THE POWER OF SYNERGISTIC INTERACTIONS

Concrete examples of the power of this synergy were first demonstrated when samples of individual Talent Profiles were used in a staff development workshop on "Differentiating Curriculum in the Classroom" for elementary teachers. The teachers' response to two of these profiles provides some insight into the effectiveness of individual Talent Records in daily practice. For this exercise, the categories of talent fields and the level of achievements in that field were left blank so that only replication of the existing data usually found in a school record was now offered through the lens of an instructional model for talent development to illustrate the shift in perception. Here are the instructions the teachers were given:

> These Descriptive Records profile observed talents in children. Imagine this tool as part of a child's cumulative folder and that these children will be in your class next year. What curriculum modifications might you consider to tap into these students' talent areas?[3]

Table 11.1

Sample Talent Profile #1

Grade	Description
1	RC "wonderful writer"
	SOI: 3 out of 3 Gifted
	(Semantic, symbolic + spatial divergent production)

Key: Second Column 2:
RC = Report Card comment from teacher
SOI stands for Structure of Intellect, an assessment designed by Mary Meeker, a student of Guilford's, to measure the many aspects of intelligence delineated in his theory of intelligence. A version of the three divergent thinking subtests remains available although different from the originals used here.

As you may or may not surmise, Talent Profile #1 describes the potential of a creatively gifted child emerging.

In first grade, the teacher noted on the report card that he showed skill for writing.[4] In second grade, the Structure of Intellect (SOI) "Creativity" test was administered. Out of the three subtests given for divergent production of ideas (semantic-words, symbolic-numbers, spatial-figures), this student performed at the gifted level on all three.[5] Also in second grade, this student performed at the 94th percentile on the advanced mathematics subscore (MA) of the Iowa test of mathematical achievement.[6]

Immediate feedback to this exercise by classroom teachers yielded a variety of written responses:[7]

Teacher 1: For this student, I would have him create a Class Math Diary. Each week he would have to pick a new activity/concept we have learned, write a brief description of it and provide his/her own example of each concept (one they have created). It can be an open-ended question so that children of the class could solve it. This diary could be printed monthly and the new activities added to it. By the end of the year we would have a diary with 40 math activities created by the student.

Teacher 2: A child with immense creativity and writing ability. For this child, I would provide additional time for him to take part in an on-going Internet writing project. The project would allow him to interact with various students locally, as well as, globally while being engaged in a cooperative project with students who have similar strengths.

Teacher 3: I would like to pair this boy with a "wonderful artist" to create LA [language arts] products. I would have him share some of his favorite books (good writers are good readers) with the class. Doing people study of favorite authors, reading several books by the same author, comparing one author's books, comparing favorite authors' books, etc. I would also give him "names" for some of his skills in writing that he may have but not know what they are called—alliteration, metaphors, similes, analogies, etc. Then let him look for these same techniques in other writings. Which techniques are used in literature and nonfiction writing?

As he has good skills in math concepts, he may be very good at creating story problems for classmates and/or younger students; writing a "math novel", counting books, mystery story with numbers, etc.

While the first teacher concentrated on enriching mathematical content by employing the student's ability in writing, the second teacher focused solely on the child's writing talent. One could comment that any personalized enrichment is better than none and that the Talent Profile initiates possibilities. In fact, this is true. All of the teachers welcomed the insights provided by this tool.

However, the qualitative difference of the response of the third teacher also merits discussion. The first two responses (from a seasoned and a first year teacher, respectively) each provide one answer to the question whereas the third response (from a special education teacher) lists a variety of modifications to the content, processes, and products potentially available to enrich the child's curriculum.

The fact that content modifications include the study of people and the need to address the organization of content by providing "names" for specific writing skills such as metaphors is juxtaposed with requiring the student to use higher level thinking skills when identifying these techniques in various contexts is worth noting. Sharing the result of the student's efforts with real audiences and inviting the student to explore a product transformation by writing a "math novel" are also learning strategies applauded in gifted education.[8] This awareness of multiple layers necessary to the modification of the students' curriculum is a qualitative difference in teacher perception and/or training. What was left unsaid here, but characteristic of this teacher, was her intent to offer these multiple options to the child who then chose the best fit with personal interest. This is an important problem-defining skill for the child to develop as well.

Another Talent Profile (#3) presented to the classroom teachers highlights academic and artistic achievements of an entering third grader.

Table 11.2

Sample Talent Profile #2 Reflects Academics and the Arts

Grade	Description
K	1st place Visual Arts: PTA Reflections contest
1	1st place music PTA Reflections
	1st place visual arts PTA Reflections
	1st place photography PTA Reflections
	2nd place literature PTA Reflections
	1st place State PTA Reflections Contest
2	SOI 1 out of 3 in gifted range (Semantic)
	128 V CogAT (ability test)
	123 Q CogAT
	150 NV CogAT
	99th percentile DRP (Degrees of Reading Power achievement test)
	96th percentile M Iowa Math (achievement test)
	97th percentile MA Iowa Math

The most common teacher response in reviewing this Talent Profile was the perceived need to enlist the expertise of arts specialists in planning for this child's year. Although art teachers would be thrilled, the academic talents of this student were, at first glance, overlooked by most.

Again, the teacher trained to address individual differences with curriculum modifications presented multiple ideas that attended to pacing of academic content, variety of learning processes, and unusual products for real audiences (e.g., photograph angles throughout the school and group into obtuse, right, and acute or use them to make up problems for classmates). In addition to these adjustments, this teacher also mentioned seeking the expertise of art specialists to assess and adequately address the next step in the development of artistic talents.[9]

Several general observations surfaced through discussion of a small sample of Talent Profiles. Quite emphatically teachers remarked on their surprise in finding that these students are so different from one another. Exposure to only a few profiles yielded recognition of the heterogeneity of these high-end learners.

Second, most of the teachers commented on their perception that this was the first time standardized test scores held some meaning and purpose for their classroom practice. In fact, several teachers hesitantly admitted that they had no knowledge of the significance of these tests other than as a tool administrators use to place students in appropriate remediation when performance levels were too low. Learning that students who obtain a score in the 99 percentile may have "hit the ceiling" of a test requiring another level of the test to accurately assess their actual level of achievement was shocking to too many classroom teachers.

This lack of understanding of the usefulness of a standardized test as a tool to guide instruction also might explain a trend to eliminate standardized testing. A tool designed to inform is excluded from the repertoire of information available about some students because instruction on the implementation is lacking.[10] If the application of this information is missing from practice, there is less information on each student. The usefulness of national normative data is especially highlighted with the Talent Record system when including rankings of these achievements among and between all of the available tests.[11]

Raising the level of awareness of teachers is a worthy goal in and of itself, but the truly invigorating response was the intense energy and interest these teachers directed at meeting the needs of these students by embracing their role as a developer of talents. The joy and satisfaction felt by teachers attracted to connections between the curriculum and individual talents is an exciting initial stage of engagement.

The creative enterprise of matching curriculum with student interest is a natural tendency for concerned teachers with or without specific training in talent development. To go beyond these minor revisions or enrichment activities, teachers also need knowledge of various instructional models.[12] For many, these Talent Records inspire interest in gaining expertise to meet the needs of each teacher's annual set of students.

This small synergistic burst magnifies with additional entries. Yet, this simple example illustrating active differentiation planning[13] based on demonstrated talent of incoming students for the following September demonstrates a degree of worthiness to Talent Records. As a communication tool they invite conversations and investigations that develop personally meaningful growth for students and teachers in real time. Of course, amplification occurs when the entries include designations of the talent area and level of accomplishment; when they are built across time; and when they are provided by sources within and outside of the school. This synergy can multiply exponentially when everyone essentially becomes a "talent scout."

Role of Schools as Talent Scouts

In our effort to leave no child behind, we are failing the high-ability children who are the most likely to become tomorrow's scientists, inventors, poets, and entrepreneurs—and in the process we risk leaving our nation behind. (Finn, 2014, p. 50)

(Scherer) Why do you say that the most important thing to know about a child is his or her strengths?

(Levine) If we want to prepare kids for adulthood, one of the most important things we can do is to celebrate their strengths, those assets with which they're going to find meaning in life and be able to make contributions. For the most part, adults who are leading worthy lives are doing so by mobilizing their strengths and affinities. What we should seek is a consonance between a student's education and his future career. (Scherer, 2006, p. 8)

Talent development is a complex process that requires an educational model that supports it in schools[14] and out. Natural talents require education and education is one of the environmental factors found to significantly contribute to an individual's success (see chapter 1). A strong national public education system, as demonstrated by Finland, has the skeletal structure to build the rest of the bridge to achieve the goal of being a curator and potential catalyst to talent development. This includes providing the scaffolds for the economically disadvantaged and any other supports required for the emotional well-being of young adults.[15]

In addition to adopting an educational model that supports talent development in each domain, the interface between domains needs to be woven. Appreciation of other domains and the accomplishments attained occur by assimilation when viewed in the context of each child's profile. Much like a picture is worth a thousand words, this chart immediately portrays much that no longer requires additional time and attention. For example, seeing that a math student is ranked at the national level in an achievement recognized by the mathematical field becomes comparable to the tennis player nationally ranked or qualifying for the U.S. Open tennis tournament. The additional work of the institution then can become breaking down any real or perceived barriers to implementation of a talent development model that celebrates the diversity of talent domains by cultivating the institutional attitudes needed to support these facts.

Although a formidable task, these efforts are minor when viewed against the immediate gains from most educators who have viewed more than one Talent Profile. Schools adopting a talent development instructional model and providing cumulative Talent Records for every student, face the undeniable fact that each child is an individual and requires very different modifications—a fact that appears much simpler to 'see' through this tool.

School systems could do more than adopt a framework and unite the disciplines and domains available through school resources. They also could be a bridge between school life, communities, families and the student. This requires both building and system fortifications beyond teachers. Teachers will add their own observations to the Talent Profiles of their students. The time, opportunity, expertise and training needed to evaluate, chronicle and make accurate entries require designated resources, human and otherwise. When these experts come from within the school, school employees more readily embrace the complexity as the implementation is designed to specifically compliment the context and environment they know as a team.

Schools are being called upon to develop 21st-century skills. An examination of these skills suggests they are designed to help students know what they do well and what they can contribute to a team. This, in other words, is a call to career development embedded as skill development. Given the tendency for many secondary students to divorce themselves from any memory of childhood pursuits, a record of all talents observed throughout a lifetime enhances the possibility of finding an accurate synthesis of developed interests.

Even when the efforts of younger years are treasured by the individual, career development ideas are mostly discussed informally around the junior year among family and friends, and perhaps also a teacher or two, pointing out what is seen as a person's demonstrated strengths rather than looking at the person's pool of strengths to lasso many possibilities. Other than the New Yorker article on Alec Baldwin's preschool report card[16] written for laughs, significant early childhood qualities that distinguish the child at the time may anticipate, even help define adult success.

The rich research available from the studies of expertise and the decades of research on students demonstrating achievements in academic and other talent domains has not been assimilated into the general knowledge of those faced with cultivating these talents in children/adolescents on a daily basis. Available reference resources reflect the same situation: a 335-page book on career finding specifically for young people dedicated 15 pages to Natural Talents, while a 372-page book on career finding for adults dedicated 22 pages to that topic.[17] This certainly emphasizes the need for a tool that synthesizes relevant research knowledge and continually updates the information base that new research provides.

With this common platform and language, and an authentic invitation to expand the sources of contributions to include those outside of the school system, schools could use the Talent Record to unify every faction of a child's world. As curator of this cohesive collaboration of family, various kinds of communities, talent domains, and resources mixed in with the school's resources, schools return to being comprehensively meaningful community leaders.

Community Members as Talent Scouts: Honoring Strengths Offers Societal/Cultural Equalities

> Strengths-based approaches, which have taken root in the field of social work, psychiatry, and business, make the case that drawing on the strengths of individuals is the best way to reduce the negative and increase the positive in individuals and families. (Kana'iaupuni, 2005, p. 35)

Sometimes a community can make up for that which is unavailable in a family. Holloway's research has found that community, like family, profoundly impacts the development and learning of children.[18] A supportive community "can mitigate the harmful effects of economic disadvantage on student achievement"[19] so policymakers seeking improvement should not focus only on classrooms but look at "how to increase the community's capacity to support its children and youth so that students' experiences outside school will enhance the teaching and learning that goes on inside school."[20]

Psychologists have suggested that knowing one's strengths allows children to develop resiliency and confidence.[21] In Bloom's study of talented young people he summarized his observations:

The parents were typically models of the work ethic and applied it to their own work and lives. They raised their children to believe in the importance of doing something well, to place work and duties before pleasure, to believe in the importance of hard work, and to strive for future goals.[22]

There *are* successful orphans or those without these support mechanisms in the home who must have learned the values from someone else in their community. These 'others' can inspire and be emulated. Acknowledging accomplishments within a child's community (social, religious, peer) on a school record that informs instruction benefits all involved.

A strengths-based approach has been promoted to address social policy.[23] According to these experts, "The goal of strengths-based approaches is not simply to reduce pathology, but to promote positive behavior and healthy development."[24] Facilitating talent development and the acquisition of degrees of expertise is one way of focusing on individual strengths and cultivating them.

Religious organizations or cultural associations can offer specific insights. How many stories have been told about a man of the cloth working with the strengths of a child of poverty or violence to get the resources needed to help that one child succeed? Or imagine, if you will, notification from a Rabbi that a child who was enrolled in training to be a Rabbinical scholar is transferring to your school district as a tenth grader. This, like many very specialized achievements, may require further decoding from experts in that religious community. Learning the academic as well as leadership qualities of a person chosen for this path is important to know as are any other leadership positions afforded young people in any other religious community.

In fact, imagine accomplishments from all religious and cultural institutions objectively ranked and listed for schools to locate on a master list. This kind of knowledge can serve to unite diversities through appreciation of commonalities.

Role of Government as Talent Scout

It is well to remember with Plato that "What is honored in a country will be cultivated there."

—E. Paul Torrance (Nelson & Psaltis, 1967)

If this cumulative record of a child's notable behaviors and achievements would be supported (in every sense of that word) at the federal level, it could buttress the federal definition with further resources and research. Envisioning the possibility of establishing a cross-disciplinary working committee of experts to review and add missing elements as research unveils them would be a powerful contribution to improving the lives of students everywhere.[25]

Specifically, the collaboration between experts in each of these fields and a national clearing house would especially enhance and keep updated the Reference Set of Possible behaviors and achievements initiated here. If a Talent Record for each child became a standard feature of educational records, over time it might also serve as a rich resource for educational researchers to deepen our knowledge of developing expertise and identify our nation's natural resources.

There is a more immediate use to a nationally standardized cumulative record of observed behaviors and achievements. This portable 'dynamic assessment' encourages a thread of constancy for children who have transient relationships with schools in various states. With families moving across the country, a cumulative record of known talents could easily be transferred electronically to the new school with immediacy. Imagine the caregiver's copy of the school's official Talent Record being provided by the family member at registration, tooling the new teachers, guidance counselors and administration with an important guideline while they wait the standard six to eight weeks to receive the former school's official records on the child.

This alone could help make a move become a replanting of the student into similar programs rather than the current uprooting. In that the official record would include the official copy of the child's Talent Record updated with final teacher comments, the path for a cumulative assessment would be uninterrupted.

This is particularly cogent for children whose families' travel across the country for military or seasonal work. They could benefit immediately from a record of previous achievements and behaviors and so would their teachers:

> Elise is one of thousands of children on the move through the education system. There are so many it's become a problem for educators.
>
> But Elise is an exception to the mobility rule: She adapts well and learns quickly. Maybe Elise could be enrolled in a program for gifted and talented students, but she's never around long enough for anyone to really know her.[26]

Identifying, recording and communicating emerging strengths and talents is just the beginning. But it is a beginning with massive potential.

Like a child's Individual Education Plan in special education, a child's participation in other programs such as a specialized gifted program could be standardized at the national level. The caveats within the specific details of what each locally defined gifted program offers would need to be nationally standardized based on identification procedures linked to demonstrated talents. For example, a child who was identified as being in the top 15%

academically in one gifted program would be placed in comparable opportunities in the new school which might be very different. A clear situation of readjustment might be that the new school only identifies the top 5% to 7% for gifted programming or only provides acceleration options for fostering extreme academic talent. In these cases, community resources (actual or virtual) could be found to match the child's demonstrated level of expertise.

This level of synergy requires a moral gatekeeper institution fashioned like the National Association of Secondary School Principals group which has spent the last several decades evaluating the submitted student opportunities and recommending only those designed in the best interests of children. Perhaps a think tank or applied research center with invited interdisciplinary experts: practitioners/scholars in education, educational researchers in expertise within each of the talent domains, educational measurement specialists/statisticians and businesses cultivating opportunities for developing leadership, entrepreneurs, and so on, to become a collaborative team to ensure authenticity, productivity, and leadership that encompasses all that is necessary to address developing talents and expertise with each child's best interests in mind.

Including an advisory council of experts and gatekeepers representing each field could address issues that come up in new research along the continuum to the highest level of elite talent. These experts are best at identifying critical innate abilities such as charisma or musicality that have been defined as essential at the elite musical talent level. They also identify observable skills such as "teachability" for all those cultivating early talent development.[27] Uniting perspectives among experts along the continuum can only help everyone remain grounded in realistic expectations.

If we assess what is relevant to student growth, a major change in evaluation tools in education will be necessary. Looking at what students do well could be one of these tools. The Talent Record, even if used simply as a communication tool, has the potential to unify every faction of and every contributor to a child's world. It could be far more comprehensive if a national system were in place. The substantially increased value education could have (once again) as a curator of a cohesive, creative collaboration of family, community, talent domains, and resources to meet the needs of all children's developing expertise would please efficiency experts as well.

Role of Parents/Legal Guardians as Talent Scouts

Providing an introduction to the expectations of a field in addition to the objective support by those gatekeepers directly involved in the pursuit benefits everyone, but most especially parents and their children. Parenthood has a huge impact on a child's life at any age and most parents/guardians want what is best for their children.[28] The child that happens to be interested in and demonstrates a talent in an area familiar to the parent might have a built—in mentor. However, supporting an offspring's interest and strengths in unfamiliar talent domains is a somewhat greater challenge for parents.

Having a direct picture of the general knowledge from the field of expertise to work from might help either situation for there are many minefields for the parent of a child with advancing talent. Most importantly, nurturing the child's talents based on that child's interest is a pivotal skill parents might develop by following hints that come directly from the child. Identifying the difference between developing persistence or "grit" and pushing a child in an unproductive direction most often requires the help of the objective expertise from others, including a trained coach/mentor. As mentioned earlier, a child's talent does not automatically include the intense and genuine interest required for the later stages of talent development.

One researcher describes "a rage to master" as an identifying characteristic of the passion required to realize exceptional talent, but not all students who exhibited that characteristic have all that it takes to realize achievement in the area of intense interest.[29] As important, it has not yet been established that this rage to master exists or is evident in all stages of talent development.[30]

Complicating matters, many children seek the approval of their parents by truly believing they are interested in something because a parent(s) would very much like them to be, only to find out later this was not really the case. It is only by matching actions and words that parents can convince a child that the support and interest in her/his chosen area of talent development is sincere.

To be resourceful though, this desire to please parents can be usefully directed in places where parents are in the best position to reinforce healthy routines and attitudes for the child's successful talent development. For example, the nurturing of an approach to competition as that of seeking one's personal best rather than competing with others is a skill that parents are in the best position to consistently reinforce on a daily basis and over the long term, once they know to do so. Developing the intense work ethic, mastering the social constructs of the situations to be encountered, and helping the child attend to the support systems like nutrition and mental/emotional strength needed to support the intensity of the pursuit are critical as well.

Many parents have said this Talent Record system was very useful as a tool in their toolkit. Adding other voices that reflect multiple observations about a child's behaviors when compared to a set of known behaviors helps everyone identify useful information to help guide informed decision-making. Parents especially appreciated the interface with the school record, as those past accomplishments shared with a kindergarten teacher currently do not have a place to formally follow a child throughout their schooling. Unfortunately, the parents of the child who was playing solo concerts on the violin before school life began, are not going to continue to share this fact and the complicated life that demands, for more than the first one or two years of school. Often by second grade, teachers are no longer provided this kind of "unrelated" information unless they ask.

Although much research is included for the lists of behaviors and accomplishments found in the previous chapters, these lists are not comprehensive. They will never be if research continues to contribute to knowledge in this area. To address this fact as well as accurately situate significant family observations, a child's behaviors need to be illustrated with specific examples describing each event and the context of the event to be useful. Just checking off the behaviors as something witnessed is not relevant to the cause. Like the entries from others, every entry needs the context described. So, if family members see a child 'make unusual connections', the description of that event, stated as close to possible to the exact words/actions the child used, is what is most relevant.

The "so what?" with regard to parents is substantial. Young parents (or a grandparent) might keep a log of the moments that surprised/amazed at least one of them during a child's development. Date and circumstances of the event are critical too, as well as witnesses. These do not need to be identified with any specific talent domain unless it is clearly observed in only one. The actual talent domain may become evident later. A prolific child's work requires documenting. For example, a parent can take (dated) photos of any three-dimensional work created (sculptures/building blocks/sandbox cities/ science experiments). Dating the writing or drawings with an old-fashioned date stamp is a simple, yet profoundly useful, strategy.[31]

Teaching children to do this for themselves as quickly as possible in the pre school years helps the child innately learn about the importance of accurate documentation in productivity. As the child develops, whether interests change, evaporate or intensify, there is a comprehensive record of the useful observations and past accomplishments for the student to use to make his/her future choices.

THE SYNERGY OF A COMMUNITY OF TALENT SCOUTS

There is no stronger weapon against inequality and no better path to opportunity than an education that can unlock a child's God-given potential.

—President Barack Obama[32]

There are more potential high achievers among our 55 million students than are currently getting the opportunity to thrive. And plenty of them are hiding in plain sight in neighborhoods and schools where adults are unaccustomed to recognizing such potential and are ill-equipped to challenge such students.

—Finn, 2014, pp. 62–63

For all we know, there may be as many late bloomers[33] as there are early beginners. With a cumulative record for each child, the timing of the initial observation is far less crucial an issue than the number or degree of accomplishments, relevant behaviors, proclivities, resource pools, and intrapersonal variables such as motivation and interests that are noted by others. Whether the talent emerges in first grade or eleventh, the purpose of the Talent Record is the same.

A talent scout form can be standardized or it can consist of a brief letter. The important elements to be included are the name, grade and school of the child, the name and the relationship between the scout and the child (boy or girl scout leader, priest or rabbi, older sibling) and the date and behavior or achievement that appears remarkable to that scout. Sometimes, a reflective letter from a parent or grandparent who has just spent time reviewing a scrapbook or photo album provides a wealth of information. Sometimes it is useful to provide a parent workshop or community leadership meeting with a list of potential behaviors and achievements that outline ideas so families understand what information is useful.

Ironically, this focus on each individual's strengths can be useful in guiding every individual away from either self-aggrandizement or fears of not measuring up to their peers. Knowing what one does well is given a context in which to set sights for improvement in areas of personal interest, empowering students with options and direction to focus on their own growth. Perhaps, with guidance, it can provide many with an antidote to some of the anxiety attributed to teen life now enhanced by social media.[34]

With so many small and large physical communities suffering from lack of cohesiveness and stability, having them become a virtual community made up of all of the positive aspects of a child's life, might be a welcome lifeboat for all to nurture potential in authentic and meaningful ways.

NOTES

1 Passow, 1988, p. 27.

2 Tannenbaum, 2000, p. 24.

3 Kay, 1997.

4 When completed, this type of anecdotal evidence would be listed under the field of academics [AC] with the subcategory of language [AC.l] and receive a score of 5 unless the reference to writing was specifically addressing creative writing. If this were the case, the field identified would be Creativity.

5 This entry would be identified as creative aptitude [CR] and given a level 3 rating.

6 The coding for this achievement would be AC.m at level 4.

7 Permissions were obtained for all teacher responses after the in-service course was completed and graded.

8 Kanevsky, 1996; Maker & Nielson, 1996.

9 Some might worry that a bias for not seeing mathematical potential in a female student might be at play with the first teacher. In fact if this were to be the case, missed chances with several students would make a bias evident to the individual or his or her colleagues potentially leading to personal and significant staff development.

10 This was discussed with E. Hagen at length.

11 This does not yet exist.

12 Coleman, 1985; Passow, 1982; Van Tassel-Baska, 1994.

13 Borland, 1989; Kanevsky, 2011, 2017.

14 Coleman, 1985, 2006; Subotnik & Coleman, 1996.

15 Coleman, 2005; Coleman & Cross, 2005.

16 As imagined by Rudnick, 2014.

17 Lore, 1998, 2008.

18 Holloway, 2004.

19 Holloway, 2004, p. 90.

20 Holloway, 2004, p. 90.

21 Conway, 2001.

22 Bloom, 1985, p. 539.

23 Maton, et al., 2004.

24 Solarz, et al., 2004, p. 345.

25 Of course, just providing funding opportunities to conduct the research would as well.

26 Schweizer, 1997, p. 4.

27 Subotnik, Jarvin, Moga & Sternberg, 2003.

28 Olszewski-Kubilius, Limburg-Weber & Pfeiffer 2003. A pillar of this work is that of Roeper, 1995; see Olszewski, Kulieke, & Buescher (1987) for a literature review of important early work on the topic, also see A Rockefeller's rules for raising (financially) responsible children (Lawson, 2004).

29 Winner, 1996a, b.

30 Talent Records could help answer these questions.

31 Kay, 2003.

32 United States Department of Justice (2015). Assistant Attorney General Bill Baer delivers remarks before the National Asian American Coalition and National Diversity Coalition, October 23, 2015, Retrieved May 28, 2018, from https://www. justice.gov/opa/speech/assistant-attorney-general-bill-baer-delivers-remarks-national-asian-american-coalition

33 Gladwell, 2009; Winner, 1996a.

34 Twenge, 2017.

Autobiographical Talent Records: Extrapolation Examples for Constructing Talent Record of Characteristics and Achievements from Autobiographical Sources

Letters from family and community members will require decoding skills by the assessor creating the Talent Record. Success with this method was experienced with teachers as assessors gleaning information from school records and multiple perspectives gathered from home.

The following examples, although retrospective (tainted by selective memory and inherent bias of only the individual's perspective), can introduce the richness found in conversations with the individual as one constructs a Talent Record or chooses a biographical questionnaire to garner direct information from the individual child. Profiling talents requires openness to potential for any talent to emerge in any form, at any time. Identifying the degree or worthiness of that accomplishment is calculated later. All behaviors or characteristics are regarded as qualitative – there is or there isn't an observation as evidence of the behavior found to be characteristic in a talent field. Recording direct quotes from the child (or other source) solidifies the observation for further analysis.

Steve Wozniak

The autobiographical talents of the co-developer (with Steve Jobs) of the Apple computer are reported through the following quotes and information from Wozniak, S. with Smith, G. (2006) *iWoz*. New York: W.W. Norton.

Sample text in book:
p. 12 "The other thing my dad taught me was a lot about electronics. Boy, do I owe a lot to him for this. He first started telling me things and explaining things about electronics when I was really, really young – before I was even four years old. One of my first memories is his taking me to his workplace on a weekend and showing me a few electronic parts, putting them on the table with

me so I got to play with them and look at them. . . . And I remember sitting there and being so little, and thinking: Wow, what a great, great world he's living in."

p. 13 "A couple of years later – I was six, maybe seven – I remember Dad demonstrating another piece of equipment for a bunch of people at his company. . . .

Talent Profile Record for S. Wozniak
b.1950, m (retrospective personal memory only)

Grade	Talent Area	Description
Age 4	PK	Enjoys playing with electronic parts (Parent entry)
1	PK	Age 6: built crystal radio; always building projects
3	AC.s	Won 1st science competition in school: working flashlight
4	AC.s	Understands how resistors work (Parent entry) school science fair competition: Which liquid conducts electricity best?
	AC.l	Loves to read (e.g. Tom Swift series) (p.25)
	L	de facto leader of neighborhood club: Electronics Kids
5	AC.s	Reading dad's old engineering journals re: computers (p.22); 1st place school science fair competition: working electronic model of atoms/electrons in periodic table
	AC.m	Loved logic of computers (p.34)
	L	Elected student body vice president of school
	PK	Considered best runner, best baseball player according to teammates, top athlete in school; All-Stars in Little League
6	IA	200+ reported IQ score
	AC.m	Advanced in math
	AC.s	Advanced in science; school science fair competition: Computerized tic-tac-toe machine that works by logic
	PK	Licensed ham radio operator
8	AC.s	School science fair competition: Adder/Subtracter machine (close to a computer) top award from Air Force at Bay Area Science Fair
9	AC.m	Won the math award from junior high graduation (p.49)
HS Yrs.	AC.m	Won yearly math awards
	AC.s	Internship at Sylvania on Fridays to learn program computer; given book that "solved a search I'd been on since fourth grade to discover what a real computer was inside." (p.54)
1975		Joined Homebrew Computer Club (neighborhood club)

Key: Constructed by author solely from Wozniak, S. with Smith, G. (2006) *iWoz*. New York: NY W.W. Norton.

And my Dad, even though I was just a kid, told me I would be the one to get to throw the switch to turn it on. He said I had to do it at the exact right time."

p. 14 "But there were also lessons from my Dad, serious lessons that got me an incredibly early start in engineering. These lessons would always start because I'd ask a question. And I had a lot of questions." I remember we actually spent weeks and weeks talking about different types of atoms and then I learned how electrons can actually flow through things – like wires. Then, finally, he explained to me how the resistors work –not by calculations, because who can do calculations when you're a second grader, but by real commonsense pictures and explanations. You see, he gave me classical electronics training from the beginning. For engineers, there's a point in life when you understand things like how a resistor works. Usually it comes much later for people than it did for me. By the fourth grade, I really did understand things like that."

p. 15 "I have to point out here that at no time did my dad make a big deal about my progress in electronics. . . . By the sixth grade, I was really advanced in math and science, everyone knew it and I'd been tested for IQ and they told us it was 200 –plus."

On C.S. Lewis

The following notes/quotes for practice in constructing a Retrospective Talent Record are from C.S. Lewis' (1956) *Surprised by Joy*. New York: Harcourt Brace.

"I never read an autobiography in which the parts devoted to the earlier years were not far the most interesting." viii

p. 5 "In addition to good parents, good food, and a garden (which then seemed large) to play in, I began life with two other blessings. One was our nurse, Lizzie Endicott, in whom even the exacting memory of childhood can discover no flaw – nothing but kindness, gaiety, and good sense." [2nd was his older, by 3 years, brother who was "very different"]

p. 6 "Our earliest pictures (and I can remember no time when we were not incessantly drawing) reveal it. His were of ships and trains and battles; mine, when not imitated from his, were of what we both called 'dressed animals' – the anthropomorphized beasts of nursery literature. His earliest story – as my elder he preceded me in the transition from drawing to writing – was called *The Young Rajah*. He had already made India 'his country'; Animal-Land was mine. I do not think any of the surviving drawings date from the first six years of my life which I am now describing, but I have plenty of them that cannot be much later. From them it appears to me that I had the better talent. From a very early age I could draw movement – figures that looked as if they were really running or fighting – and the perspective is good. But nowhere, either in my brother's work or my own, is there a single line drawn in obedience to an idea, however crude, of beauty. There is action, comedy, invention; but there is not even the germ of a feeling for design, and there is a shocking ignorance of natural form. Trees appear as balls of cotton wool stuck on posts, and there is nothing to show that either of us knew the shape of any leaf in the garden where we played almost daily."

p. 7 "Once in those very early days my brother brought into the nursery the lid of a biscuit tin which he had covered with moss and garnished with twigs and flowers so as to make it a toy garden or a toy forest. That was the first beauty I ever knew. What the real garden had failed to do, the toy garden did. It made me aware of nature – not, indeed, as a storehouse of forms and colors but as something cool, dewy, fresh, exuberant. I do not think the impression was very important at the moment, but it soon became important in memory. As long as I live my impression of Paradise will retain something of my brother's toy garden."

p. 8 "My bad dreams were of two kinds, those about specters and those about insects. The second were, beyond comparison, the worse; to this day I would rather meet a ghost than a tarantula."

p. 9 "Much later, in my teens, from reading Lubbock's *Ants, Bees, and Wasps*, I developed for a short time a genuinely scientific interest in insects. Other studies soon crowded it out, but while my entomological period lasted my fear almost vanished, and I am inclined to think a real objective curiosity will usually have this cleansing effect."

p. 11 (before boarding school age) "I, meanwhile, was going on with my education at home – French and Latin from my mother and everything else from an excellent governess, Annie Harper."

p. 12 "What drove me to write was the extreme manual clumsiness from which I have always suffered. I attribute it to a physical defect which my brother and I both inherit from our father; we only have one joint in the thumb."

p. 12 "But whatever the cause, nature laid on me from birth an utter incapacity to make anything. With pencil and pen I was handy enough, and I can still tie as good a bow as ever on a man's collar; but with a tool or a bat or a gun, a sleeve link or a corkscrew, I have always been unteachable. It was this that forced me to write. I longed to make things, ships, houses, engines. Many sheets of cardboard and pairs of scissors I spoiled, only to turn from my hopeless failures in tears. As a last resource, as a *pis aller,* I was driven to write stories instead; little dreaming to what a world of happiness I was being admitted. You can do more with a castle in a story than with the best cardboard castle that ever stood on a nursery table."

p. 12 "I soon staked out a claim to one of the attics and made it 'my study.' Pictures of my own making or cut from the brightly colored Christmas numbers of magazines, were nailed to the walls."

p. 13 "Here my first stories were written, and illustrated, with enormous satisfaction. They were an attempt to combine my two chief literary pleasures – 'dressed animals' and 'knights in armor.' As a result, I wrote about chivalrous mice and rabbits who rode out in complete mail to kill not giants but cats."

p. 13 "The Animal-Land which came into action in the holidays when my brother was at home was a modern Animal-Land; it had to have trains and steamships if it was to be a country shared with him. It followed, of course, that the medieval Animal-Land about which I wrote my stories must be the same country during an earlier period; and of course the two periods must be properly connected. This led me from romancing to historiography; I set upon writing a full history of Animal-Land."

pp. 13–14 "From history it was only a step to geography. There was soon a map of Animal-Land – several maps, all tolerably consistent. Then Animal-Land had to be geographically related to my brother's India, and India consequently lifted out of its place in the real world. . . . And those parts of the world which we regarded as our own -Animal-Land and India – were increasingly peopled with consistent characters."

p. 14 "Of the books I have read at this time very few have quite faded from memory, but not all have retained my love." [did not retain his love: Conan Doyle's *Sir Nigel* & Mark Twain's *A Connecticut Yankee in King Arthur's Court*]

pp. 14–15 "Much better than either of these was E. Nesbit's trilogy, *Five Children and It, The Phoenix and the Wishing Carpet,* and *The Amulet.* The last did most for me. It first opened my eyes to antiquity, the "dark backward and abysm of time. I can still reread it with delight. *Gulliver* in an unexpurgated and lavishly illustrated edition was one of my favorites, and I pored endlessly over an almost complete set of old *Punches* which stood in my father's study. Tenniel gratified my passion for 'dressed animals' with his Russian Bear, British Lion, Egyptian Crocodile, and the rest, while his slovenly and perfunctory treatment of vegetation confirmed my own deficiencies. Then came the Beatrix Potter books, and here at last beauty.

"It will be clear at this time – at the age of six, seven, and eight – I was living almost entirely in my imagination; or at least that the imaginative experience of those years seems to me more important than anything else."

pp. 15–16 "Invention is essentially different from reverie; if some fail to recognize the difference that is because they have not themselves experienced both. Anyone who has will understand me. In my daydreams I was training myself to be a fool; in mapping and chronicling Animal-Land I was training myself to be a novelist. Note well a novelist; not poet. My invented world was full (for me) of interest, bustle, humor, and character; but there was no poetry, even no romance in it. It was almost astonishingly prosaic.[1] For reader's of my children's books, the best way of putting this would be to say that Animal-land had nothing whatever in common with

---

1 "For reader's of my children's books, the best way of putting this would be to say that Animal-land had nothing whatever in common with Narnia except the anthropomorphic beasts. Animal-Land, by its whole quality, excluded the least hint of wonder."

Narnia except the anthropomorphic beasts. Animal-Land, by its whole quality, excluded the least hint of wonder. Thus if we use the word imagination
in a third sense, and the highest sense of all, this invented world was not
imaginative."

pp. 16–17 [Lewis goes on to describe the first three experiences he associates with imagination: the "memory of a memory" of the toy garden his
brother brought in to their nursery that resurfaces later with certain sensory
experiences Beatrix Potter's Squirrel Nutkin, and poetry, specifically a few
lines from the unrhymed translation of *Tegner's Drapa* regarding Balder. He
unites them for the reader:]

pp. 17–18 "The reader who finds these three episodes of no interest need
read this book no further, for in a sense the central story of my life is about
nothing else. For those who are still disposed to proceed I will only underline
the quality common to the three experiences; it is that of an unsatisfied desire
which is itself more desirable than any other satisfaction. I call it Joy, which
is here a technical term and must be sharply distinguished both from Happiness and from Pleasure. Joy (in my sense) has indeed one characteristic, and
only one, in common with them; the fact that anyone who has experienced it
will want it again. Apart from that, and considered only in its quality, it might
almost equally well be called a particular kind of unhappiness or grief. But
then it is a kind we want. I doubt whether anyone who has tasted it would
ever, if both were in his power, exchange it for all the pleasures in the world.
But then Joy never is in our power and pleasure often is."

More Practice Constructing Talent Records

There are at least two significant problems with looking at autobiographies
for the raw material to construct a retrospective Talent Record: (1) like psy-
chobiography or biographies we are looking at one interpretation and (2) there
is no empirical evidence that the hindsight revealed is comprehensive in a
way that is useful for generalization of any kind.

Biographies are equally fraught with bias and lack of information. The
childhood of eminent individuals is often "that part of life for which the
empirical evidence is sparsest." (Wallace, p. 38) In a book, *Creative People
at work*, the author describes the child-adult continuum as addressed by the
case study method:

> In this book the case studies are concerned primarily with the evolution of the
> mature work. There are several reasons for this. First, our interest includes
> establishing the development of the person and understanding continuity in the
> career. But the career only rarely begins before adolescence. The case of Picasso
> is one of the very few that comes close to providing enough data to consider

childhood as part of a continuous lifelong developmental process. The beginning of creative work in adolescence is much less rare. The organic chemist R. B. Woodward was on his way in early adolescence. (p. 38, Wallace & Gruber)

Imagine if "enough data to consider childhood as part of a continuous lifelong developmental process" was available for all, where that might lead. How much wider might that path be when this lens can include biographical data on those as accomplished but without published autobiographies?

With some basic skills in analyzing the presented material on the two autobiographical samples provided, a case study method of accumulating authentic material would provide you with the beginnings of a child's Talent Record. Doing this exercise with a partner or a small team would bring out biases and/ or concerns that are worthy of discussion.

References

Abramo, P. C. (1996). Adventurous spirit leads to discovery. *The Cornwall Local*, July 31, 2, 13.

Alvin Ailey Junior Division Brochure (n.d.) now available:https://www.theai leyschool.edu/sites/default/files/TheAileySchool_JrDivision-brochure.pdf

Amabile, T. M. (1993). The role of motivation in talent development: Some thoughts for Future research. In N. Colangelo, S. G. Assouline, & D. E. Ambroson(Eds.), *Talent Development: Proceedings from the 1993 Henry B. and Jocelyn Wallace National Research Symposium in Talent Development*, 123–125. Dayton, OH: Ohio Psychology Press.

Amabile, T. & Kramer, S. (2011). *The progress principle: Using small wins to ignite joy, engagement, and creativity at work*. Boston, MA: Harvard Business Review Press.

American Academy of Achievement, (no date) 37th Annual Salute to Excellence program, p. 6.

Assouline, S. G. & Lupkowski-Shoplik, A. (2011). *Developing math talent: A comprehensive guide to math education for gifted students in elementary and middle school* (2nd ed.), Waco, TX: Prufrock.

Baldus, C., Blando, C., Croft, L., & Hirsch, C. M. (Eds.) (2005). *Invent Iowa Curriculum Guide*. Iowa City, IA: The Connie Belin & Jacqueline N. Blank International Center for Gifted Education & Talent Development, The University of Iowa.

Baldwin, L., Omdal, S. N., & Pereles, D. (2015). Beyond stereotypes: Understanding, recognizing, and working with twice-exceptional learners. *TEACHING Exceptional Children*, XX(X), 1–10.

Bamberger, J. (1986). Cognitive issues in the development of musically gifted children. In R. Sternberg & J. Davidson (Eds.), *Conceptions of giftedness*, 388–416. New York, NY: Cambridge University Press.

Bartusiak, M. (2005, November). *Margaret Burbridge, Smithsonian*, 34–35.

Benbow, C. P., Perkins, S., & Stanley, J. C. (1983). Mathematics taught at a fast pace: A longitudinal evaluation of SMPY's first class. In C. P. Benbow & J. C. Stanley

(Eds.), *Academic precocity: Aspects of its development*, 51–78. Baltimore, MD: Johns Hopkins University Press.

Benbow, C. W. (1991). Mathematical talent: Its nature and consequences. In N. Colangelo, S. G. Assouline, & D. L. Ambroson (Eds.), *Talent Development: Proceedings from the 1991 Henry B. and Jocelyn Wallace National Research Symposium on Talent Development*, 95–123, Unionville, NY: Trillium Press.

Bilger, B. (2002). The riddler: Meet the Marquis de Sade of the puzzle world. *The New Yorker*, March 4, 64–71.

Bisland, A. (2004). Developing leadership skills in young gifted students. *Gifted Child Today*, *27*(1), 24–27, 57.

Bisland, A., Karnes, F. A., & Cobb, Y. B. (2004). Leadership education: Resources and web sites for teachers of gifted students. *Gifted Child Today*, *27*(1), 50–56.

Bloom, B. (Ed.) (1985). *Developing talent in young people*. New York, NY: Ballantine Books.

Borland, J. H. (1989). *Planning and implementing programs for the gifted*. New York, NY: Teachers College.

Brandt, R. S. (1985). On talent development: A conversation with Benjamin Bloom, *Educational Leadership*, September, Washington, DC: Association for Supervision and Curriculum Development.

Brewer, R. L. (Ed.) (2009). *88th Annual Edition Writer's Market 2010,*. Bluefish, OH: Writer's Digest Books.

Brewer, R. L. (Ed.) (2016). *96th Annual Edition Writer's Market 2017*. Bluefish, OH: Writer's Digest Books.

Bruer, J. T. (1993). The mind's journey from novice to expert: If we know the route, we can help students negotiate their way. *American Educator*, Summer, 6–15, 38–46.

Burton, J. M. (2017). *Dreaming, imagining, creating: On being wise and other/wise*, Invited lecture, March 21, 2017, Clark Studio Theater, Lincoln Center Institute, NY.

Cadle, C. & Selby, E. C. (April 2010). The need for thinking and problem solving development. Retrieved September 8, 2010, www.idodi.org/2010_need_for_thinking.pdf.

Cameron, J. (2001). Negative effects of reward on intrinsic motivation—A limited phenomenon: Comment on Deci, Koestner, & Ryan (2001). *Review of Educational Research*, Spring, *71*(1), 29–42.

Castillo, L. C. (1998). The effect of analogy instruction on young children's metaphor comprehension. *Roeper Review*, *21*(1), 27–31.

Catell, R. B. (1971). *Abilities: Their structure, growth, and action. Boston*, MA: Houghton Mifflin.

Ceci, E. L., Koestner, R., & Ryan, R. M. (2001). Extrinsic rewards and intrinsic motivation in education: Reconsidered once again. *Review of Educational Research*, Spring, *71*(1), 1–27.

Ceci, S. J., Barnett, S. M., & Kanaya, T. (2003). Developing childhood proclivities into adult competencies: The overlooked multiplier effect. In R. J. Sternberg &

E. Grigorenko (Eds.), *The psychology of abilities, competencies, and expertise*, 70–92. New York, NY: Cambridge University Press.

Chadwick, D. (2005, November). *Daphne Sheldrick, Smithsonian*, 51.

Chi, M. T. H. (2006). Two approaches to the study of expert's characteristics. In K. A. Ericsson, N. Charness, P. J Feltovich, & R. R. Hoffman (Eds.), *The Cambridge handbook of expertise and expert performance*, 21–30. New York, NY: Cambridge University Press.

Chi, M. T. H., Feltovich, P., & Glaser, R. (1981). Categorization and representation of physics problems by experts and novices. *Cognitive Science, 5*, 121–152.

CHSN (Clarkstown High School North), English Department. (1994). *Fifth Annual Writers in Residence Writing Festival and English Honor Society Induction program*, June 1, New City, NY: Clarkstown High School.

Clark, B. (1979). *Growing up gifted*. Columbus, OH: Charles E. Merrill.

Clark, R. C. (2008). *Building expertise*. San Francisco, CA: John Wiley & Sons.

Clinkenbeard, P. R. (2012). Motivation and gifted students: Implications of theory and research. *Psychology in the Schools, 49*, 622–630.

Clinkenbeard, P. R. (2014). Motivation and goals. In C. Callahan & J. Plucker (Eds.), *Critical issues and practices in gifted education: What the research says* (2nd ed.). Waco, TX: Prufrock Press. Pre-publication draft.

Conway, F. (2001). Raising resilient kids. *Newsweek*, May 14, 64.

Code.com (2017). Hour of Code business campaign to bring computer science to classrooms. Retrieved June 2, 2017 from https://hourofcode.com/files/hoc-one-pager.pdf

Cole, K. C. (2003). Fun with Physics. *The New Yorker*, June 2, 48–50, 55–57.

Coleman, L. (1985). *Schooling the gifted*. Menlo Park: CA: Addison-Wesley.

Coleman, L. (2005). *Nurturing talent in high school: Life in the fast lane*. New York, NY: Teachers College, Columbia University.

Coleman, L. (2006). Talent development in economically disadvantaged populations. *Gifted Child Today, 29*(2), 22–27.

Coleman, L. J. & Cross, T. L. (2000). Social-emotional development and the personal experience of gifted children. In K. A. Heller, F. J. Monks, R. J. Sternberg, & R. F. Subotnik (Eds.), *International handbook of giftedness and talent* (2nd ed.), 203–212, Oxford, UK: Elsevier Science.

Coleman, L. J. & Cross, T. L. (2005). *Being gifted in school* (2nd ed.). Waco, TX: Prufrock Press.

Connell, M. W., Sheridan, K., & Gardner, H. (2003). On abilities and domains. In R. J. Sternberg & E. L. Grigorenko (Eds.). *The psychology of abilities, competencies, and expertise*, 126–155, Cambridge, UK: Cambridge University Press.

Cronbach, L. J. (1963). Course Improvement through evaluation. *Teachers College Record, 64*, 672–683.

Cropley, A. J. (2000). Defining and measuring creativity: Are creativity tests worth using? *Roeper Review, 23*(2), 72–79.

Cross, T. L., Van Tassel-Baska, J. L., & Olenchak, F. R. (2009). Creating gifted lives: Concluding thoughts. In J. L. Van Tassel-Baska, T. L. Cross, & F. R. Olenchak (Eds.), *Social-emotional curriculum with gifted and talented students*, 361–372. Waco, TX: Prufrock.

Csikszentmihalyi, M. (1990). *Flow: The psychology of optimal experience.* New York, NY: Harper Collins.

Csikszentmihalyi, M. Rathunde, K., & Whalen, S. (1993). *Talented teenagers: The roots of success & failure.* Cambridge, NY: Cambridge University.

Davidson, J. E., & Sternberg, R. J. (1984). The role of insight in intellectual giftedness. *Gifted Child Quarterly, 28*(2), 58–64.

Davidson, L., & Scripp, L. (1994). Conditions of giftedness: Musical development in the preschool and early elementary years. In R. F. Subotnik & K. D. Arnold (Eds.), *Beyond Terman: Contemporary longitudinal studies of giftedness and talent.* Norwood, NJ: Ablex.

Davis, C. (Ed.) (2001). NAEA Policy on contests and competitions—adopted March 2001. *Advisory NAEA,* Summer 2001. Reston, VA: National Art Education Association.

DeGroot, A. (1965). *Thought and choice in chess.* New York, NY: Basic books.

Dembo, A., Hartz, D., Kay, S. I., Samuelson, S. E., & Tate, J. (1981). *A description of E.X.P.A.N.D.: Exceptional Pupils Adding New Dimensions—A multi-faceted secondary program for gifted and talented youth.* Central Valley, NY: Monroe-Woodbury Central School district.

Dewey, J. (1938). *Experience and Education.* New York: Macmillan.

Doskoch, P. (2005). The winning edge. *Psychology Today,* November–December, 42–52.

Duke University Talent Identification Program. (1997). *1997 Educational Opportunity Guide: A Directory of programs for the gifted.* Duke University Talent Identification Program: Durham, NC (published annually via internet now).

Dunning, D., Heath, C., & Suls, J. M. (2005). Picture imperfect. *Scientific American Mind,* 20–27.

Dutton, D. (2009). *The art instinct.* New York, NY: Bloomsbury.

Dweck, C. S. (1999). Caution—Praise can be dangerous. *American Educator,* Spring, 4–9.

Dweck, C. S. (2007). *Mindset: The new psychology of success.* New York, NY: Ballantine.

Eadie, F., Sutton-Smith, B., & Griffin, M. (1983). Filmmaking by "young filmmakers." *Studies in Visual Communications,* 65–75.

Erickson, J. B. (1994). *1994–1995 Directory of American youth organizations* 5th ed. Minneapolis: Free Spirit.

Erickson, J. B. (1998). *Directory of American youth organization: A guide to 500 Clubs, groups, troops, teams,* 7th ed. Minneapolis, MN: Free Spirit.

Ericsson, K. A. (1996). The acquisition of expert performance: An introduction to some of the issues, In *The Road to Excellence: The Acquisition of Expert Performance in the Arts and Sciences, Sports, and Games,* 1–50. Mahwah, NJ, Lawrence Erlbaum.

Ericsson, K. A. & Charness, N. (1997). Cognitive and developmental factors in expert performance. In P. J. Feltovich, K. M. Ford, & R. R. Hoffman (Eds.), *Expertise in context,* 3–41, Cambridge, MA: Massachusetts Institute of Technology.

Ericsson, K. A., Krampe, R. T., & Tesch-Römer, C. (1993). The role of deliberate practice in the acquisition of expert performance. *Psychological Review, 100*(3), 363–406.

Ericsson, K. A., Perez, R. S., Eccles, D. W., Lang, L., Baker, E. L., Bransford, J. D., Vanlehn, K., & Ward, P. (2009). The measurement and development of professional performance: An introduction to the topic and a background to the design and origin of this book. In K. A. Ericsson (Ed.), *Development of professional expertise: Toward measurement of expert performance and design of optimal learning environments*, 1–24. New York, NY: Cambridge University Press.

Ericsson, K. A. & Pool, R. (2017). *PEAK—Secrets from the new science of expertise*. New York, NY: Houghton Mifflin Harcourt.

Feldhusen, J. F. (1991). Saturday and summer programs. In N. Colangelo & G. A. Davis (Eds.) *Handbook of gifted education*, 197–208. Boston: Allyn & Bacon.

Feldhusen, J. F. (1995). *Talent identification and development in education (TIDE)* (2nd ed.). Sarasota, FL: Center for Creative Learning.

Feldhusen, J. F. (2001). *Talent development in gifted education*. ERIC Digest, EDO-EC-01–5. A U.S. Office of Educational Research and Improvement (OERI) publication.

Feldhusen, J. F., Hoover, S. M., & Saylor, M. F. (1990). *Identifying and educating gifted students at the secondary level*. Monroe, NY: Trillium Press.

Feldhusen, J. F. & Kennedy, D. M. (1988). Preparing gifted youth for leadership roles in a rapidly changing society. *Roeper Review, 10*(4), 226–230.

Feldhusen, J. F. & Pleiss, M. K. (1992). Leadership: A synthesis of social skills, creativity, and histrionic ability? *Roeper Review*, June 1994, 293–294.

Feldman, D. H. (1986). *Nature's gambit: Child prodigies and the development of human potential*. New York, NY: Basic Books.

Feltovich, P. J., Spiro, R. J., & Coulson, R. L. (1997). Issues of expert flexibility in contexts characterized by complexity and change. In P. J. Feltovich, K. M. Ford, & R. R. Hoffman (Eds.), *Expertise in context*, 125–146. Cambridge: Massachusetts Institute of Technology.

Finn, C. E. Jr. (2014). Gifted, talented, and underserved. In *National Affairs*, 18, Winter, 50–62. Retrieved March 17, 2017 from https://www.nationalaffairs.com/publications/detail/gifted-talented-and-underserved.

Fleming, E. S. & Hollinger, C. L. (1981). The multidimensionality of talent in adolescent young women. *Journal for the Education of the Gifted, IV*(3), 188–199.

Fraioli, J. & Kay, S. I. (2000). Advisory—A successful first year. *In Transition—Journal of the NYS Middle School Association, XVIII*(1),18–20.

Friedman, T. L. (2007). *The world is flat*, 3rd ed. New York, NY: Farrar, Strauss & Giroux.

Gagné, F. (1993). Constructs and models pertaining to exceptional human abilities. In K. A. Heller, F. J. Mönks, & A. H. Passow (Eds.), *International Handbook of Research and Development of Giftedness and Talent*, 69–87. Oxford: Pergamon Press.

Gagné, F. (1995). The differentiated nature of giftedness and talent: A model and its impact on the technical vocabulary of gifted and talented education. *Roeper Review, 18*, 103–111.

Gagné, F., Neveu, F., Simard, L., & St Père, F. (1996). How a search for multitalented individuals challenged the concept itself. *Gifted and Talented International*, 11, 4–10.

Gardner, H. (1985). *Frames of mind.* New York, NY: Basic Books.

Getzels, J. W. & Csikszentmihalyi, M. (1964). *Creative thinking in art students: An exploratory study* (Cooperative Research Project No. E-008). Chicago: The University of Chicago.

Getzels, J. W. & Csikszentmihalyi, M. (1976). *The creative vision: A longitudinal study of problem finding in art.* New York, NY: John Wiley and Sons.

Gladwell, M. (1999). The physical genius. *The New Yorker,* August 2, 57–65.

Gladwell, M. (2008). *Outliers.* New York, NY: Little, Brown, & Co.

Gladwell, M. (2009). *What the dog saw.* New York, NY: Little, Brown, & Co.

Goldsmith, L. T. (2000). Tracking trajectories of talent: Child prodigies growing up. In R. C. Friedman & B. M. Shore (Eds.), *Talents unfolding cognition and development: Selected proceedings of 1992 Esther Katz Rosen Symposium,* 89–122. Washington, DC: American Psychological Association.

Gourley, T. J. & Micklus, C. S. (1982). *Problems! Problems! Problems!—Discussions and activities designed to enhance creativity.* Glassboro, NJ: Creative Competitions, Inc.

Greene, M. (1995). *Releasing the Imagination: essays on education, the arts, and social change,* San Francisco, CA: Jossey-Bass.

Gross, M. U. M. (1995, November). *Early scholar award presentation.* Paper presented at the meeting of the National Association for Gifted Children, Tampa, Florida.

Gross, M. U. M., MacLeod, B., Drummond, D. & Merrick, C. (2001). *Gifted students in primary schools: Differentiating the curriculum.* Sydney, NSW, Australia: GERRIC, University of New South Wales.

Gross, M. U. M., Sleap, B., & Pretorius, M. (1999). *Gifted students in secondary schools: Differentiating the curriculum,* Sydney, Australia: GERRIC, University of New South Wales.

Gruber, H. E. (1978). Emotion and cognition: Aesthetics and science. In S.S. Madeja (Ed.), *The Arts, Cognition, and Basic Skills.* St. Louis, MO: Cemrel.

Gruber, H. E. & Richard, L. (1990). Active work and creative thought in university classrooms. In M. Schwebel, C. A. Maher, & N. S. Fagley (Eds.), *Promoting cognitive growth over the life span,* 137–164. Hillsdale, NJ: Lawrence Erlbaum Associates.

Guilford, J. P. (1956). The structure of the intellect, *Psychological Bulletin, 53,* 276–293.

Hagen, E. P. (1980), *Identification of the gifted.* New York, NY: Teachers College Press.

Harari, O. (2002). Open doors: Colin Powell's seven laws of power. *Modern Maturity,* January/February, 49–50.

Haroutounian, J. (2000). The delights and dilemma of the musically talented teenager. *The Journal of Secondary Gifted Education, 12*(1), 3–16.

Hayes-Jacobs, H. (1996). *Developing an integrated curriculum unit with outcomes, standards, and assessment.* Rye, NY: Curriculum Designers.

Hirsch, E. D. (2016). *Why knowledge matters: Rescuing our children from failed educational theories.* Cambridge, MA: Harvard University Press.

Hitt, J. (2007). The amateur future of space travel. *New York Times Magazine*, July 1, 40–47, 66, 80.

Ho, W. (1989). *Yani—The brush of innocence*. New York, NY: Hudson Hills Press.

Hoekman, K., McCormick, J., & Barnett, K. (2005). The important role of optimism in a motivational investigation of the education of gifted adolescents. *Gifted Child Quarterly, 49*(2), 99–110. Retrieved June 18, 2015, from gcq.sagepub.com at UNSW Library.

Hoekman, K., McCormick, J., & Gross, M. U. M. (1999). The optimal context for gifted students: A preliminary exploration of motivational and affective considerations. *Gifted Child Quarterly, 43*(4), 170–193. Retrieved May 24, 2016, from gcq.sagepub.com at UNSW Library.

Holloway, J. H. (2004). Research link/How the community influences achievement. *Educational Leadership, 61*(8), 89–90.

Howe, M. J. A. (1996). The childhoods and early lives of geniuses: Combining psychological and biographical evidence, In K. A. Ericsson (Ed.), *The Road to Excellence: The Acquisition of Expert Performance in the Arts and Sciences, Sports, and Games*, 225–270. Mahwah, NJ: Lawrence Erlbaum.

Howe, M. J. A., Davidson, J. W., & Sloboda, J. A. (n.d., prepublication draft). *Innate gifts and talents: Reality or myth?*

Howe, M. J. A. & Sloboda, J. (1992). Early signs of talents and special interest in the lives of young musicians. *European Journal for High Ability, 2*, 102–111.

Hurwitz, A. (1983). *The gifted and talented in art: A guide to program planning*. Worcester, MA: Davis Publications.

Hurwitz, A. & Day, M. (2007). *Children and their art: Methods for the elementary school, eighth edition*. Belmont, CA: Thomson Wadsworth.

Imagine Editor. (1999). The joys of competition. *Imagine*, September/October, 4–5. Baltimore, MD: Johns Hopkins Center for Talented Youth.

Imagine Editor. (2017). Engineering. *Imagine*, May/June, *24*(5). Baltimore, MD: Johns Hopkins Center for Talented Youth.

Jarvin, L. & Subotnik, R.F. (2005). Understanding elite talent in academic domains: A developmental trajectory from basic abilities to Scholarly Productivity/Artistry. In F. Dixon & S. Moon (Eds.), *The handbook of secondary gifted education*, 203–220. Waco, TX: Prufrock Press.

Jarvin, L. & Subotnik, R. F. (2010). Wisdom from conservatory faculty: Insights on success in classical music performance, *Roeper Review, 3*(2), 78–87.

Johns Hopkins University Center for Talented Youth. (2003). *Imagine: Focus on visual arts, 10*(5), 12–13, 18–19. Baltimore, MD: Johns Hopkins University.

Jolly, J. & Kettler, T. (2004). Authentic assessment of leadership in problem-solving groups. *Gifted Child Today*, 27(1), 32–39.

Kanaʻiaupuni, S. M. (2005). Kaʻakālai Kū Kanaka: A call for strengths-based approaches from a native Hawaiian perspective. *Educational Researcher, 34*(5), 32–38.

Kanevsky, L. (1996). Applying the principles in an elementary school classroom. In C. J. Maker & A. B. Nielson (Eds.), *Curriculum development and teaching strategies for gifted learners*, 181–218. Austin, TX: Pro-ed.

Kanevsky, L. (2011). Deferential differentiation: What types of differentiation do students want? *Gifted Child Quarterly, 55*(4), 279–299.

Kanevsky, L. (2017). *Tool kit for high end curriculum differentiation.* Vancouver, BC, Canada: Author. Free download available at tinyurl.com/TKHED2017

Kanevsky, L. & Kay, S. I. (1998). Differences in gifted and non-gifted students' learning preferences. In *Research Briefs, 12.* Research & Evaluation Division, Washington, DC: NAGC.

Kanevsky, L. & Kay, S. I. (2006). Student voices in curriculum reform: Learning preferences and curriculum differentiation. Presentation at The Ninth Biennial Wallace National Research Symposium on Talent Development. University of Iowa, Iowa City, Iowa. May 22.

Kaplan, S. N. (1979). *Inservice training manual: Activities for developing curriculum for the gifted/talented.* Los Angeles, CA: National/State Leadership Training Institute on the gifted and talented.

Karnes, F. A. & Bean, S. M. (1995). *Leadership for students: A practical guide for ages 8–18.* Waco, TX: Prufrock.

Karnes, F. A. & Bean, S. M. (1997). *Girls and young women entrepreneurs: True stories about starting and running a business, plus how you can do it yourself.* Minneapolis, MN: Free Spirit.

Karnes, F. A. & Chauvin, J. C. (1985). *Leadership skills inventory.* East Aurora, NY: DOK.

Karnes, F. A. & Chauvin, J. C. (2005). *Leadership development program manual* (2nd ed.). Scottsdale, AZ: Great Potential Press.

Karnes, F. A. & Riley, T. L. (1996). *Competitions: Maximizing your abilities.* Waco, TX: Prufrock Press.

Karnes, F. A. & Riley, T. L. (2005). *Competitions for talented kids: Win scholarships, big prize money, and recognition.* Waco, TX: Prufrock Press.

Karnes, M. B. (1978a). *Music checklist.* ERIC Document No. ED 160 226.

Karnes, M. B. (1978b). *Nurturing talent in the visual and performing arts in early childhood: Art and music.* ERIC Document No. ED 161 533.

Karnes, M. B. & Associates. (1978). *Preschool talent checklists record booklet.* Urbana, IL: Institute for Child Behavior and Development.

Kay, S. (1990). Cognitive theory—An element of design for art education. *Design for Arts Education, 92*(2), 10–20.

Kay, S. (1991). *Think! — A Guide of Ideas for the Classroom (Grades 4–6).* Team leader/consultant for curriculum guide jointly sponsored by Ulster BOCES Board of Education and the New York State Education Department.

Kay, S. I. (1989). *Differences in figural problem-solving and problem-finding behavior among professional, semiprofessional, and non-artists.* UMI. Unpublished doctoral dissertation.

Kay, S. I. (1994). From theory to practice—Promoting problem-finding behavior in children. *Roeper Review, 16*(3), 195–197.

Kay, S. I. (1996). The Talent Profile—Translating theory into practice. *Gems of AGATE, 20*(1), 4.

Kay, S. I. (1997). *From novice to expert: Student perceptions on developing talents.* Presentation at the 44th National Association for Gifted Children conference. Little Rock, Arkansas, November.

Kay, S. I. (1999). The Talent Profile as a curricular tool for academics, the arts, and athletics. In S. Cline & K. T. Hegeman (Eds.), *Gifted education in the 21st century: Issues and concerns,* 47–60. New York, NY: Winslow Press.

Kay, S. I. (2000). On the nature of expertise in visual art. In R. C. Friedman & B. M. Shore (Eds.), *Talents unfolding cognition and development: Selected proceedings of 1992 Esther Katz Rosen Symposium,* 217–232. Washington, DC: American Psychological Association.

Kay, S. I. (2001a). A Talent Profile for facilitating talent development in schools. *Gifted Child Quarterly, 45*(1), 45–53.

Kay, S. I. (2001b). From novice to expert: A pilot study of students' perceptions of developing talents. In N. Colangelo & S. Assouline (Eds.), *Talent Development IV: Proceedings of the Fourth Biennial Wallace National Symposium on Talent Development.* University of Iowa, 363–367. Scottsdale, AZ: Great Potential Press.

Kay, S. I. (2001c). Identifying and nurturing talent in the visual arts. *Duke Gifted Newsletter—A Newsletter for Parents of Gifted Children, 1*(4), 1–2.

Kay, S. I. (2002). An Interview with Abraham J. Tannenbaum: Innovative programs for the gifted and talented. *Roeper Review, 24*(4), 186–190.

Kay, S. I. (2003). Recognizing and developing early talent in the visual arts. In P. Olszewski-Kubilius, L. Limburg-Weber, & S. Pfeiffer (Eds.), *Early gifts—Recognizing and nurturing children's talents,* 125–138. Waco, TX: Prufrock Press.

Kay, S. I. (2008). Nurturing Visual Arts Talent. In S. I. Kay (Ed.) *Gifted Child Today* (31) 4, 19–23.)

Kay, S. I. (2013). Designing elegant problems for creative thinking. In F. Reisman (Ed.), Creativity: Process, product, personality, environment & technology, 28–36, KIE Conference Book Series, 2013 International Conference on Knowledge, Innovation & Enterprise, Cambridge, England.

Kay, S. I. (2016.) Serious Play with Elegant Problems, p. 112–115 invited contribution to Singapore Teachers' Academy for the aRts Serious Play: Perspectives on Art Education, Ministry of Education, 2 Malan Road, Singapore, 109433.

Kay, S. I., & Gagné, F. (1997). Brief overview of the Talent Profile. In *1996 NAGC Conference Proceedings,* Research & Evaluation Division, NAGC, Washington, DC: NAGC.

Kay, S. I. & Subotnik, R. F. (1994). Talent beyond words: Unveiling spatial, expressive, kinesthetic, and musical talent in young children. *Gifted Child Quarterly,* 38(2), 70–74.

Kelly, R. (2012). *Educating for creativity: A global conversation.* Calgary, Canada: Brush Education.

Kerr, B. (Ed.) (2009). *Encyclopedia of giftedness, creativity, and talent,* Vol. 1 & 2, Thousand Oaks, CA: Sage.

Kitano, M. K. (1990). A developmental model for identifying and serving young gifted children. *Early Child Development and Care, 63,* 19–31.

Kitano, M. K. & Kirby D. F. (1986). *Gifted education: A comprehensive view.* Boston, MA: Little Brown & Co.

Kogan, L. (2003). *Creativity centenarians.* Baltimore, MD: American Visionary Art Museum, 18–23.

Kohn, A. (1993). *Punished by rewards.* New York, NY: Houghton Mifflin.

Kough, J. & DeHaan, R. F. (1955). *Volume I: Identifying children with special needs.* Chicago, IL: Science Research Associates.

Krampe, R. T. & Ericsson, K. A. (1996). Maintaining excellence: Deliberate practice and elite performance in young and older pianists. *Journal of Experimental Psychology: General, 125,* 331–359.

Lawson, D. M. (2004). Who wants to be a billionaire?—A Rockefeller's rules for raising responsible children. *Smithsonian,* June, 136.

Lemley, B. (2005). The Super Bowl of smart. *Discover,* February 2005, 55–59.

Levy, S. (2002). Great minds, great ideas. *Newsweek,* May 27, 56–59.

Levy, S. (2005). The mind of an inventor. *Newsweek,* October 10, 48–54.

Lewis, C.S. (1956). *Surprised by Joy.* New York, NY: Harcourt Brace.

Lohman, D. F. (2005a). Beliefs about differences between ability and accomplishment: From folk theories to cognitive science. Pre-publication draft for *ROEPER Review.*

Lohman, D. F. (2005b). *Developing academic talent: The roles of experience, mentoring, motivation, and volition.* Paper presented at the Henry B. & Jocelyn Wallace National Research Symposium on Talent Development, Iowa City, Iowa, May.

Lohman, D. F., Gambrell, J., & Lakin, J. (2008). The commonality of extreme discrepancies in the ability profiles of academically gifted students. *Psychology Science Quarterly, 50*(2), 269–282.

Lohman, D. F. & Hagen, E. P. (2001). *CogAT Form 6: Interpretive guide for school administrators.* Itasca, IL: Riverside.

Lohman, D. F., Korb, K. A., & Lakin, J. M. (2008). Identifying academically gifted English-language learners using non-verbal tests: A comparison of the Raven, NNAT, and CogAT, *Gifted Child Quarterly, 52*(4), 275–296.

Lore, N. A. (1998). *The Pathfinder: How to choose or change your career for a lifetime of satisfaction and success.* New York, NY: Fireside Simon & Schuster.

Lore, N. A. (2008). *Now what? The young person's guide to choosing the perfect career.* New York, NY: Fireside Simon & Schuster.

Maker, C. J. & Nielson, A. B. (1996). *Curriculum development and teaching strategies for gifted Learners* (2nd ed.). Austin, TX: PRO-ED.

Manning, S. (2005). Young leaders: Growing through mentoring. *Gifted Child Today, 28*(1), 14–20.

Marland, S. P. (1972). *Education of the gifted and talented: Report to the Congress of the United States by the U.S. Commissioner of Education.* Washington, DC: U.S. Government Printing Office.

Marsh, H. W. (1987). The big-fish-little-pond effect on academic self-concept. *Journal of Educational Psychology, 79*(3), 280–295.

Mathews. B. (2000). Get with the program: The USA Computing Olympiad. *Imagine,* March/April, 10–11.

Maton, K. I., Dodgen, D. W., Leadbeater, B. J., Sandler, I. N., Schellenbach, C. J., & Solarz, A. L. (2004). Strength-based research and policy: An introduction. In K. I. Maton, C. J. Schellenbach, B. J. Leadbeater, & A. L. Solarz (Eds.), *Investing in children, youth, families, and communities*, 3–12, Washington, DC: American Psychological Association.

McDonald, M. (1982). *Teachers' messages for report cards, Revised Edition*, Fearon Teacher Aids. Torrance, CA: Frank Schaffer Publications.

Meeker, M. (1977). *Teaching gifted children music in grades one through six*. ERIC Document No. ED 152 022.

Milbrath, C. (1995). Germinal motifs in the work of a gifted child artist. In C. Golomb (Ed.), *The development of artistically gifted children: Selected case studies*, 101–134, Hillsdale, NJ: Lawrence Erlbaum Associates.

Morell, V. (2005, November). *Richard Leakey, Smithsonian*, 40–41.

Mullich, J. (August/September 2004). All I ever needed to know about business . . . I learned in my childhood. *My Business*, 37–38.

Mumford, M. D., Friedrich, T. L., Caughron, J. J., & Antes, A. L. (2009). Leadership development and assessment: Describing and rethinking the state of the art. In K.A. Ericsson (Ed.), *Development of professional expertise: Toward measurement of expert performance and design of optimal learning environments*, 84–107. New York, NY: Cambridge University Press.

Murphy, S. E. & Johnson, S. K. (2011). The benefits of a long-lens approach to leader development: Understanding the seeds of leadership. *The Leadership Quarterly*, 22, 459–470.

My Business. (2004). Superstar students. *My Business*, August/September, 34–35.

National Foundation for Teaching Entrepreneurship, Inc. (2000). *Entrepreneurs in profile*. Franklin Lakes, NJ: Career Press.

National Inventive Thinking Association. (1998). *Young Inventors & Creators Competition* (Brochure). Richardson, Texas.

Nebraska State Department of Education (Anne Campbell, Commissioner of Education) (n.d.). *Identification Supplement to Rule 3: Ideas for identification of gifted/talented in the areas of: Creativity, leadership, visual and performing arts, psychomotor ability*. Lincoln, NE: Nebraska State Department of Education.

Nelson, L. & Psaltis, B. (1967). *Fostering creativity*. New York, NY: Associated Educational Services Corp.

Newsweek. (2005). Capturing Kong. *Newsweek*, December 5, 63–67.

Nichols, T. (2017). *The death of expertise: The campaign against established knowledge and why it matters*. New York, NY: Oxford University Press.

Nieuwenhuis, C. F., Spamer, E. J., & Rossum, J. H. A. (2002). Prediction function for identifying talent in 14- to 15-year-old female field hockey players, *High Ability Studies*, *13*(1), 22–33.

Office of Development and External Affairs. (Summer 2004). The last lesson. *TC Today: The Magazine of Teachers College, Columbia University*, 22–24.

Olszewski, P., Kulieke, M., & Buescher, T. (1987). The influence of the family environment on the development of talent: A literature review. *Journal for the Education of the Gifted*, *11*, 6–28.

Olszewski-Kubilius, P., Limburg-Weber, L., & Pfeiffer, S. (2003). *Early gifts—Recognizing and nurturing children's talents.* Waco, TX: Prufrock.

Orfalea, P. (2005). Copy that! *Fortune Small Business,* September, 91–94.

Ozturk, A. & Debelak, C. (2008). Affective benefits from academic competitions for middle school. *Gifted Child Today, 31*(2), 48–53.

Partnership for 21st Century learning (2007). Framework for 21st C. Learning. http://www.p21.org/our-work/p21-framework.

Passow, A. H. (1977). Forward for *A new generation of leadership: Education for the gifted in leadership.* Ventura, CA: Office of the Ventura County Superintendent of Schools.

Passow, A. H. (1982). *Differentiated curricula for the gifted/talented.* Committee report to the National/State Leadership Training Institute on the Gifted and Talented. Ventura County, CA: Office of the Superintendent of Schools.

Passow, A. H. (1988). The educating and schooling of the community of artisans in science. In Brandwein, P. F. & Passow, A. H (Eds.), *Gifted Young in Science: Potential through Performance*, 27–38. Washington, DC: National Science Teachers Association.

Patel, V. L. & Ramoni, M. F. (1997). Cognitive models of directional inference in expert medical reasoning. In P. J. Feltovich, K. M. Ford, & R. R. Hoffman (Eds.), *Expertise in context*, 67–99. Cambridge, MA: Massachusetts Institute of Technology.

Patrick, C. (1935a). Creative thought in poets. *Archives Psychology, 26,* 178.

Patrick, C. (1935b). Creative thought in artists. *Journal of Psychology, 4,* 35–73.

Plagens, P. (2003). Transitions—The line kings exit the stage. *Newsweek,* February 3, 12.

Qualifications and Curriculum Authority. (2006). National curriculum of the United Kingdom: *Guidance on teaching the gifted and talented—Design and technology.* Retrieved September 14, 2006 from http://www.nc.uk.net/gt/design/index.htm

Renzulli, J. S. (1978). What makes giftedness? Reexamining a definition. *Phi Delta Kappan, 60,*180–184, 261.

Renzulli, J. S. (1986). The three-ring conception of giftedness: A developmental model for creative productivity. In R. J. Sternberg & J. E. Davidson (Eds.), *Conceptions of giftedness*, 53–92; Cambridge, England: Cambridge University Press.

Renzulli, J. S. & Smith, L. H. (1979). A practical model for designing individualized education programs (IEP's) for gifted and talented students, summary article for *A guidebook for developing individualized education programs (IEP's) for gifted and talented students.* Mansfield Center, CT: Creative Learning Press.

Renzulli, J. S., Smith, L. H., White, A. J., Callahan, C. M., & Hartman, R. K. (1976). *Scales for rating the behavioral characteristics of superior students.* Mansfield Center, CT: Creative Learning Press.

Resnick, L. B. (1999). From aptitude to effort. *American Educator,* Spring, 14–17.

Richardson, C. P. (1990). Measuring musical giftedness. *Music Educators Journal, 76*(7), 40–49.

Riggio, R. E. & Mumford, M. D. (2011). Introduction to the special issue: Longitudinal studies of leadership development. *The Leadership Quarterly 22,* 453–456.

Roach, A. A., Wyman, L. T., Brookes, H., Chavez, C, Heath, S. B., & Valdes, G. (1999). Leadership giftedness: Models revisited. *Gifted Child Quarterly, 43*(1), 13–24.

Robinson, A. (2017). Developing STEM talent in the early school years: STEM Starters and its next Generation scale up. In K. S. Taber & M. Sumida (Eds.), *Teaching gifted learners in STEM subjects: Developing talent in science, technology, engineering and mathematics*, 21–30. London: Routledge.

Robinson, A., Adelson, J. L., Kidd, K., & Cunningham, C. M. (2018). A talent for tinkering: Developing talents in children from low-income households through engineering curriculum. *Gifted Child Quarterly, 62*(1). doi: 10.1171/0016986217738049

Robinson, A. & Jolly, J. L. (2014). *A century of contributions to gifted education: Illuminating lives.* New York, NY: Routledge.

Robinson, A., Kidd, K., & Adelson, J. L. (2017). Assessments for K-8 engineering: What is available and advisable for talented students? In D. Dailey & A. Cotabish (Eds.) *Engineering instruction for high-ability learners in K-8 classrooms*, 165–178. Waco, TX: Prufrock.

Robinson, N. M. & Robinson, H. B. (1982). The optimal match: Devising the best compromise for the highly gifted student. San Francisco: Jossey-Bass.

Roeper, A. (1995). *Annemarie Roeper: Selected writings and speeches.* Minneapolis, MN: Free Spirit.

Roets, L. S. (1992). *Leadership, a skills training program.* New Sharon, IA: Leadership Publishers.

Root-Bernstein, M. (2014). *Inventing imaginary worlds: from childhood play to adult creativity across the arts and sciences.* Lanham, MD: Rowman & Littlefield.

Root-Bernstein, R. (1989). *Discovering.* Cambridge, MA: Harvard University Press.

Root-Bernstein, R. (2000). Art advances science. *Nature, 407,* 134.

Root-Bernstein, R. (2011). General session keynote presentation on ways art education has impacted elite scientists, especially Nobel laureates. For the NAEA National Convention on Creativity, Imagination, & Innovation in Art Education, Seattle, WA, March 19.

Rothstein, E. (2005, November). *Julie Taymor, Smithsonian,* 52–54.

Rudnick, P. (2014). Alec Baldwin's preschool report card, *The New Yorker,* 33.

Ruenzel, D. (2000). Gold star junkies. *Teacher Magazine,* February, 25–29.

Russell, B. (1967). *The Autobiography of Bertrand Russell,* Boston, MA: Little Brown & Co.

Saffo, P. (2002). Failure is the best medicine. *Newsweek,* March 25, 53.

Sawyer, R. K. (2012). *Explaining creativity: The science of human motivation.* New York, NY: Oxford University Press.

Scherer, M. (2006). Celebrate strengths, nurture affinities: A conversation with Mel Levine. *Educational Leadership, 64*(1), 8–15.

Schneider, W. (2002). Relationships among giftedness, expertise, and (exceptional) performance: A developmental perspective. Presentation at the 8th Conference of the European Council for High Ability (ECHA), Rhodes, Greece, October 10.

Schulz, Kathryn. (2010). *Being wrong: Adventures in the margin of error.* New York, NY: Harper Collins.

Schweizer, K. (1997). Children of change: Elise's story. *The Times Herald Record,* March 24, 4–5.

Scrivani, G. (Ed.) (1988). *The collected writings of Willem de Kooning.* New York, NY: Hanuman.

Seivert, S. (2001). It's not just how we play that matters. *Newsweek, March 19, 2001,* 12.

Sheerin, J. (2009). Malawi windmill boy with big fans. *BBC News.* Retrieved October 25, 2018. from http://news.bbc.co.uk/go/pr/fr/-2/hi/africa/8257153.stm

Shore, B. M., Cornell, D. G., Robinson, A., & Ward, V. S. (1991). *Recommended practices in gifted education: A critical Analysis.* New York, NY: Teachers College.

Simonton, D. K. (1988). Creativity, leadership and chance. In R. J. Sternberg (Ed.), *The nature of creativity,* 386–426, New York, NY: Cambridge University Press.

Simonton, D. K. (1996). Creative expertise: A life-span developmental perspective, In K.A Ericsson (Ed.) *The Road to Excellence: The Acquisition of Expert Performance in the Arts and Sciences, Sports, and Games,* 227–253. Mahwah, NJ, Lawrence Erlbaum.

Simpson, J.W., Delaney, J. M., Carroll, K. L., Hamilton, C. M., Kay, S. I., Kerlavage, M. S., & Olson, J. L. (1998). *Creating meaning through art: Teacher as Choicemaker,* Upper Saddle River, NJ: Prentice Hall.

Sisk, D. (1993). Leadership education for the gifted. In K. Heller, F. Monks, & A.H. Passow (Eds.) *International handbook of research and development in giftedness and talent,* 491–505, New York, NY: Pergamon.

Sloboda, J. A. (1996). The acquisition of musical performance expertise: Deconstructing the "Talent" account of individual differences in musical expressivity, In K. A Ericsson (Ed.) *The Road to Excellence: The Acquisition of Expert Performance in the Arts and Sciences, Sports, and Games,* 107–126. Mahwah, NJ, Lawrence Erlbaum.

Small, L. M.(2005). Invention at play. *Smithsonian,* April, 14.

Snow, R. E. (1980). Aptitude and achievement. In W. B. Schrader (Ed.), Measuring *achievement: Progress over a decade: Proceedings of the 1979 ETS Invitational Conference,* 39–60. San Francisco, CA: Jossey-Bass. (New directions for testing and measurement series).

Sohn, E. (2005). When fair means superb. *Science News,* May 21, 167, 326 & 332.

Sokolove, M. (2010). From boys to pros: How a cutting edge European talent factory produces elite players, *New York Times Magazine,* June 6, 40–49, 64, 66, 68.

Solarz, A.L., Leadbeater, B. J., Sandler, I. N., Maton, K. I, Schellenbach, C. J., Dodgen, D.W. (2004). A blueprint for the future. In Maton, K. I., Schellenbach, C. J., Leadbeater, B. J., Solarz, A.L. (Eds.) *Investing in children, youth, families, and communities,* 343–353, Washington, DC: American Psychological Association.

Sosniak, L. A. (2006). Retrospective interviews in the study of Expertise and Expert Performance. In K.A. Ericsson, N. Charness, P. J Feltovich, & R.R. Hoffman (Eds.) *The Cambridge Handbook of Expertise and Expert Performance,* 287–301. New York, NY: Cambridge University Press

Spearman, C. (1927). *The abilities of man.* New York: MacMillan.

Stanley, J. C. (1998). Helping students learn only what they don't already know. In N. Colangelo & S. G. Assouline (Eds.) *Proceedings from the 1998 Henry B. & Jocelyn Wallace National Research Symposium on Talent Development*, 293–299, Scottsdale, AZ: Great Potential Press.

Sternberg, R. J. (1985). *Beyond IQ: A triarchic theory of human intelligence.* New York, NY: Cambridge University.

Sternberg, R. J. (1999). Ability and expertise. *American Educator*, Spring, 10–13, 50–51.

Sternberg, R. J. (2000). Identifying and developing creative giftedness. *Roeper Review, 23*(2), 60–64.

Subotnik, R. F. (2000). Developing young adolescent performers at Juilliard: An educational prototype for elite level talent development in the arts and sciences. In C. F. Van Lieshout & P. G. Heymans (Eds.), *Developing talent across the lifespan*, 249–276. Philadelphia, PA: Taylor & Francis.

Subotnik, R. F. (2003). A developmental view of giftedness: From being to doing. *Roeper Review, 26*, 14–15.

Subotnik, R. F. (2004). Transforming elite musicians into professional artists: A view of the talent development process at the Juilliard School. In L. V. Shavinina & M. Ferrari (Eds.), *Beyond knowledge: Extra cognitive aspects of developing high ability*. Mahwah, NJ: Lawrence Erlbaum Associates.

Subotnik, R. F., & Arnold, K. D. (Eds.). (1994). *Beyond Terman: Contemporary longitudinal studies of giftedness and talent.* Norwood, NJ: Ablex.

Subotnik, R. F. & Calderon, J. (2008). Developing giftedness and talent. In F. A. Karnes & K. R. Stephens (Eds.), *Achieving excellence: Educating the gifted and talented*, 49–61. Columbus, OH: Pearson.

Subotnik, R. F. & Coleman, L. (1996). Establishing the foundations for a talent development school: Applying principles to creating an ideal. *Journal for the Education of the Gifted, 20*, 175–189.

Subotnik, R. F., & Jarvin, L. (2005). Beyond expertise: Conceptions of giftedness as great performance. In R. J. Sternberg & J. E. Davidson (Eds.), *Conceptions of giftedness* (2nd ed.), 343–357. New York, NY: Cambridge University Press.

Subotnik, R. F., Jarvin, L., Moga, E., & Sternberg, R. (2003). Wisdom from gatekeepers: Secrets of success in music performance. *Bulletin of Psychology and the Arts*, 4, 5–9.

Subotnik, R. F.; Olszewski-Kubilius, P., & Worrell, F. C. (2011). Rethinking giftedness and gifted education: A proposed direction forward based on psychological science. *Psychological Science in the Public Interest, 12*(1), 3–54.

Talents Unlimited. (1978). *Criterion referenced tests.* Mobile, AL: Talents Unlimited.

Tannenbaum, A. J. (1983). *Gifted children.* New York, NY: Macmillan.

Tannenbaum, A. J. (2000). A history of giftedness in school and society. In K. Heller, F. Monks, R. Sternberg, & R. Subotnik (Eds.), *International handbook of giftedness and talent* (2nd ed.), 23–54. Oxford, England: Pergamon.

Terman, L. M. (1916). *The measurement of intelligence.* Boston: Houghton Mifflin.

Tharp, T. (2006). *The creative habit.* New York, NY: Simon & Schuster.

Tietz, J. (2011). Santiago's brain. *Rolling Stone*, 78–87.

Torrance, E. P. (1969). Creative positives of disadvantaged children and youth. *Gifted Child Quarterly, 13*(2), 71–81.

Torrance, E. P. & Myers, R. E. (1974). *Creative teaching and learning*. New York, NY: Dodd, Mead, & Co.

Treffinger, D. J. (1998). From gifted education to programming for talent development, *Phi Delta Kappan*, June, 752–755.

Twenge, J. M. (2017). Have smart phones destroyed a generation? *The Atlantic*, September. Retrieved October 15, 2017 from https://www.theatlantic.com/magazine/archive/2017/09/has-the-smartphone-destroyed-a-generation/534198/#article

U. S. Patent and Trademark Office. (2007). U.S. commerce secretary Carlos M. Gutierrez unveils National campaign to inspire innovation in children, April 10, 2007. *Press Release*. Retrieved August 8, 2009 from http://www.uspto.gov/web/offices/com/speeches/inspinvntunveils.htm

Van Rossum, J. H. A. (1996). Psychological characteristics of elite athletes according to top level coaches, *High Ability Studies*, *7*(1), 15–23.

Van Rossum, J. H. A. (1997). Gifted athletes and complexity of family structure: A condition for talent development, *High Ability Studies*, *8*(1), 19–29.

Van Rossum, J. H. A. (2000). Deliberate practice and Dutch field hockey: An addendum to Starkes. *International Journal of Sport Psychology*, *31*, 452–460.

Van Rossum, J. H. A. (2001). Talented in dance: the Bloom Stage Model revisited in the personal histories of dance students. *High Ability Studies*, *12*(2), 181–197.

Van Tassel-Baska, J. L. (1988). Curriculum for the gifted: Theory, research and practice. In J. Van Tassel-Baska, J. Feldhusen, K. Seeley, G. Wheatley, L. Silverman, and W. Foster (Eds.), *Comprehensive curriculum for gifted learners*. Boston, MA: Allyn and Bacon.

Van Tassel-Baska, J. L. (1989). Profiles of precocity: A three-year study of talented adolescents. In J. L. Van Tassel -Baska & P. Olszewski-Kubilius (Eds.), *Patterns of influence in gifted learners*, 29–39. New York, NY: Teachers College Press.

Van Tassel-Baska, J. L. (1994). The National Curriculum Development Projects for high ability learners: Key issues and findings. In N. Colangelo, S. G. Assouline, & D. L. Ambroson (Eds.), *Talent Development: Proceedings from the 1993 Henry B. and Jocelyn Wallace National Research symposium in Talent Development*. Dayton, OH: Ohio Psychology Press.

Van Tassel-Baska, J. L. (1998). The development of academic talent: A mandate for educational best practice. *Phi Delta Kappan*, 760–763.

Wainer, H. (1997). *Visual revelations: Graphical tales of fate and deception from Napoleon Bonaparte to Ross Perot*. NJ: Lawrence Erlbaum.

Walberg, H. J. (1995). Nurturing children for adult success. In M. W. Katzko and F. J. Monks (Eds.), *Nurturing talent: Individual needs and social ability*, 168–179. Assen, NL: Van Gorcum.

Walberg, H. J. (1988). Creativity and talent as learning. In R. J. Sternberg (Ed.), *The nature of creativity*, New York, NY: Cambridge University Press.

Wallace, D. B. (1989). Studying the individual: The case study method and other genres, In D. B. Wallace & H. E. Gruber (Eds.), *Creative People at Work*, 25–43. New York, NY: Oxford University Press.

Whitehead, A. N. (1929). *The aims of education*. New York, NY: Macmillan.

Whitmore, J. (1980). *Giftedness, conflict, and underachievement*. Boston, MA: Allyn & Bacon.

Winner, E. (1982). *Invented worlds: The psychology of the arts*. Cambridge, MA: Harvard University Press.

Winner, E. (1996a). *Gifted children: Myths and realities*. New York, NY: Basic Books.

Winner, E. (1996b). The rage to master: The decisive role of talent in the visual arts. In K. A Ericsson (Ed.) *The road to excellence: The acquisition of expert performance in the arts and sciences, sports, and games*, 271–301. Mahwah, NJ: Lawrence Erlbaum.

Wolfe, R. M. (1990). *Evaluation in education*. New York, NY: Praeger.

Worrell, F. C., Knotek, S. E., Plucker, J. A., Portenga, S., Simonton, D. K., Olszewski-Kubilius, P., Schultz, S. R., & Subotnik, R. F. (2016). Competition's role in developing psychological strength and outstanding performance. *Review of General Psychology*, July 25. Advance online publication: http://dx.doi.org/10.1037/gpr0000079

Wozniak, S. with Smith, G. (2006). *iWoz*. New York, NY: W. W. Norton.

Zakaria, F. (2006). We all have a lot to learn. *Newsweek*, January 9.

Zuckerman, H. (1977/1996). *Scientific elite: Nobel laureates in the United States*. New Brunswick, Canada: Transaction Publishers.

About the Author

Sandra I. Kay has a doctor of education in special education and master of education in instructional practices from Teachers College, Columbia University, where she remained as a visiting scholar for 10 years. Her bachelor and master of science in art education and the grounding of over 30 years of K-12 teaching directed her research focus on developing talent/expertise and on the problem-finding aspects of creative thought, visual thinking, and other habits of mind that engage the imagination and promote self-directed inquiry in children and adults.